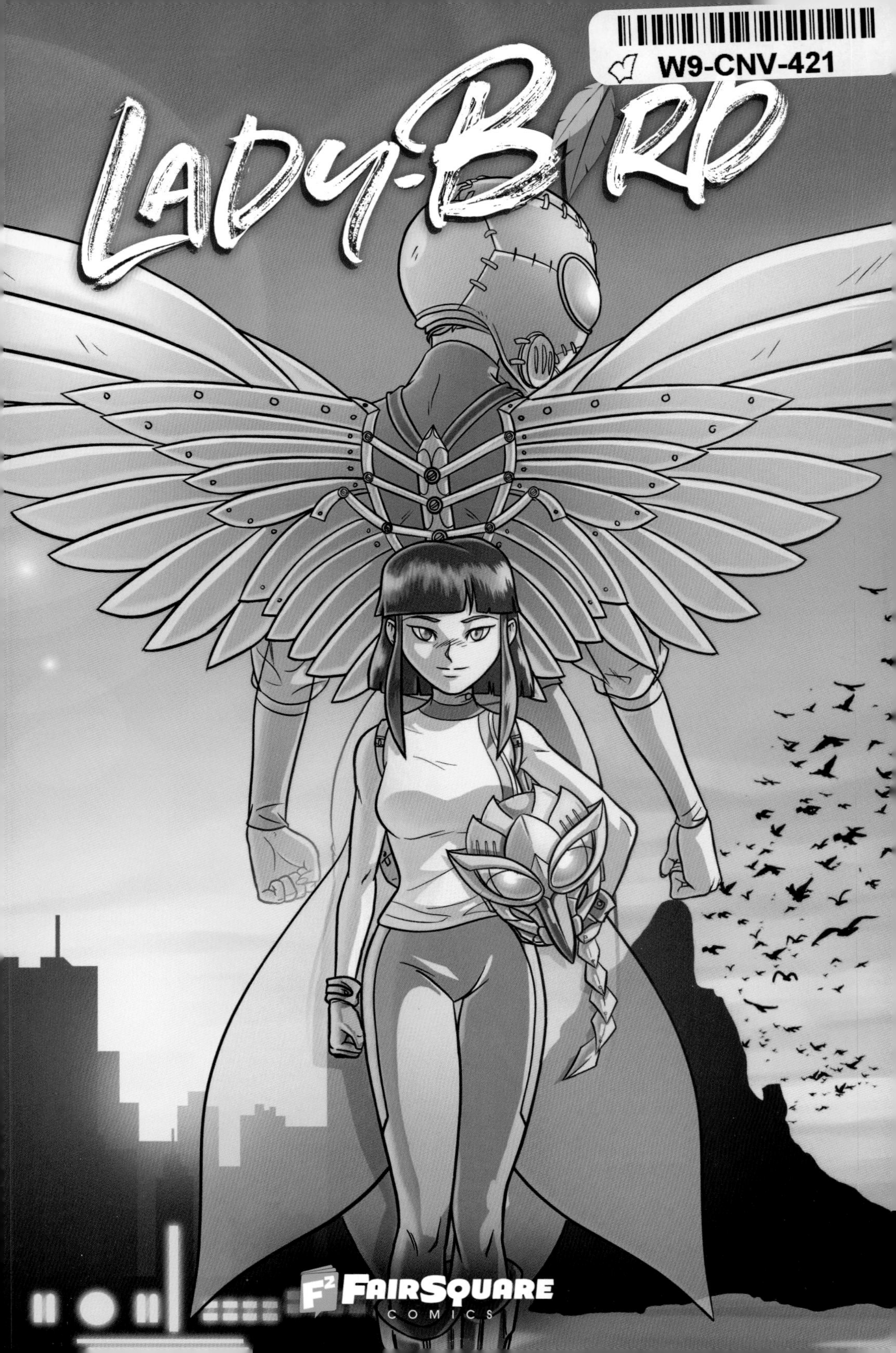
LADY-BIRD
FAIRSQUARE
COMICS

LADY-BIRD

Volume 1. First Printing.

This title is a publication of FairSquare Comics, LLC.
608S Dunsmuir Ave #207, Los Angeles, CA 90036.
Copyright © FairSquare Comics.
All Rights Reserved.

Inspired by VÉGA LA MAGICIENNE, published in
"L'indépendent du Cher" in 1911 by René D'Anjou
(Public Domain).

ISBN: 978-0-9992766-4-8

DREAM TEAM

Fabrice Sapolsky
Kristal Adams Sapolsky
Ethan Sapolsky

SPECIAL THANKS

Xavier Fournier, Will Torres, Fred Pham Chuong,
Jonathan Lang, Dario Morgante, Arianna Sabella,
Stephan Franck.

COMICS FROM THE REST OF US
WWW.FAIRSQUARECOMICS.COM

STORY
**FABRICE SAPOLSKY
AND DAWN J. STARR**

ART AND COLORS
DANIELE SAPUPPO

COLOR ASSIST (P.80-120)
DIEGO FICHERA

ADDITIONAL ARTWORK
**FRED PHAM CHUONG
WILL TORRES
FABRICE SAPOLSKY**

PROOFREADING
KATRINA ROETS

COVER
LISSA

It's a Kind of Magic!

VÉGA
LA MAGICIENNE
PAR RENÉ D'ANJOU

The fact that this story exists is actually a little miracle of its own. It starts with a short novel, "Vega La Magicienne" (Vega the Magician), written by René D'Anjou and published in "L'Indépendant du Cher", a local French newspaper, from August 17th, 1911 to December 24th of the same year.

René d'Anjou is actually a stage name. Behind the mask, there's a woman, Renée Gouraud d'Ablancourt (1853-1941), a prolific writer from the late 19th/early 20th century. In those days, it was not really easy to be a female writer in a male dominated industry. She chose to gender bend her first name and to add "d'Anjou" as a last name, to honor the town where she was born: Angers.

And in 1911, "l'Oiselle", the original Lady-Bird, was born!
Flash forward to 2018. My friend Xavier Fournier sends me the short story encouraging me to take a look at it. "L'Oiselle" being public domain, updating the concept and bringing back to life what is probably the first ever female superhero in History sounded like a no brainer. I promised to take a look at it. I must say, I wasn't really inspired, though. But I kept the file in my "In development" folder, just in case.

Early 2020, as COVID 19 spread on the world, I browsed through my files and re-read the Vega story. And I clicked. Rediscovering Lady-Bird, I imagined how her world could've been in the 21st Century.
I re-used some of the characters from the original tale: Vega De Ortega, Cleto Pizanni, Count San Remo and tweaked the place where the Lady-Birds came from (Stella Negra became Estrella Negra). Next to those, I created Mina, the new Lady-Bird, as well as Tamara, Marques and the heir to the San Remo dynasty: Daniel.
For the designs, I chose to go steampunk for Vega and more high tech for Mina, reflecting two different eras.

Dawn came quickly on-board. She had never written a comic before, but I was happy to split the writing duties so I could focus on designing our new birds (see at the end of this volume). After a long process, we found Daniele, our artist and a year later, Lissa, who drew our cover. We truly embarked on a life changing adventure. I hope you'll enjoy reading Lady-Bird as much as we all loved making it. This book is a true gem and we have more tales in store for Mina, Vega and their friends!

Fabrice Sapolsky

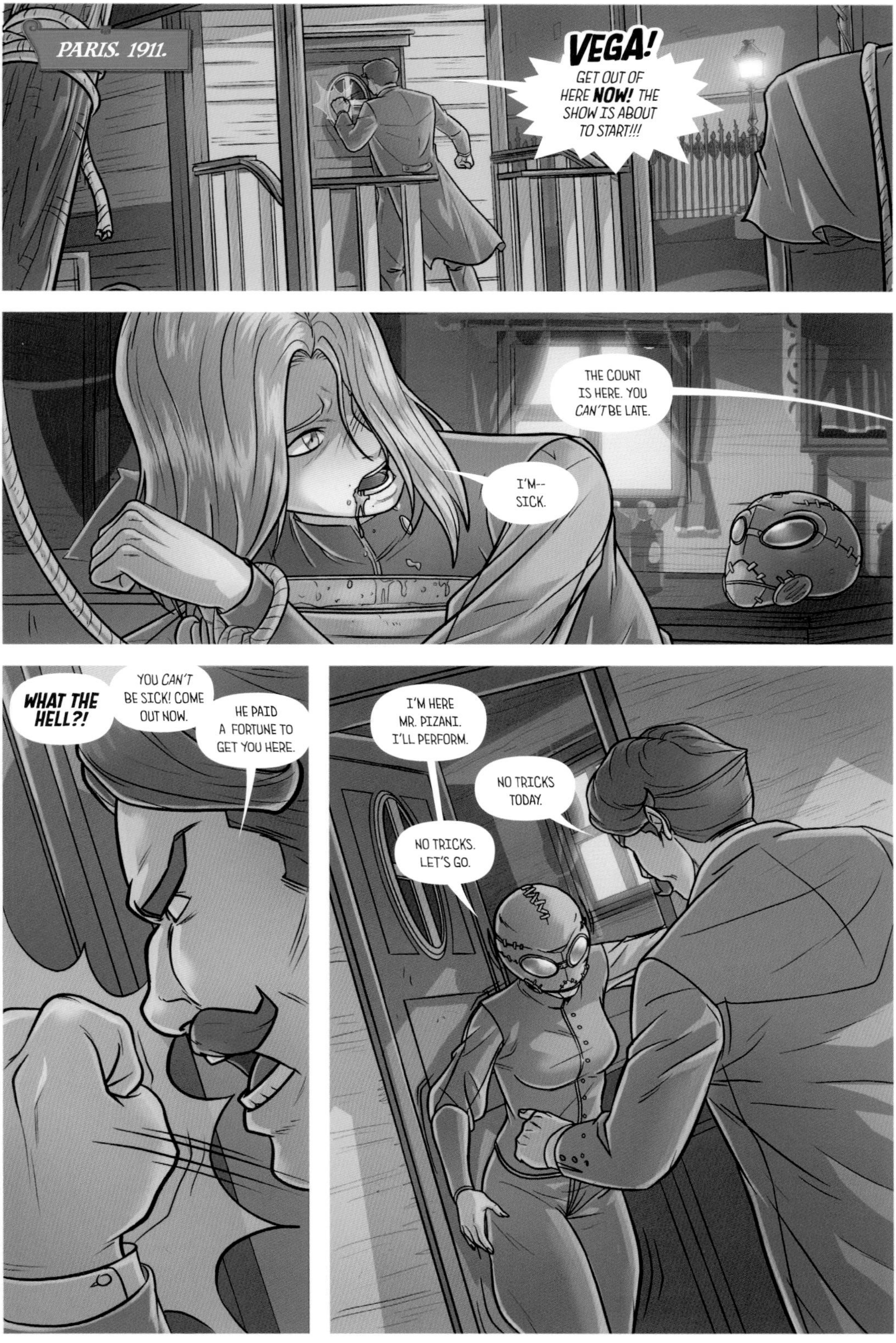
PARIS. 1911.
VEGA!
GET OUT OF HERE NOW! THE SHOW IS ABOUT TO START!!!
THE COUNT IS HERE. YOU CAN'T BE LATE.
I'M-- SICK.
WHAT THE HELL?!
YOU CAN'T BE SICK! COME OUT NOW.
HE PAID A FORTUNE TO GET YOU HERE.
I'M HERE MR. PIZANI. I'LL PERFORM.
NO TRICKS TODAY.
NO TRICKS. LET'S GO.

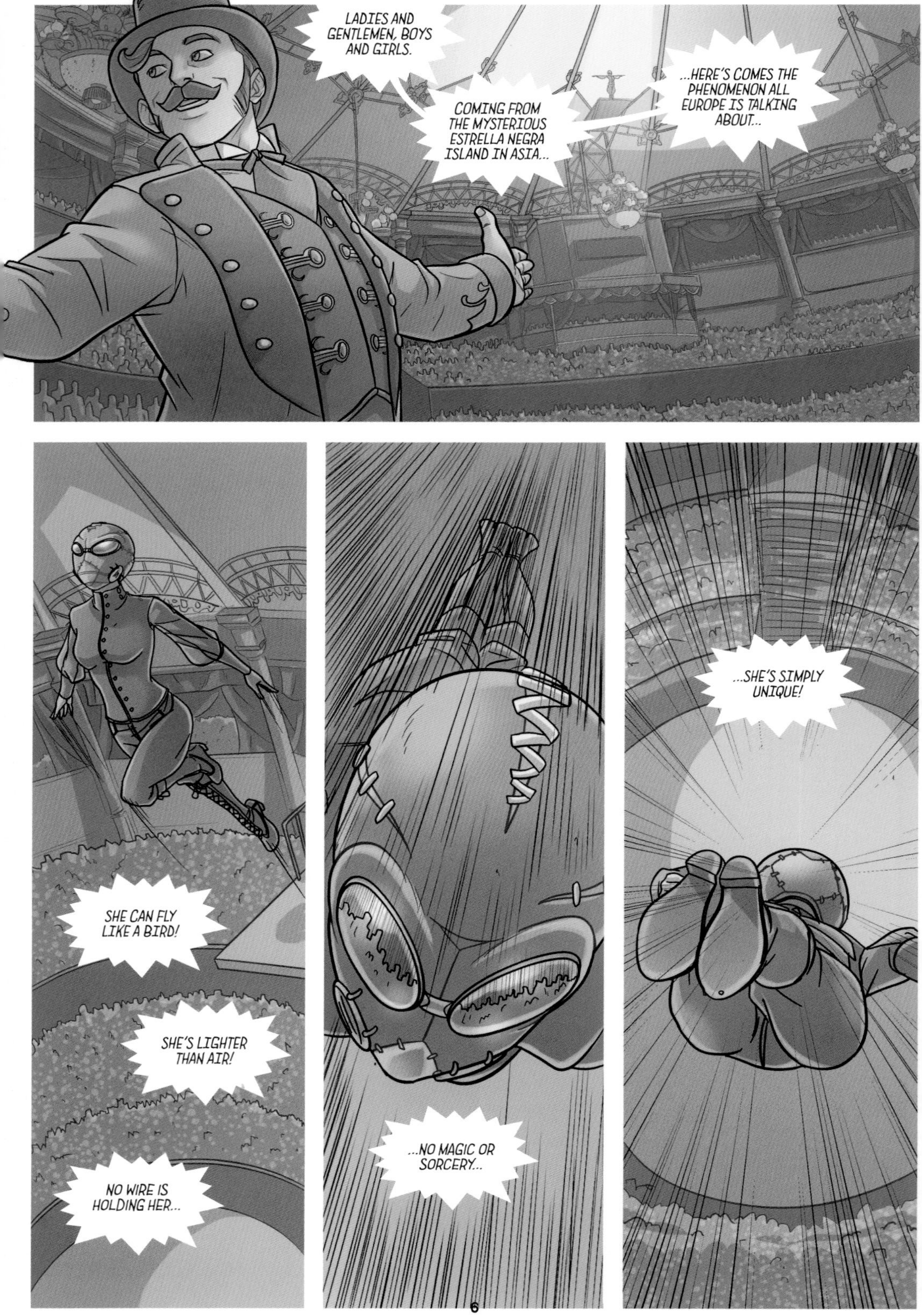
LADIES AND GENTLEMEN, BOYS AND GIRLS.
COMING FROM THE MYSTERIOUS ESTRELLA NEGRA ISLAND IN ASIA...
...HERE'S COMES THE PHENOMENON ALL EUROPE IS TALKING ABOUT...
SHE CAN FLY LIKE A BIRD!
SHE'S LIGHTER THAN AIR!
NO WIRE IS HOLDING HER...
...NO MAGIC OR SORCERY...
...SHE'S SIMPLY UNIQUE!

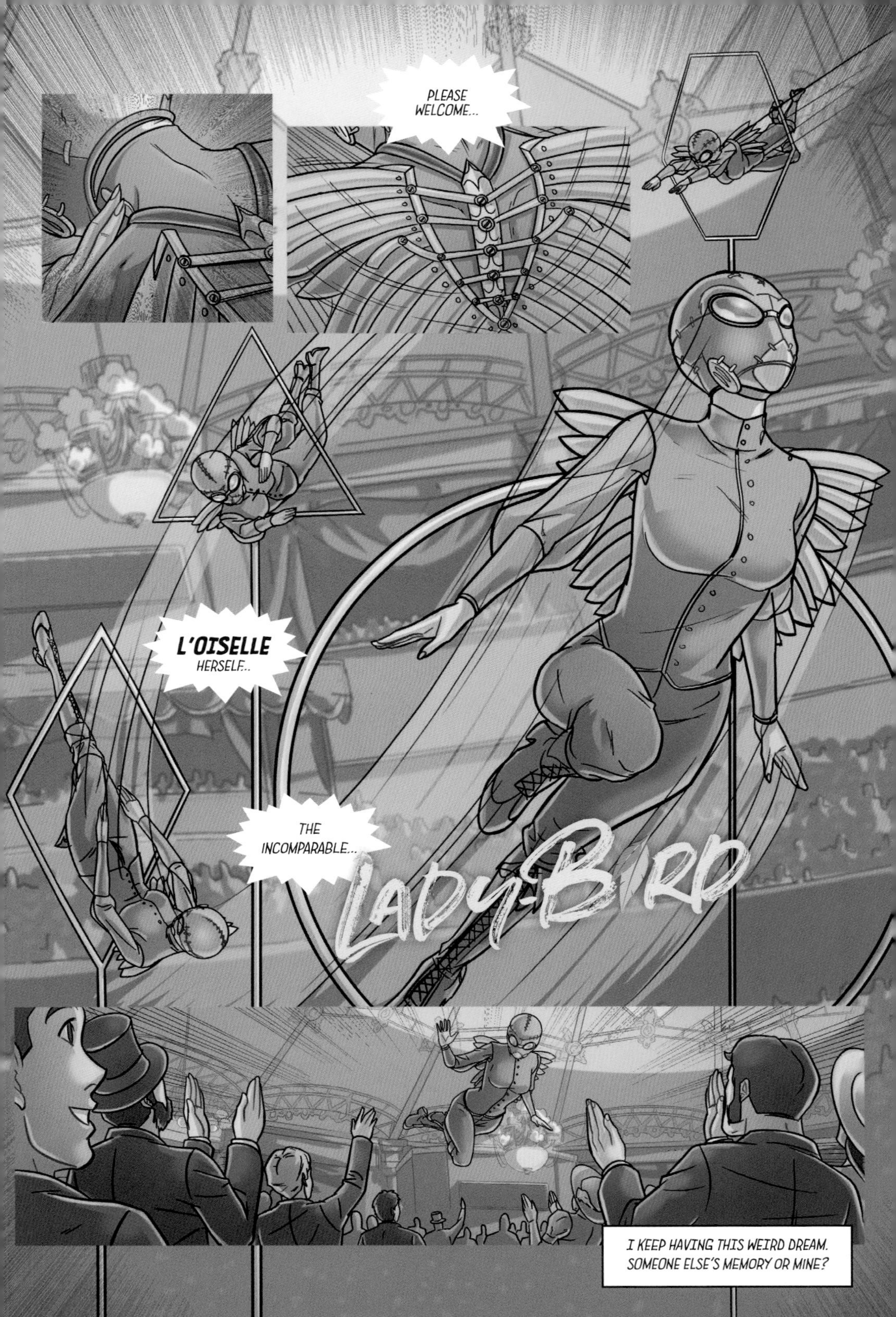
PLEASE WELCOME...
L'OISELLE HERSELF..
THE INCOMPARABLE...
LADY-BIRD
I KEEP HAVING THIS WEIRD DREAM. SOMEONE ELSE'S MEMORY OR MINE?

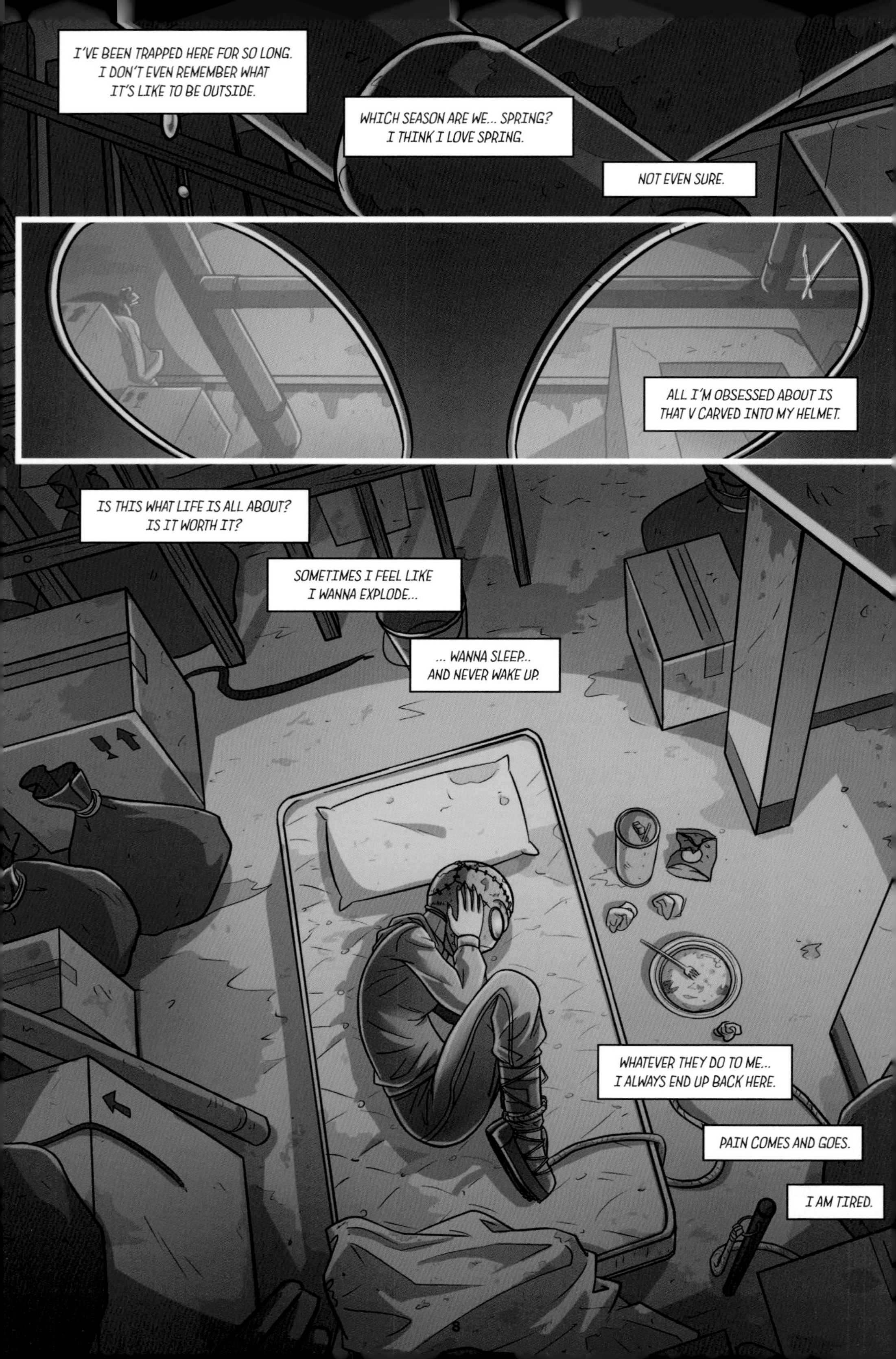
I'VE BEEN TRAPPED HERE FOR SO LONG. I DON'T EVEN REMEMBER WHAT IT'S LIKE TO BE OUTSIDE.
WHICH SEASON ARE WE... SPRING? I THINK I LOVE SPRING.
NOT EVEN SURE.
ALL I'M OBSESSED ABOUT IS THAT V CARVED INTO MY HELMET.
IS THIS WHAT LIFE IS ALL ABOUT? IS IT WORTH IT?
SOMETIMES I FEEL LIKE I WANNA EXPLODE...
... WANNA SLEEP.. AND NEVER WAKE UP.
WHATEVER THEY DO TO ME... I ALWAYS END UP BACK HERE.
PAIN COMES AND GOES.
I AM TIRED.

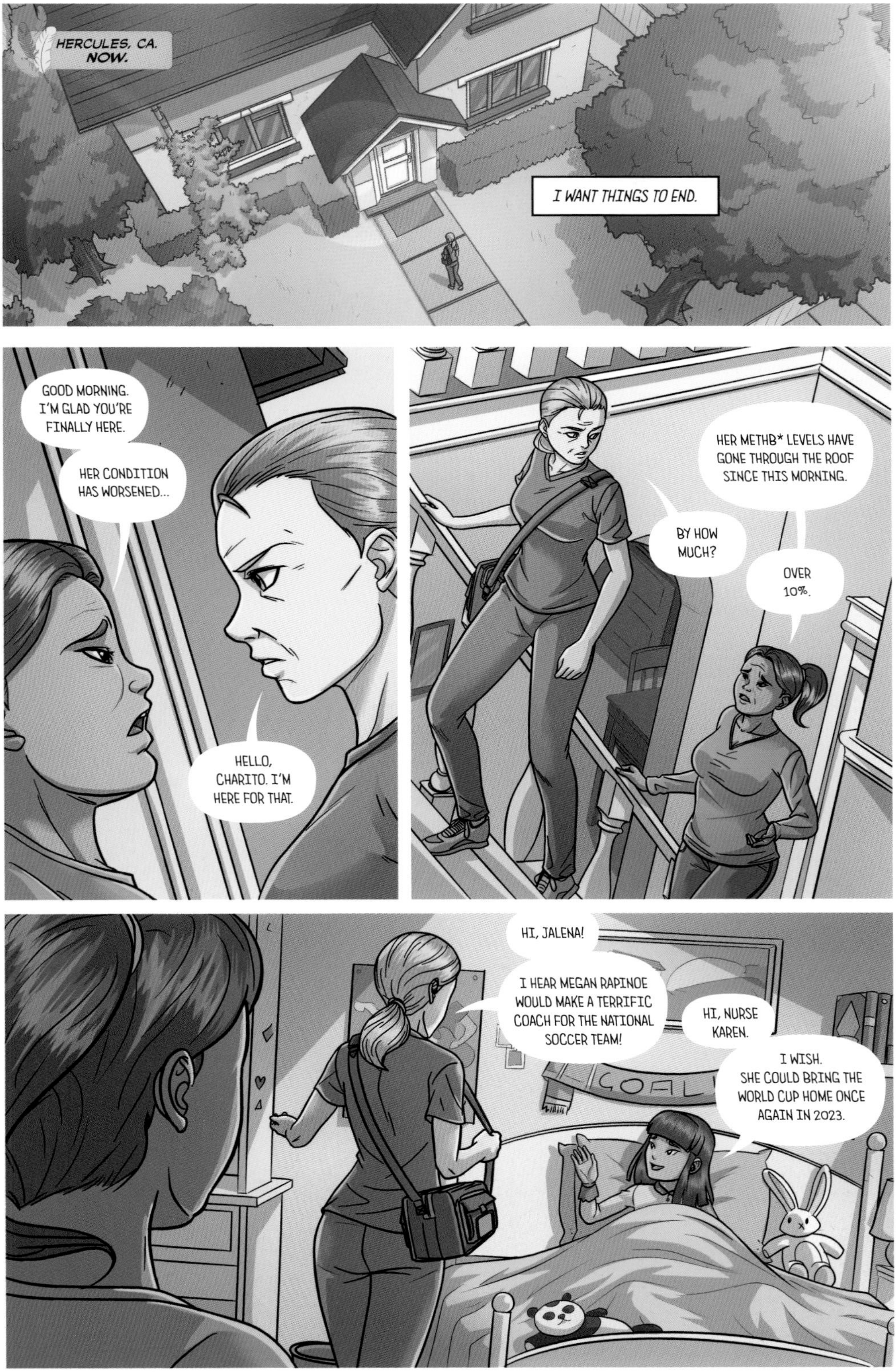
HERCULES, CA.
NOW.
I WANT THINGS TO END.
GOOD MORNING. I'M GLAD YOU'RE FINALLY HERE.
HER CONDITION HAS WORSENED...
HELLO, CHARITO. I'M HERE FOR THAT.
HER METHB* LEVELS HAVE GONE THROUGH THE ROOF SINCE THIS MORNING.
BY HOW MUCH?
OVER 10%.
HI, JALENA!
I HEAR MEGAN RAPINOE WOULD MAKE A TERRIFIC COACH FOR THE NATIONAL SOCCER TEAM!
HI, NURSE KAREN.
I WISH. SHE COULD BRING THE WORLD CUP HOME ONCE AGAIN IN 2023.
GOAL

* METHEMOGLOBIMINEMIA: IT'S A BLOOD DISORDER IN WHICH TOO LITTLE OXYGEN IS DELIVERED TO CELLS.

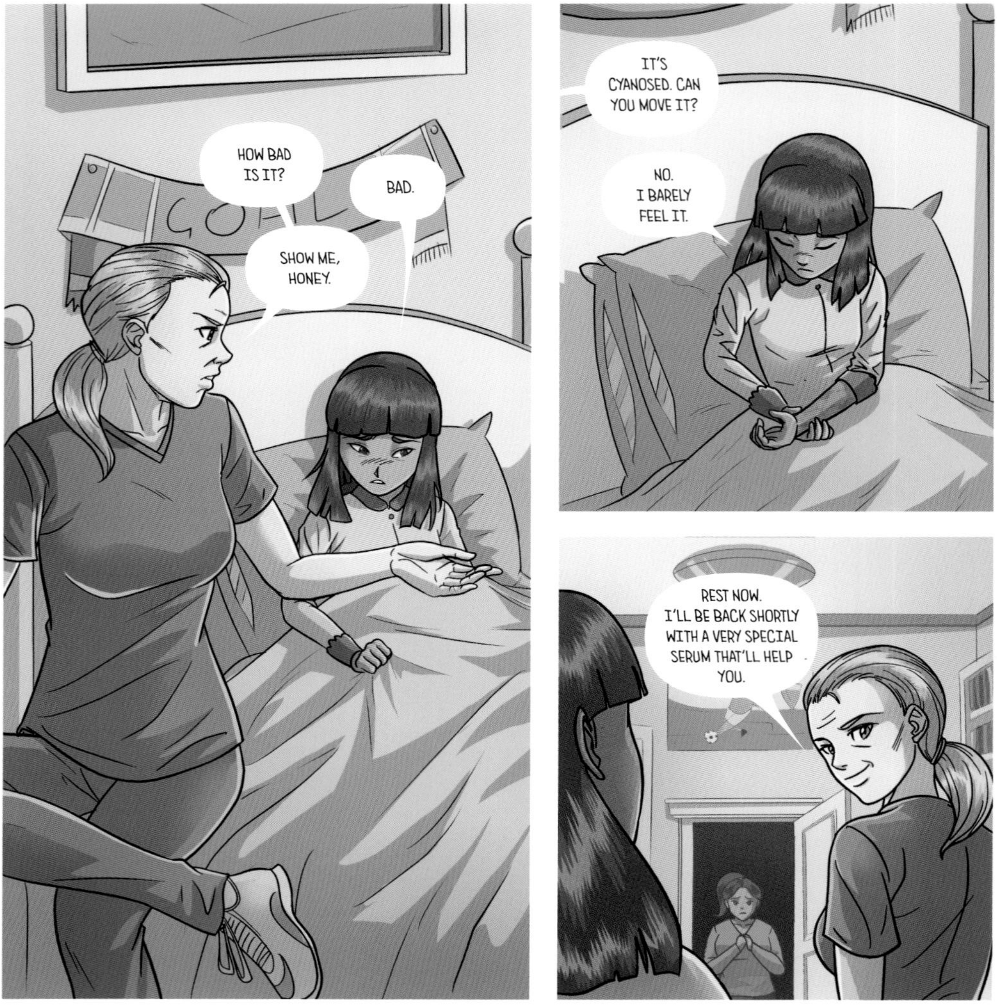
HOW BAD IS IT?
BAD.
SHOW ME, HONEY.
IT'S CYANOSED. CAN YOU MOVE IT?
NO. I BARELY FEEL IT.
REST NOW. I'LL BE BACK SHORTLY WITH A VERY SPECIAL SERUM THAT'LL HELP YOU.
FOLLOW ME.

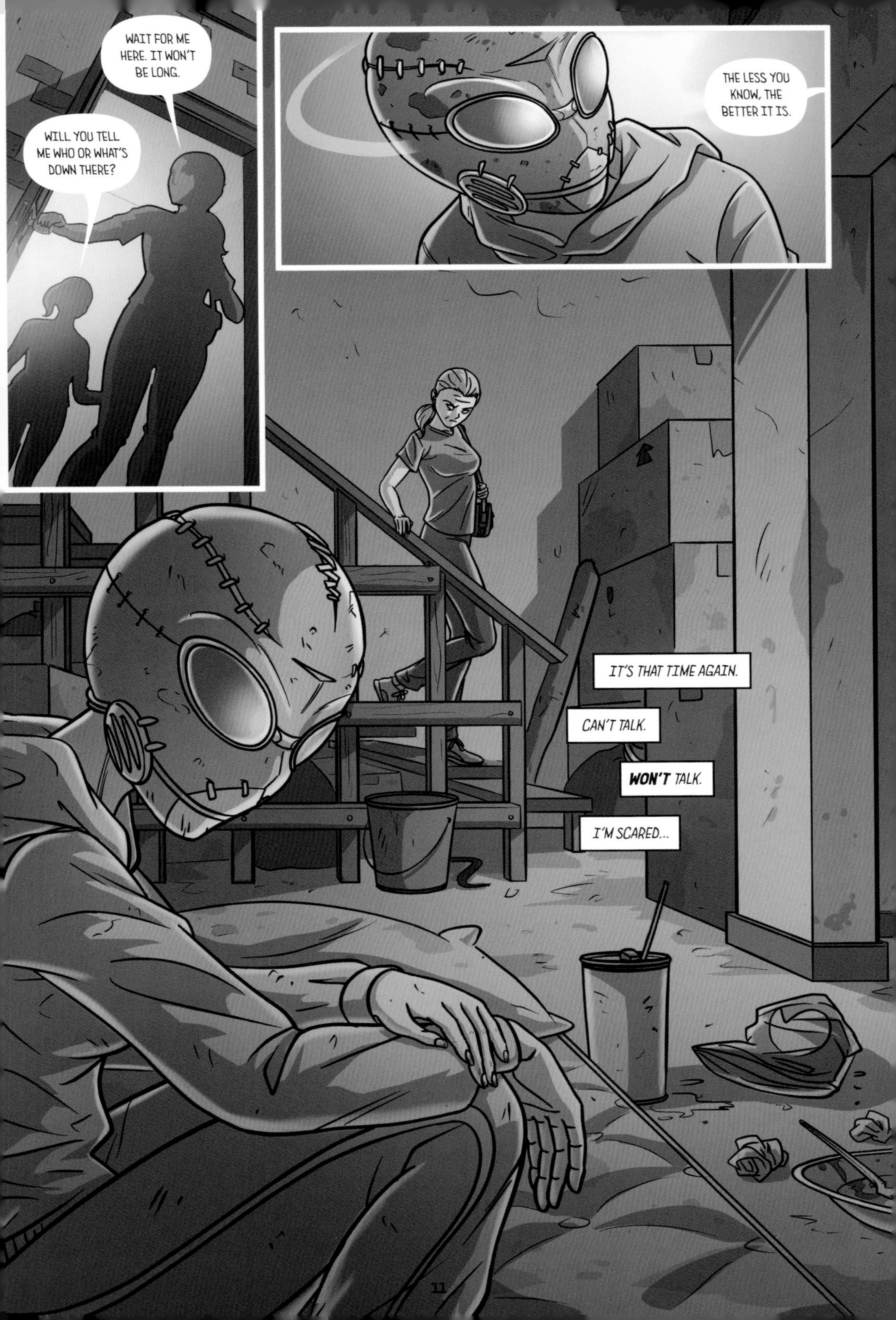
WAIT FOR ME HERE. IT WON'T BE LONG.
WILL YOU TELL ME WHO OR WHAT'S DOWN THERE?
THE LESS YOU KNOW, THE BETTER IT IS.
IT'S THAT TIME AGAIN.
CAN'T TALK.
WON'T TALK.
I'M SCARED...

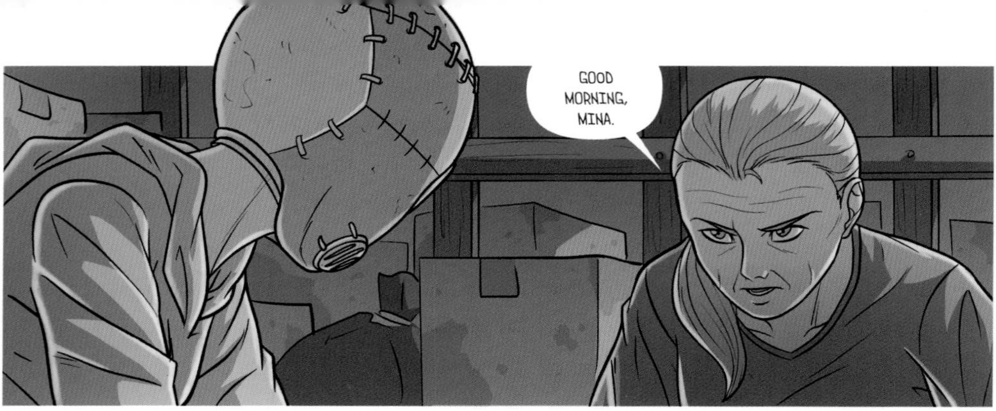
GOOD MORNING, MINA.

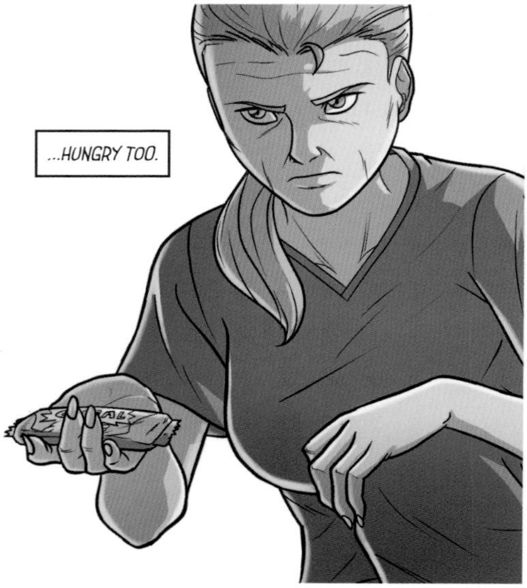
...HUNGRY TOO.

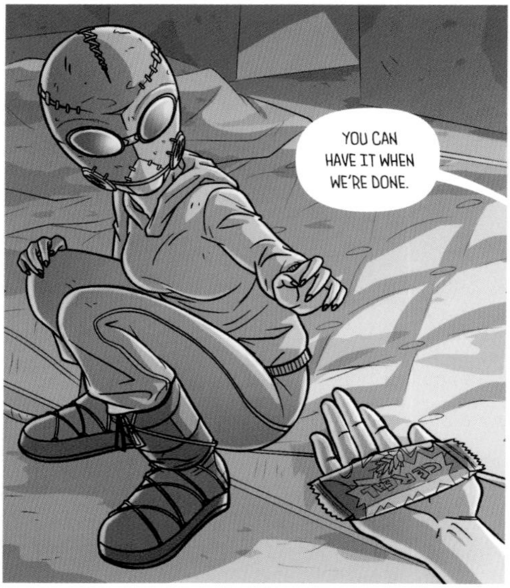
YOU CAN HAVE IT WHEN WE'RE DONE.

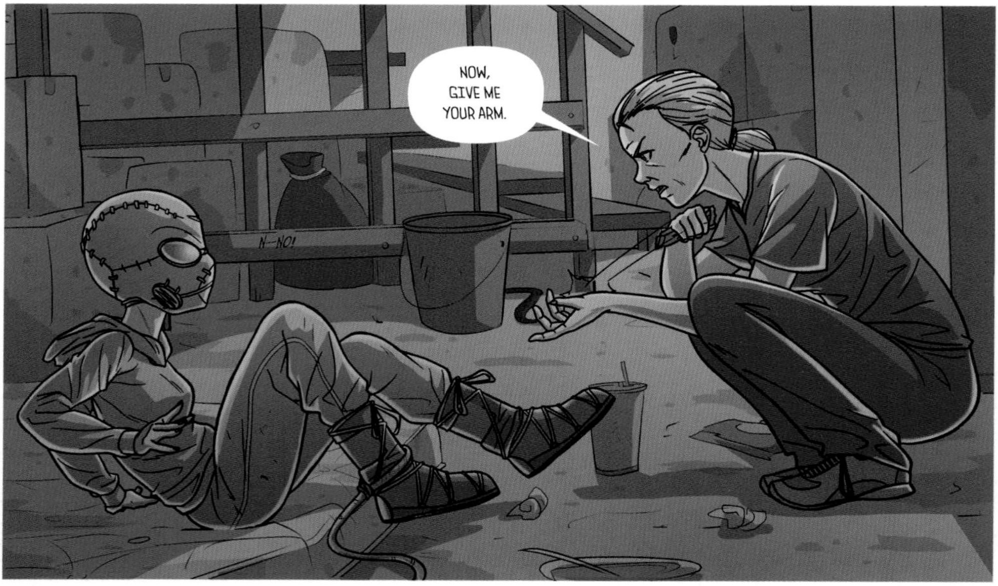
NOW, GIVE ME YOUR ARM.
N—NO!

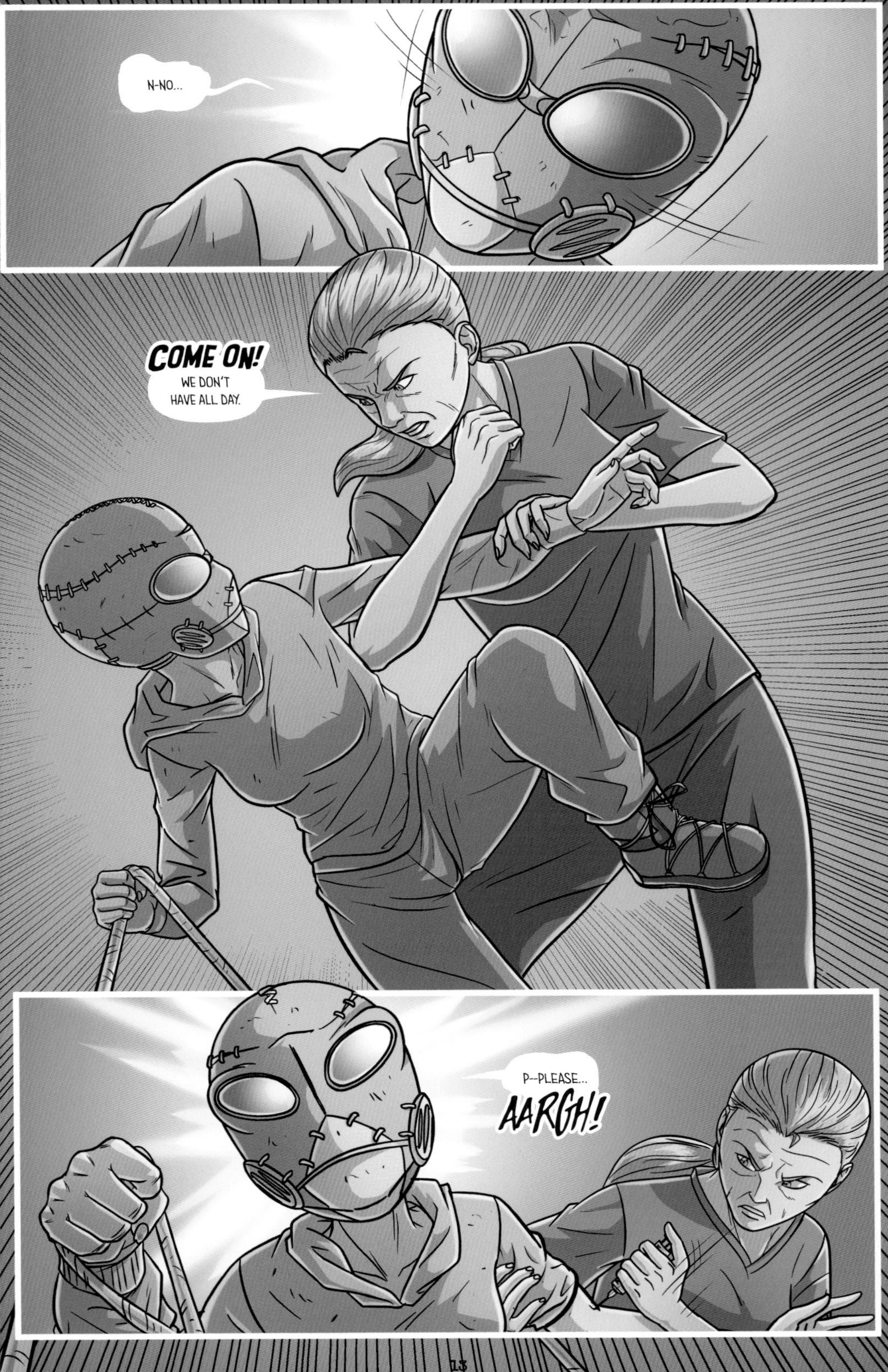
N-NO...
COME ON! WE DON'T HAVE ALL DAY.
P--PLEASE... AARGH!

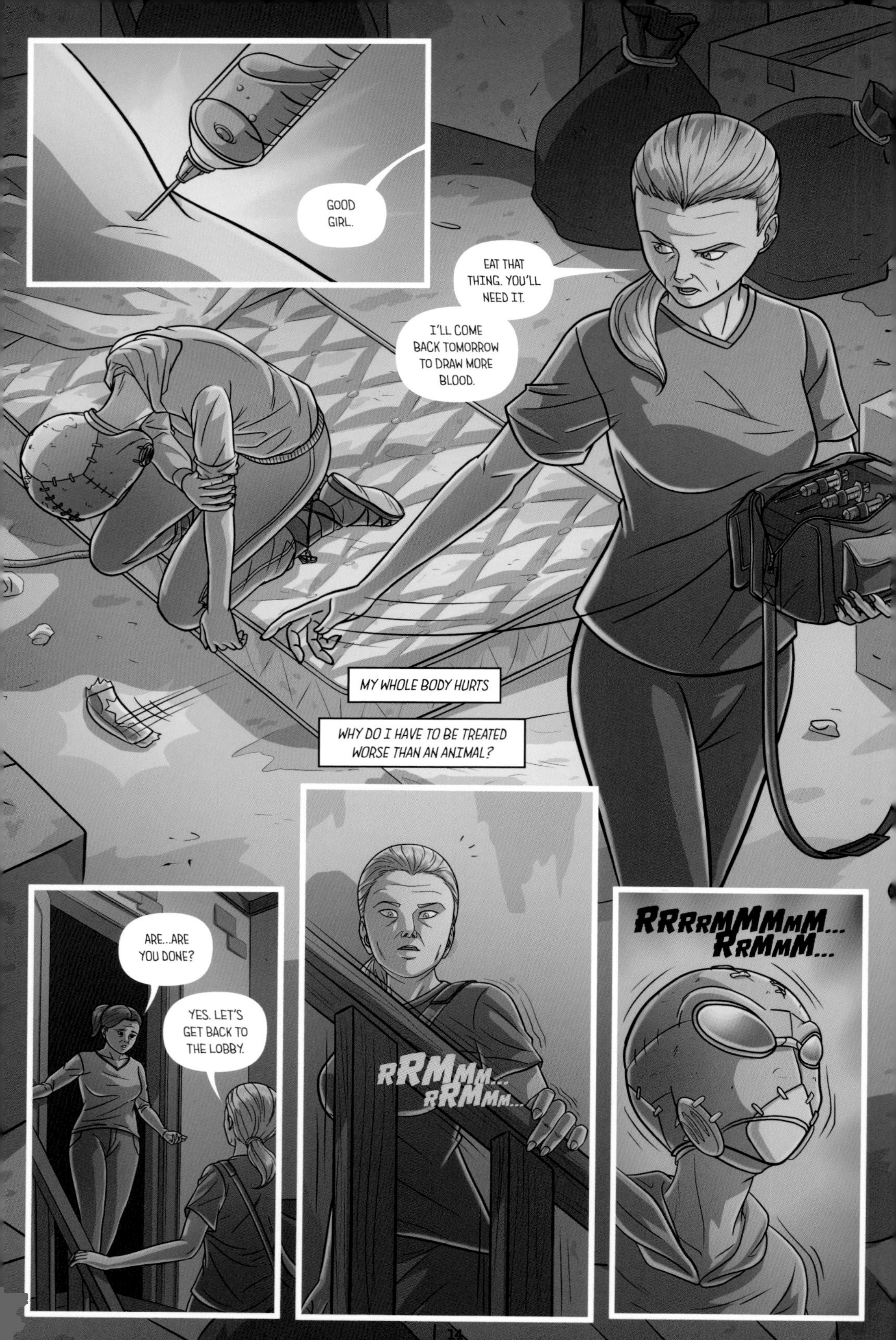

GOOD GIRL.
EAT THAT THING. YOU'LL NEED IT.
I'LL COME BACK TOMORROW TO DRAW MORE BLOOD.
MY WHOLE BODY HURTS
WHY DO I HAVE TO BE TREATED WORSE THAN AN ANIMAL?
ARE...ARE YOU DONE?
YES. LET'S GET BACK TO THE LOBBY.
RRMMM... RRMMM...
RRRRMMMMM... RRMMM...

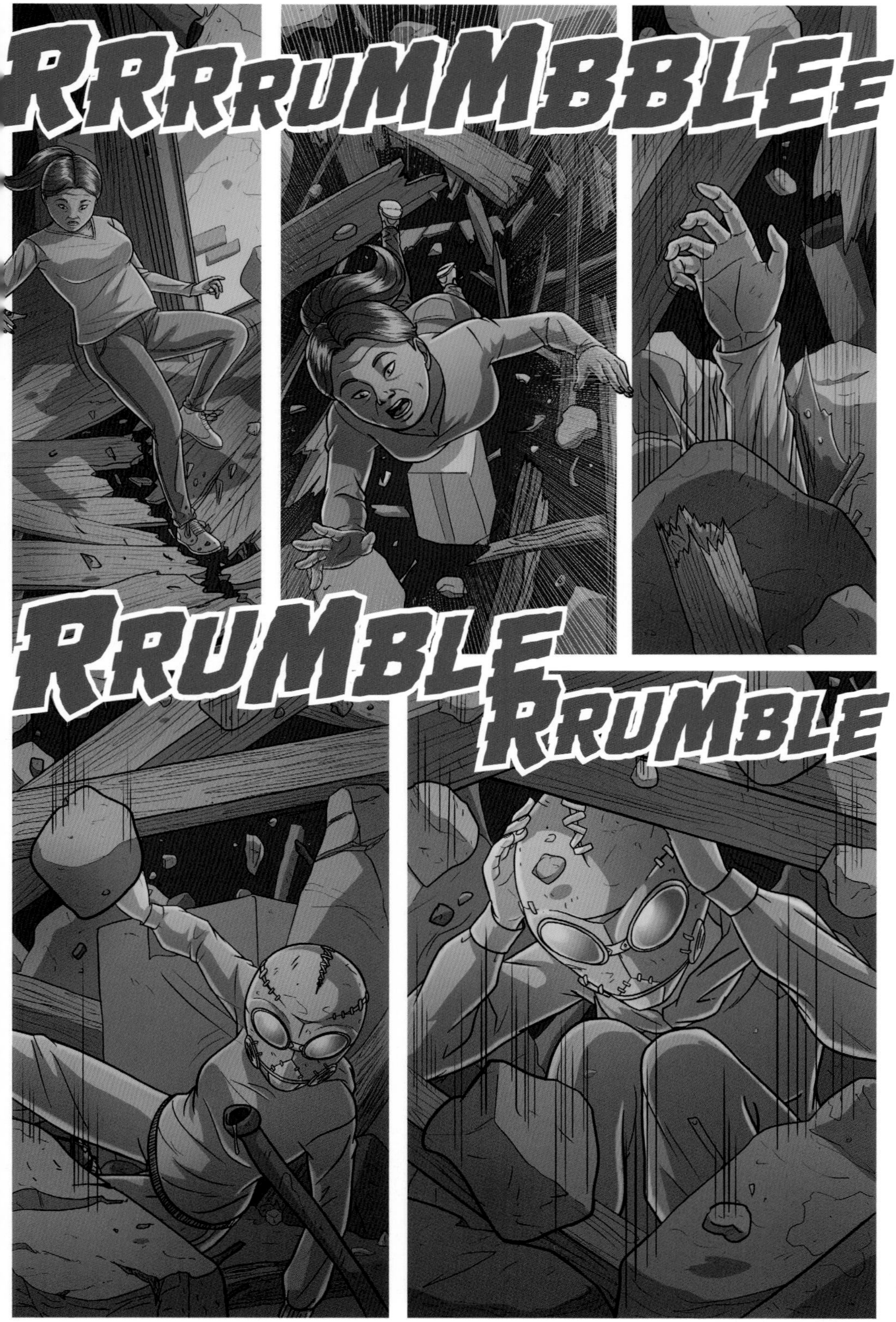
RRRRUMMMBBLEE
RRUMBLE
RRUMBLE

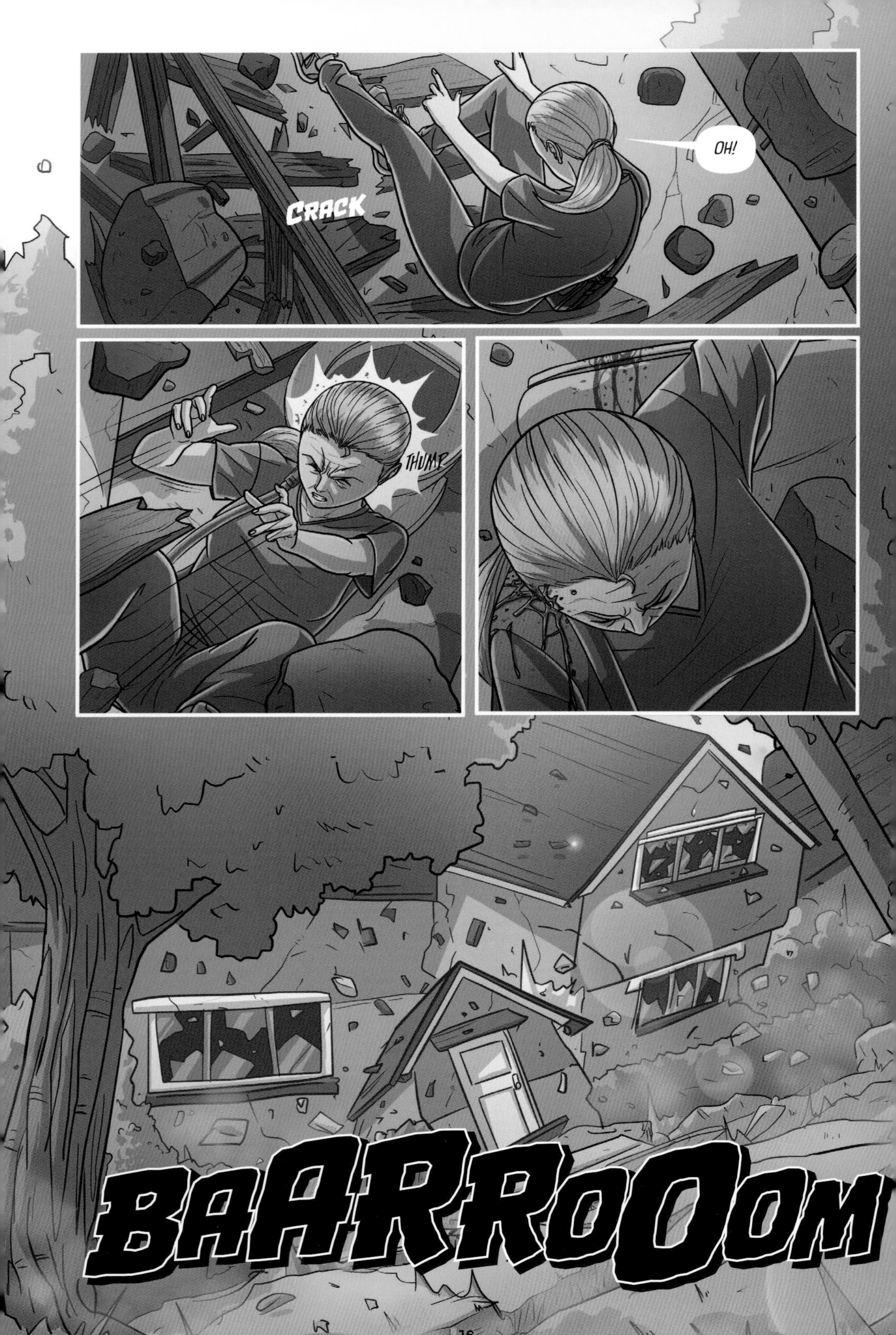
OH!
CRACK
THUMP
BAARROOOM

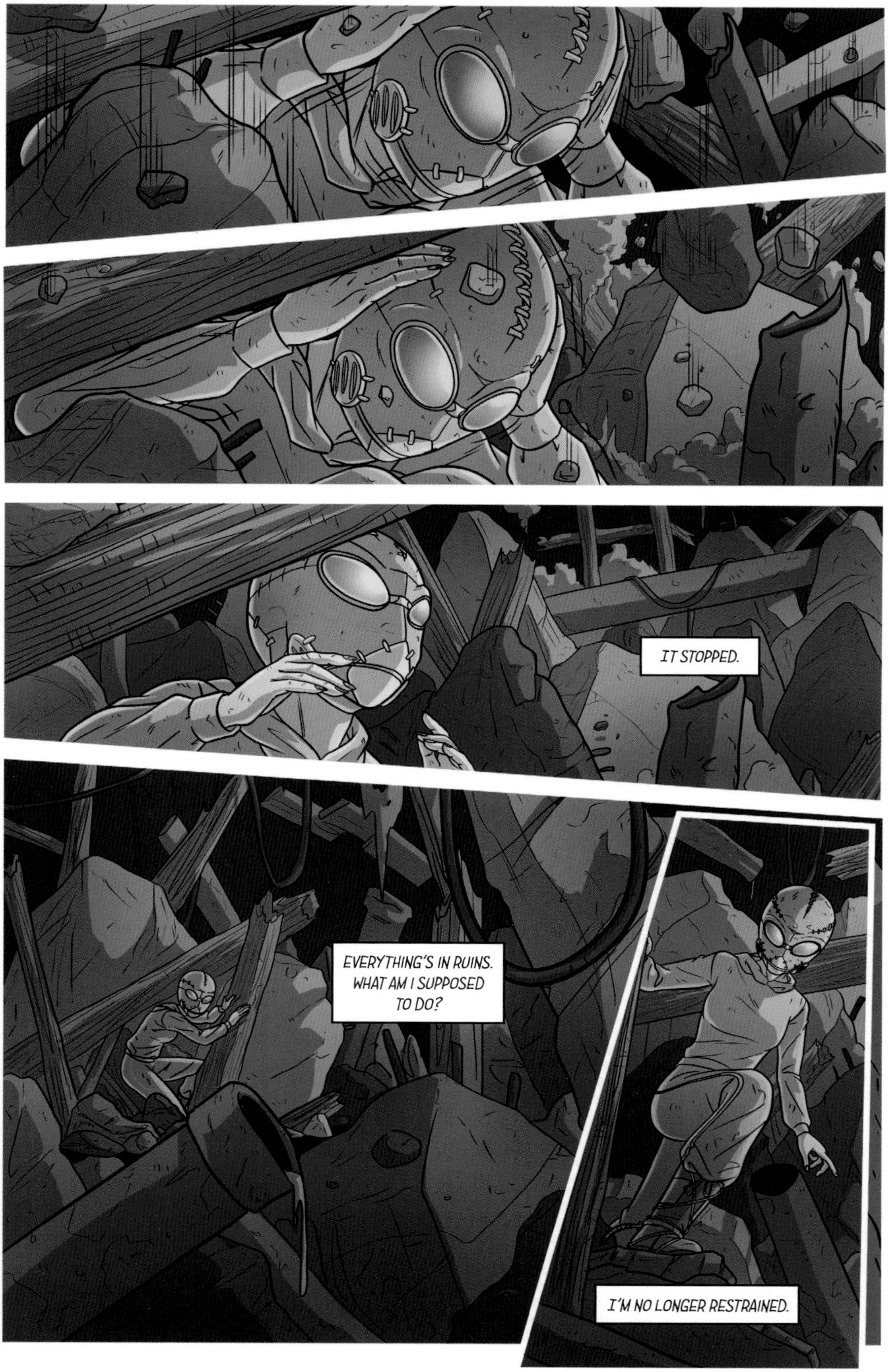
IT STOPPED.
EVERYTHING'S IN RUINS. WHAT AM I SUPPOSED TO DO?
I'M NO LONGER RESTRAINED.

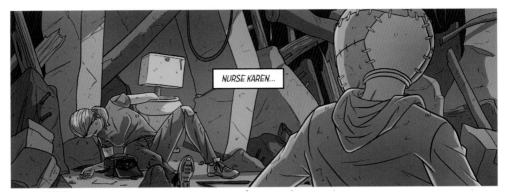

NURSE KAREN...

SHE'LL LIVE.

I'M TAKING MY BLOOD BACK.

IT'S NOT FAIR. EVIL NURSE GETS TO LIVE...

...WHILE THIS INNOCENT MOTHER DOESN'T.

THERE'S NOTHING I CAN DO. I NEED TO GET OUT.

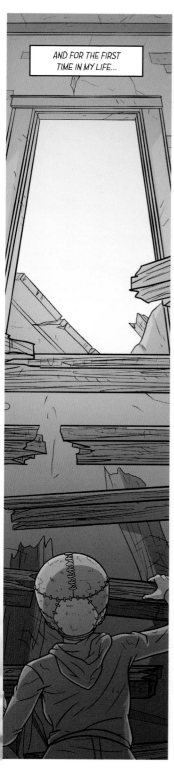

AND FOR THE FIRST
TIME IN MY LIFE...

...FOLLOW MY INSTINCTS.
AND RUN. FAR FROM HERE.

WHEREVER I MAY GO, IT CAN'T
BE WORSE THAN THIS PLACE...

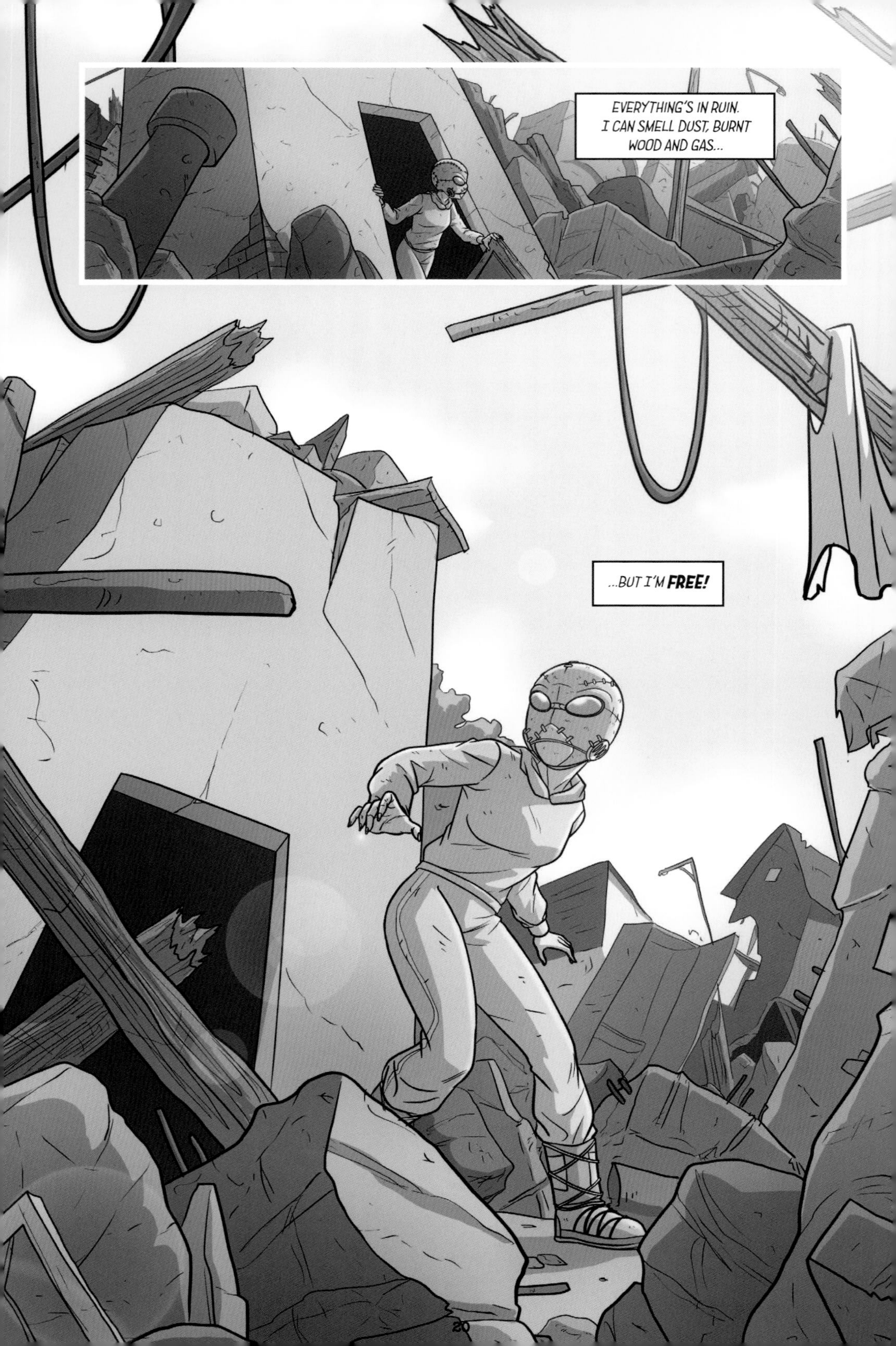
EVERYTHING'S IN RUIN. I CAN SMELL DUST, BURNT WOOD AND GAS...
...BUT I'M **FREE!**

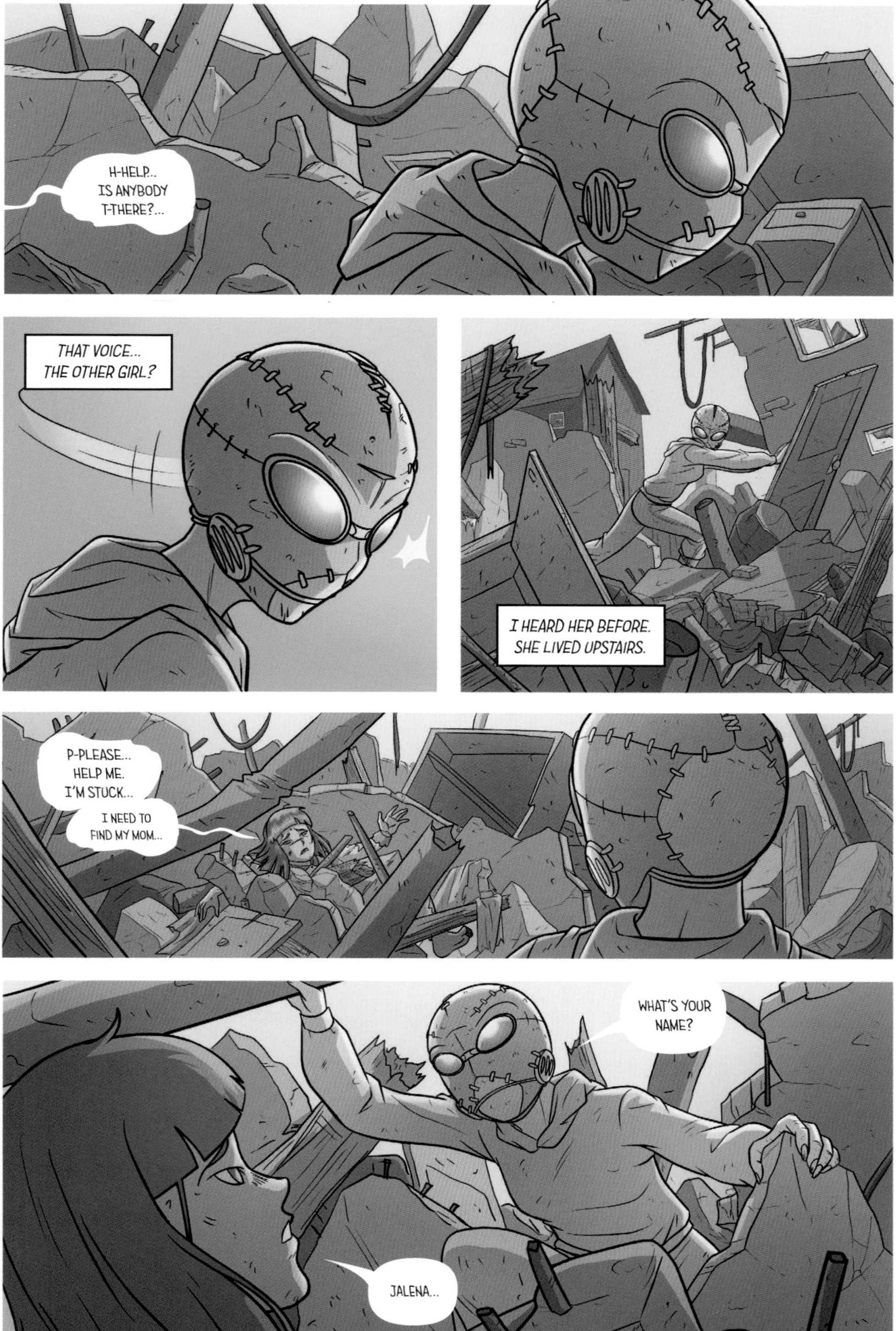
H-HELP... IS ANYBODY T-THERE?...
THAT VOICE... THE OTHER GIRL?
I HEARD HER BEFORE. SHE LIVED UPSTAIRS.
P-PLEASE... HELP ME. I'M STUCK...
I NEED TO FIND MY MOM...
WHAT'S YOUR NAME?
JALENA...

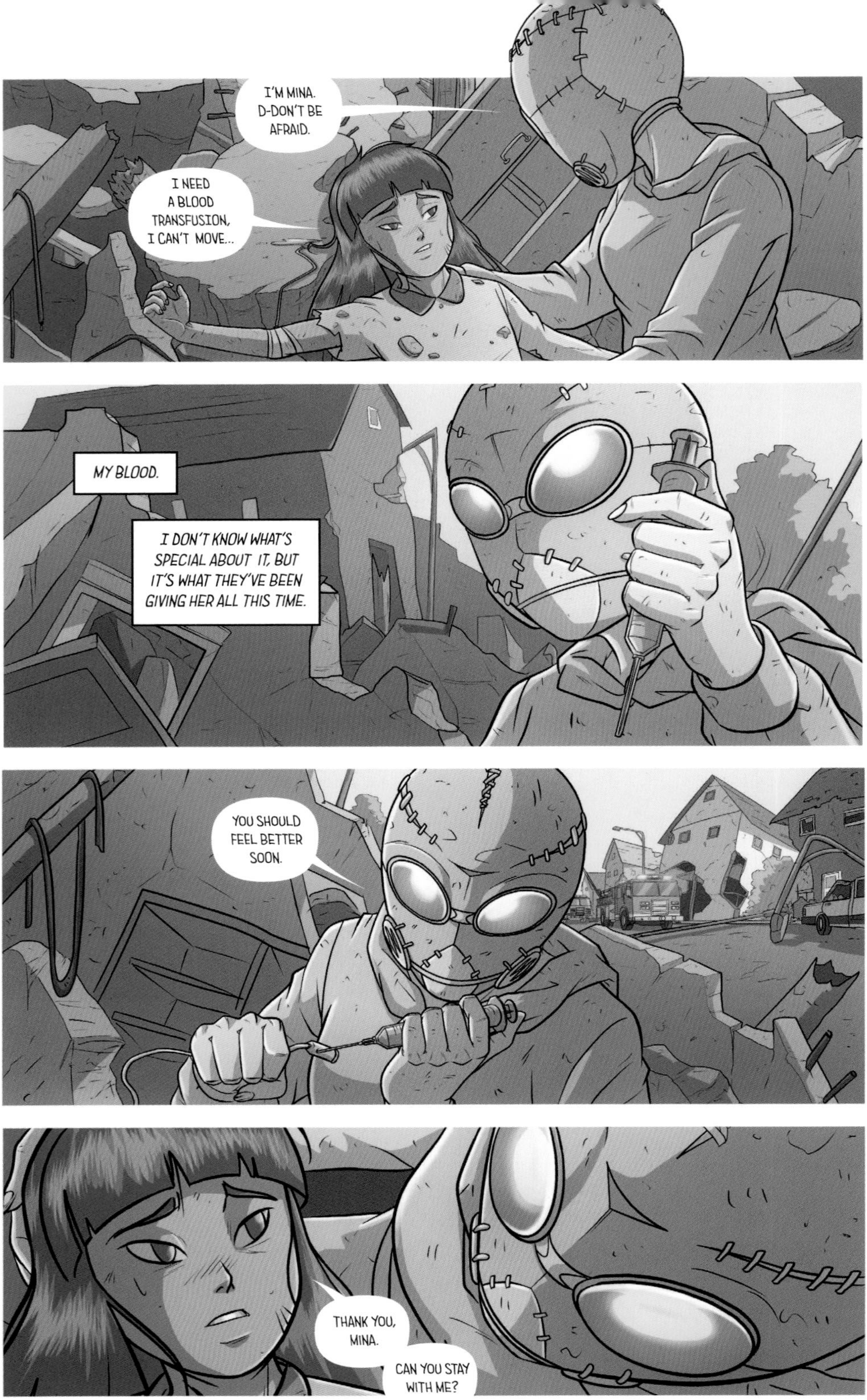
I'M MINA. D-DON'T BE AFRAID.
I NEED A BLOOD TRANSFUSION, I CAN'T MOVE...
MY BLOOD.
I DON'T KNOW WHAT'S SPECIAL ABOUT IT, BUT IT'S WHAT THEY'VE BEEN GIVING HER ALL THIS TIME.
YOU SHOULD FEEL BETTER SOON.
THANK YOU, MINA.
CAN YOU STAY WITH ME?

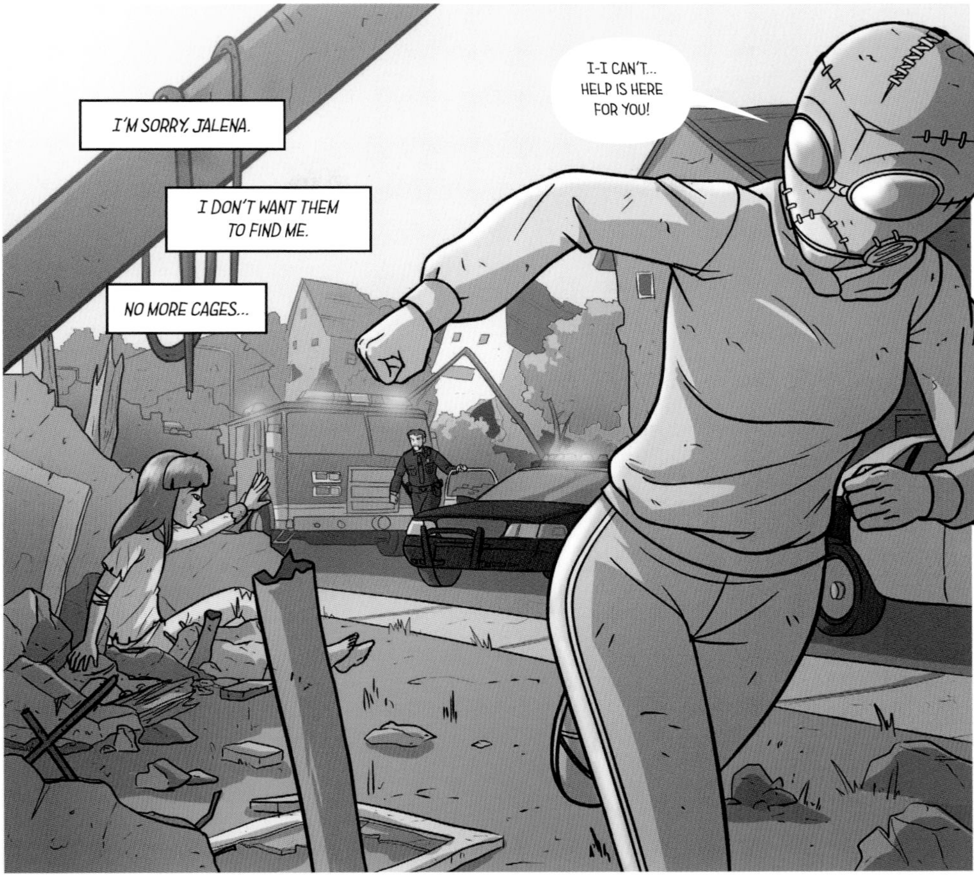
I'M SORRY, JALENA.
I DON'T WANT THEM TO FIND ME.
NO MORE CAGES...
I-I CAN'T... HELP IS HERE FOR YOU!

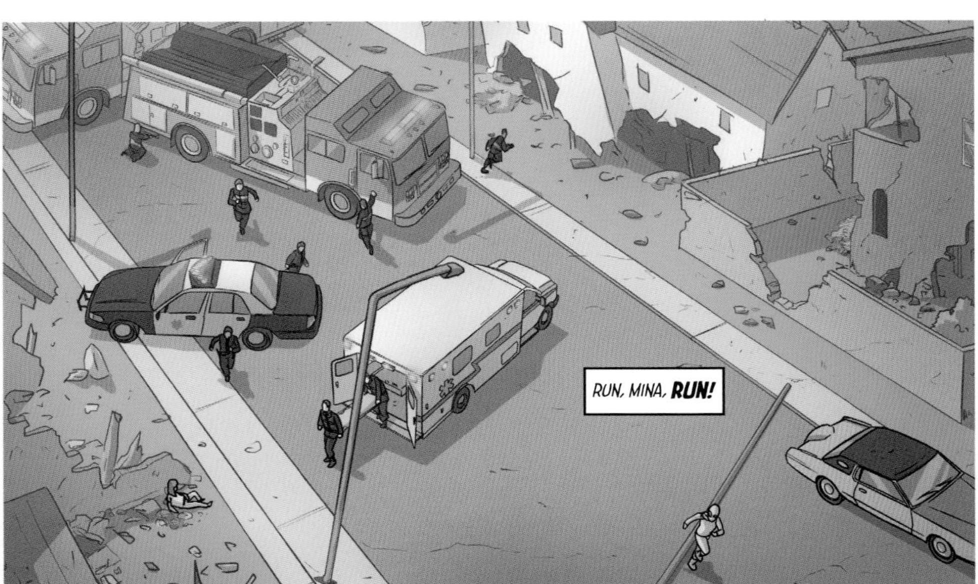
RUN, MINA, **RUN!**

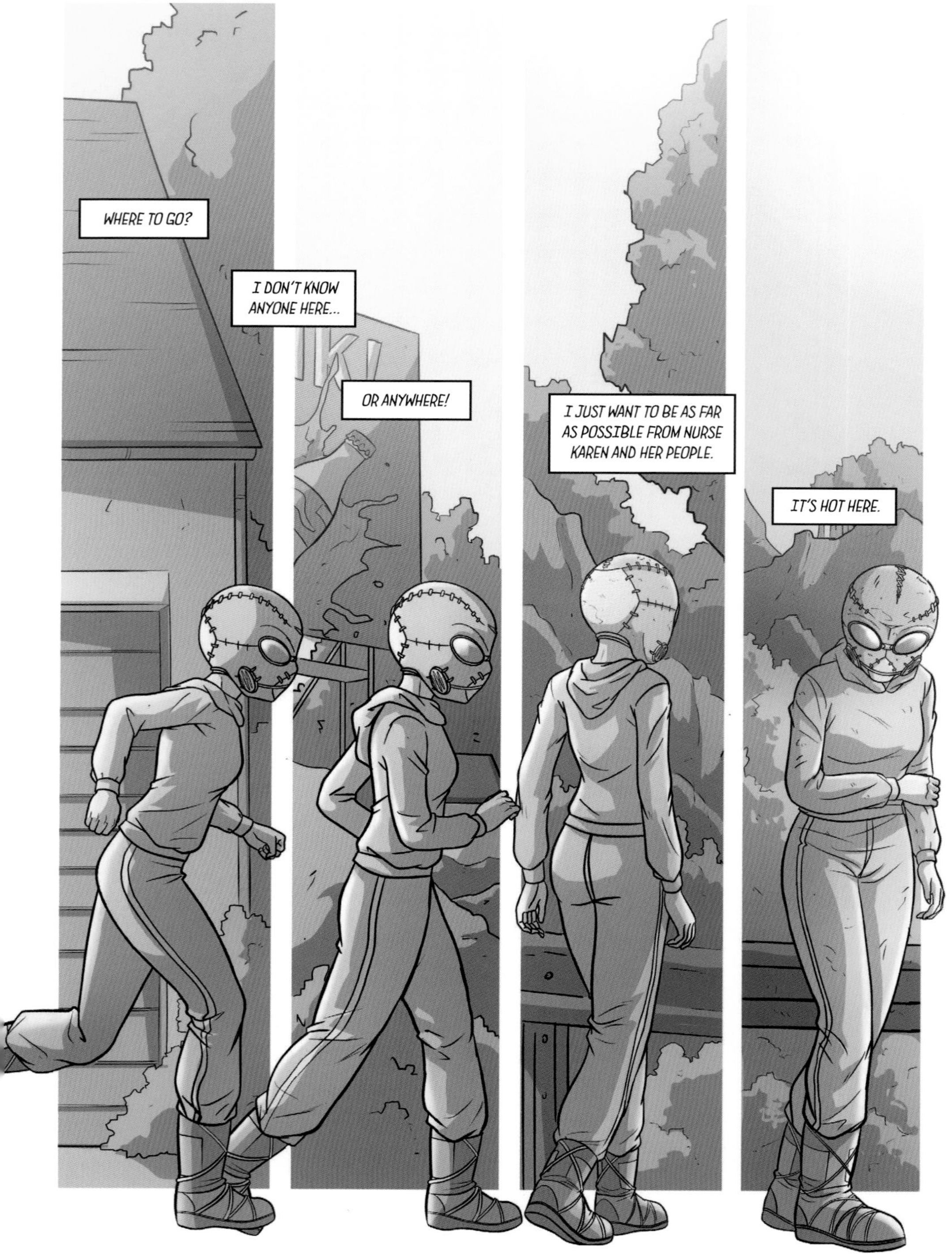
WHERE TO GO?
I DON'T KNOW ANYONE HERE...
OR ANYWHERE!
I JUST WANT TO BE AS FAR AS POSSIBLE FROM NURSE KAREN AND HER PEOPLE.
IT'S HOT HERE.

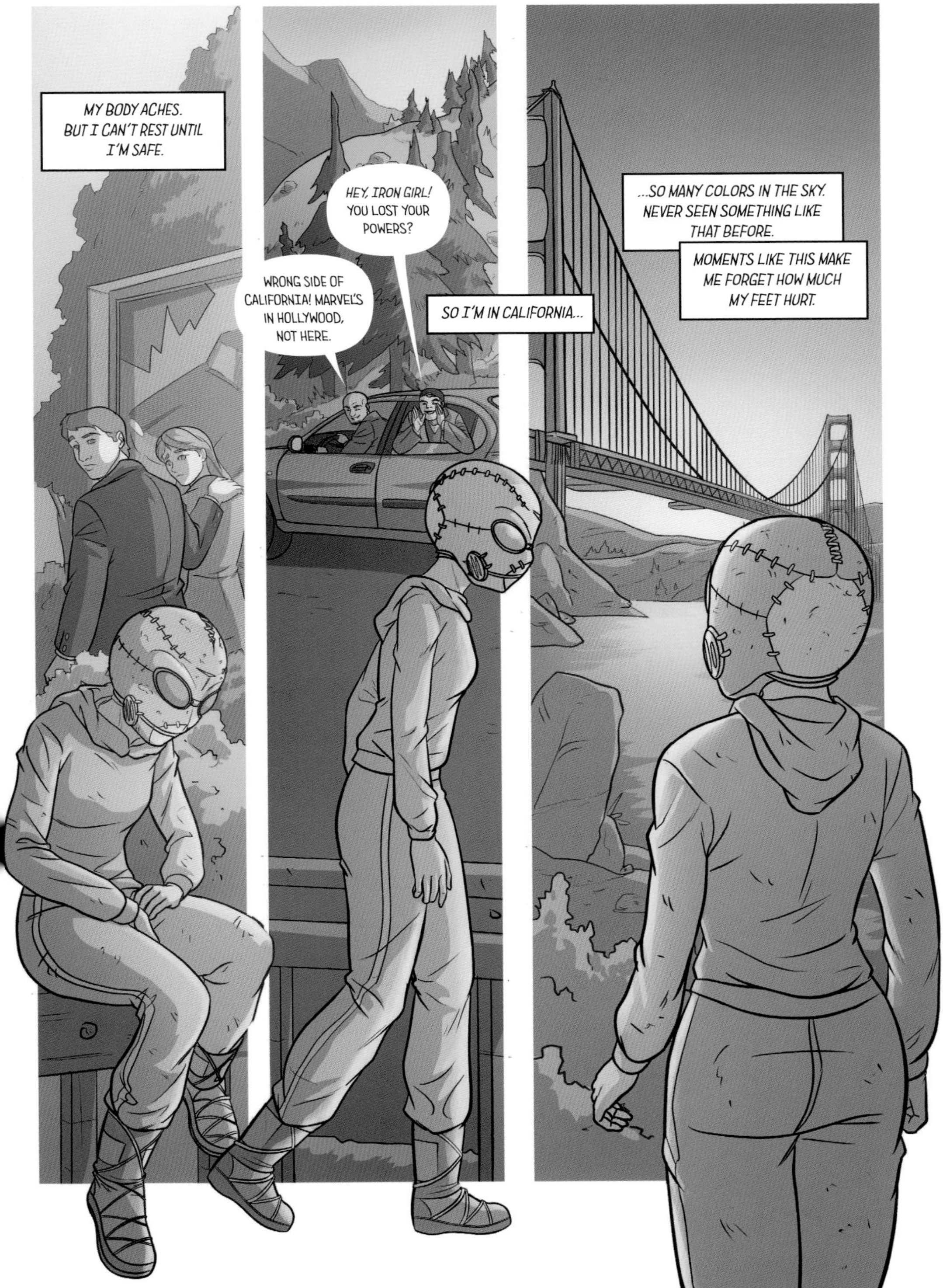
MY BODY ACHES. BUT I CAN'T REST UNTIL I'M SAFE.
HEY, IRON GIRL! YOU LOST YOUR POWERS?
WRONG SIDE OF CALIFORNIA! MARVEL'S IN HOLLYWOOD, NOT HERE.
SO I'M IN CALIFORNIA...
...SO MANY COLORS IN THE SKY. NEVER SEEN SOMETHING LIKE THAT BEFORE.
MOMENTS LIKE THIS MAKE ME FORGET HOW MUCH MY FEET HURT.

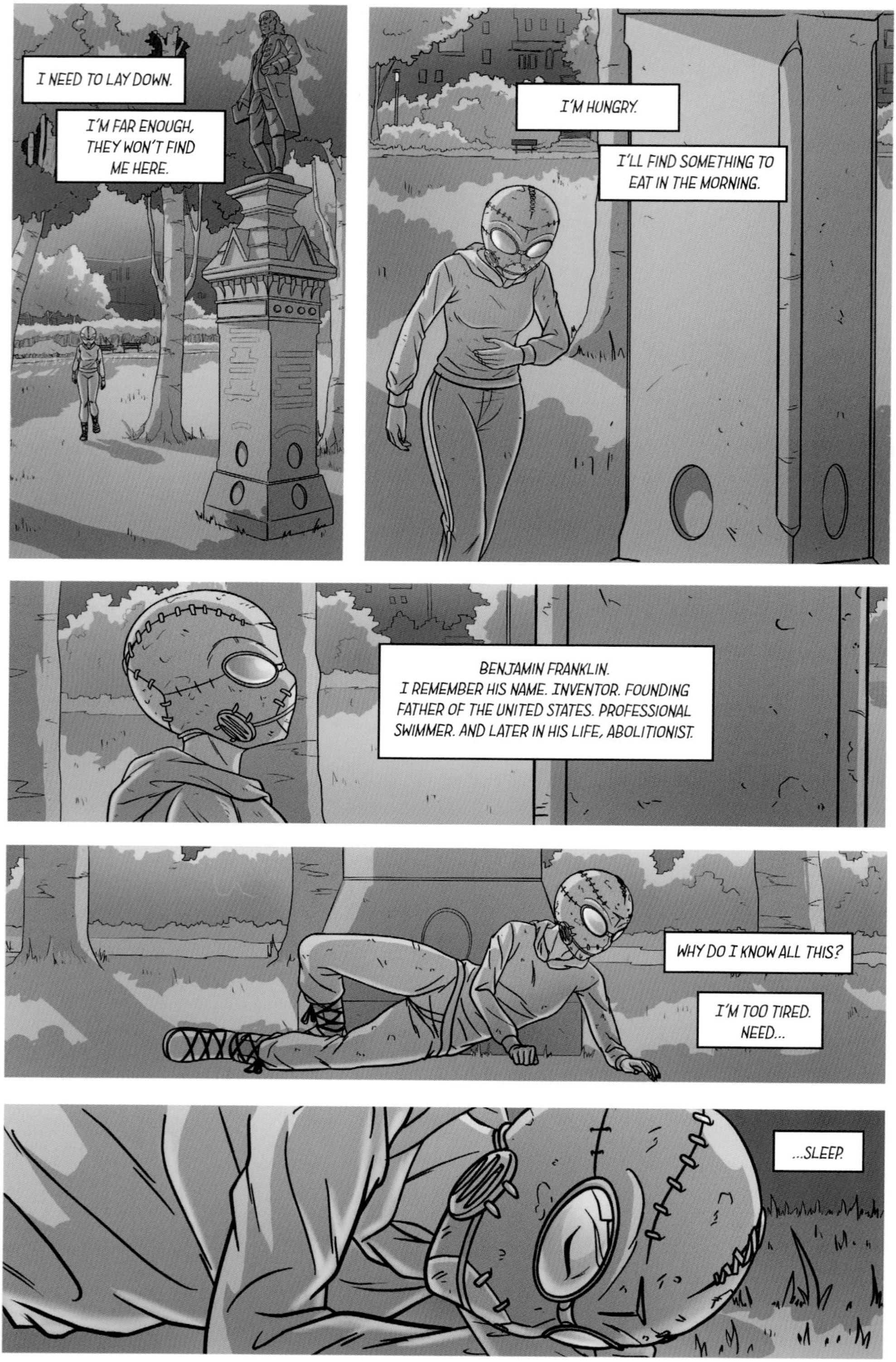
I NEED TO LAY DOWN.
I'M FAR ENOUGH, THEY WON'T FIND ME HERE.
I'M HUNGRY.
I'LL FIND SOMETHING TO EAT IN THE MORNING.
BENJAMIN FRANKLIN. I REMEMBER HIS NAME. INVENTOR. FOUNDING FATHER OF THE UNITED STATES. PROFESSIONAL SWIMMER. AND LATER IN HIS LIFE, ABOLITIONIST.
WHY DO I KNOW ALL THIS?
I'M TOO TIRED. NEED...
...SLEEP.

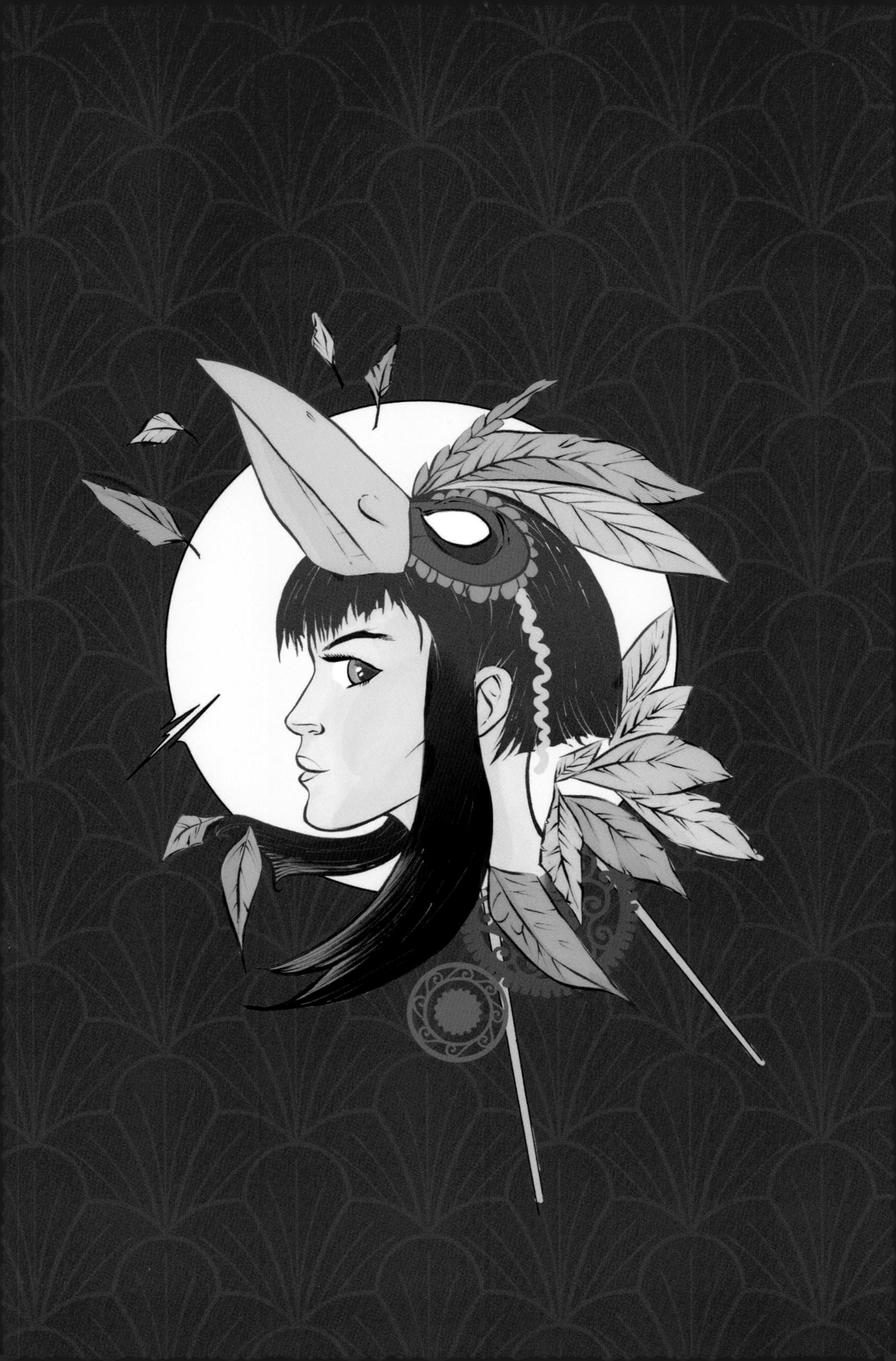

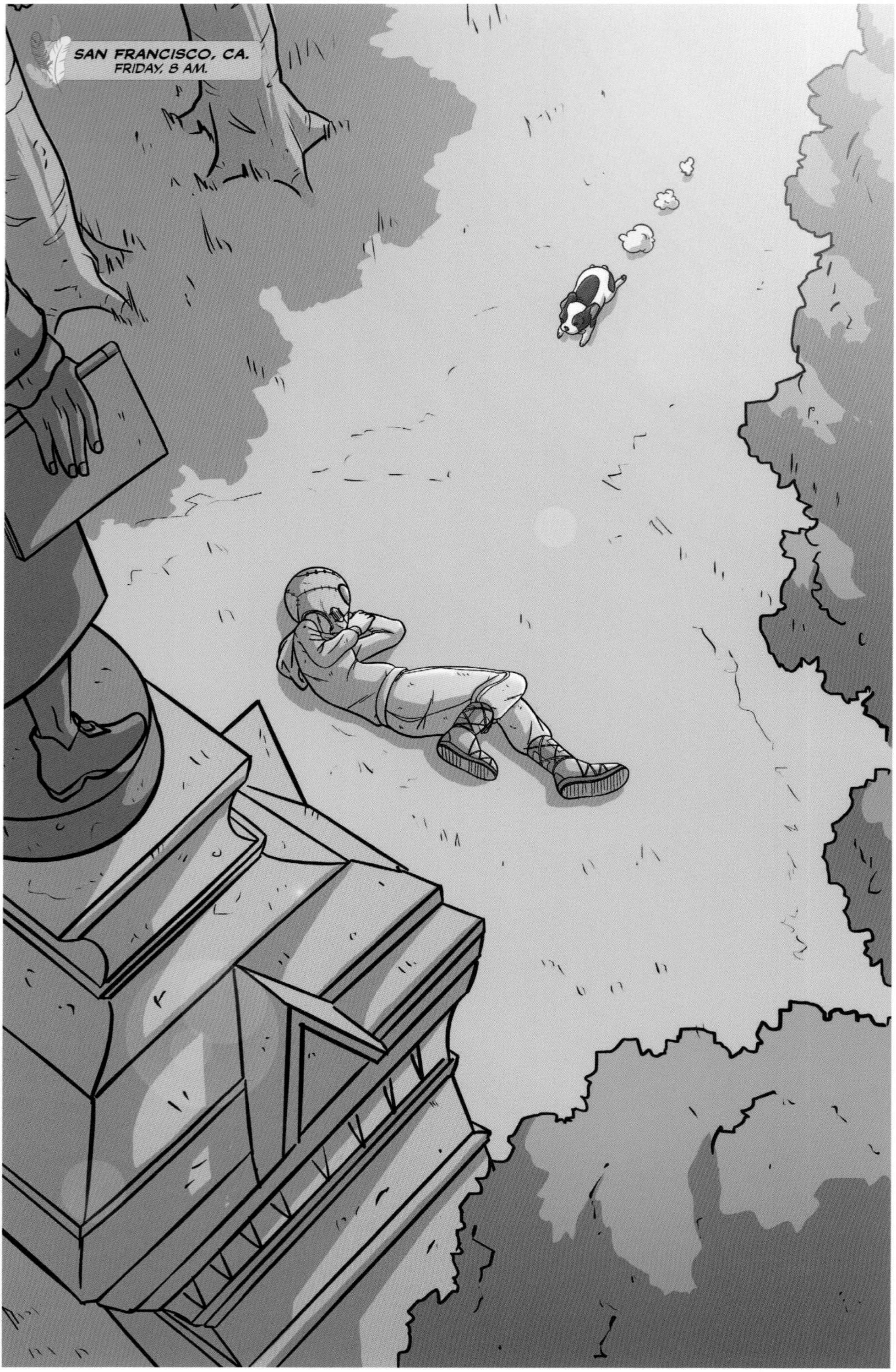
SAN FRANCISCO, CA.
FRIDAY, 8 AM.

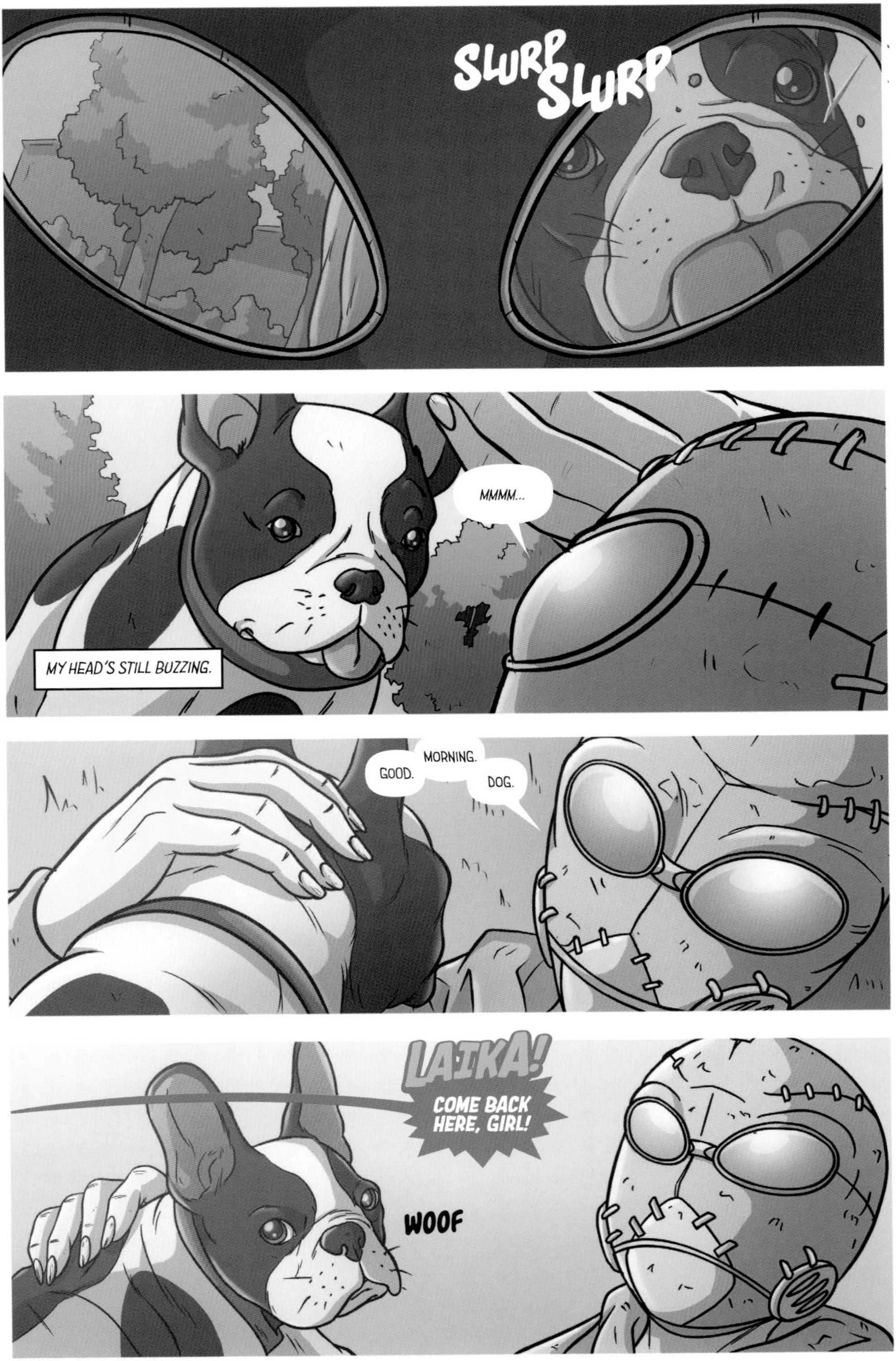
SLURP SLURP
MMMM...
MY HEAD'S STILL BUZZING.
GOOD.
MORNING.
DOG.
LAIKA!
COME BACK HERE, GIRL!
WOOF

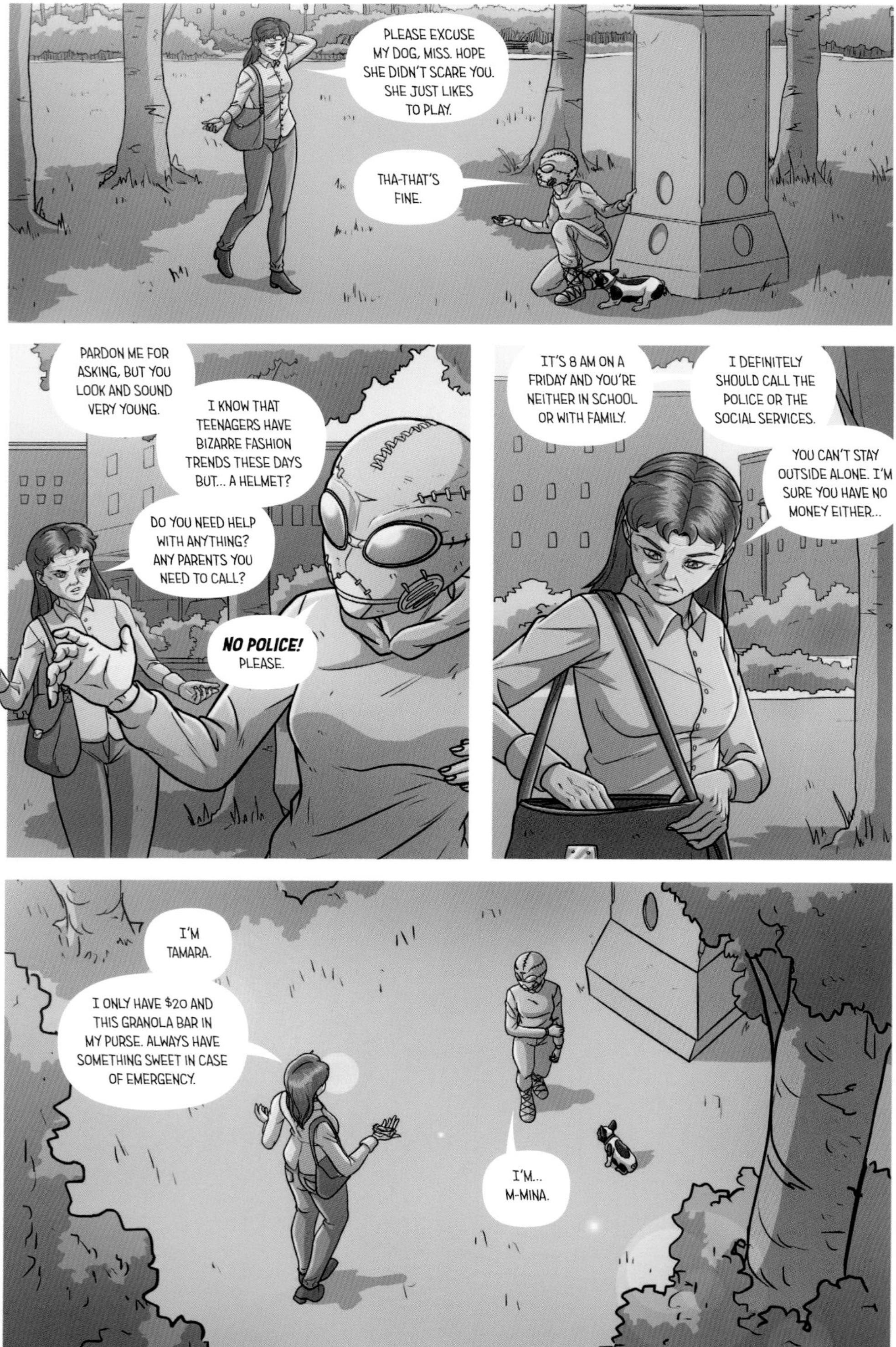
PLEASE EXCUSE MY DOG, MISS. HOPE SHE DIDN'T SCARE YOU. SHE JUST LIKES TO PLAY.
THA-THAT'S FINE.
PARDON ME FOR ASKING, BUT YOU LOOK AND SOUND VERY YOUNG.
I KNOW THAT TEENAGERS HAVE BIZARRE FASHION TRENDS THESE DAYS BUT... A HELMET?
DO YOU NEED HELP WITH ANYTHING? ANY PARENTS YOU NEED TO CALL?
NO POLICE! PLEASE.
IT'S 8 AM ON A FRIDAY AND YOU'RE NEITHER IN SCHOOL OR WITH FAMILY.
I DEFINITELY SHOULD CALL THE POLICE OR THE SOCIAL SERVICES.
YOU CAN'T STAY OUTSIDE ALONE. I'M SURE YOU HAVE NO MONEY EITHER...
I'M TAMARA.
I ONLY HAVE $20 AND THIS GRANOLA BAR IN MY PURSE. ALWAYS HAVE SOMETHING SWEET IN CASE OF EMERGENCY.
I'M... M-MINA.

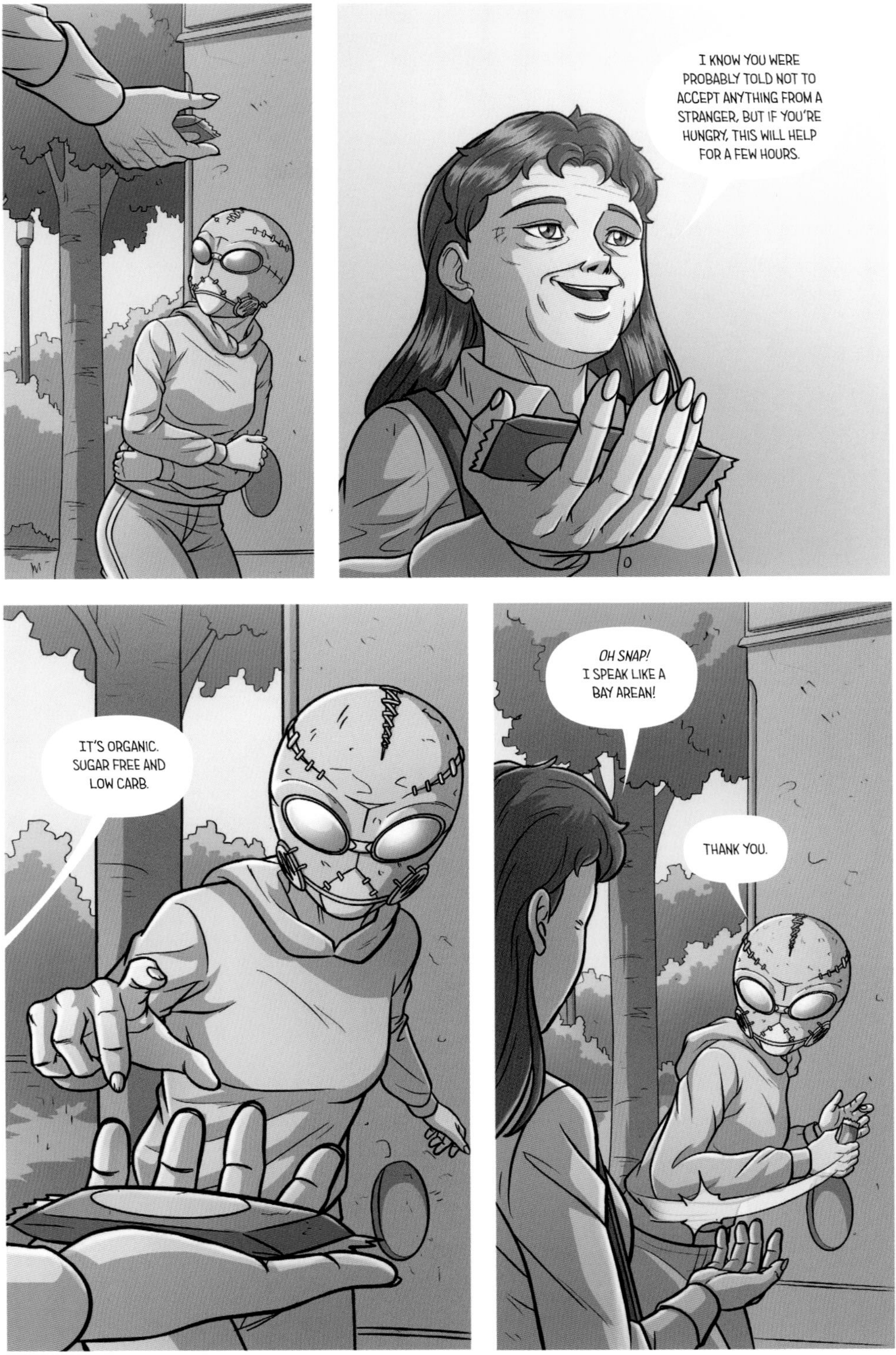
I KNOW YOU WERE PROBABLY TOLD NOT TO ACCEPT ANYTHING FROM A STRANGER, BUT IF YOU'RE HUNGRY, THIS WILL HELP FOR A FEW HOURS.
IT'S ORGANIC. SUGAR FREE AND LOW CARB.
OH SNAP! I SPEAK LIKE A BAY AREAN!
THANK YOU.

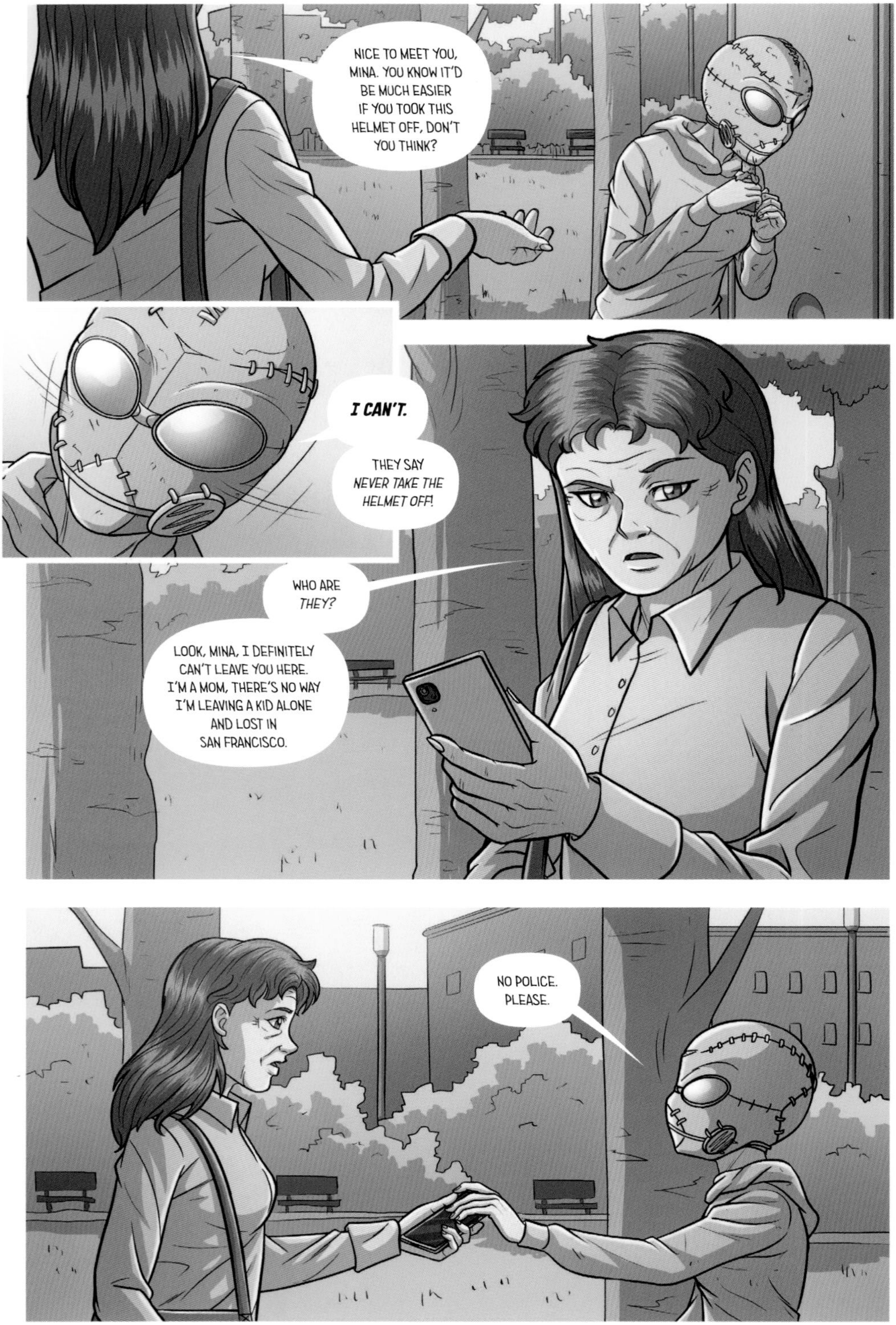
NICE TO MEET YOU, MINA. YOU KNOW IT'D BE MUCH EASIER IF YOU TOOK THIS HELMET OFF, DON'T YOU THINK?
I CAN'T.
THEY SAY *NEVER TAKE THE HELMET OFF!*
WHO ARE *THEY?*
LOOK, MINA, I DEFINITELY CAN'T LEAVE YOU HERE. I'M A MOM, THERE'S NO WAY I'M LEAVING A KID ALONE AND LOST IN SAN FRANCISCO.
NO POLICE. PLEASE.

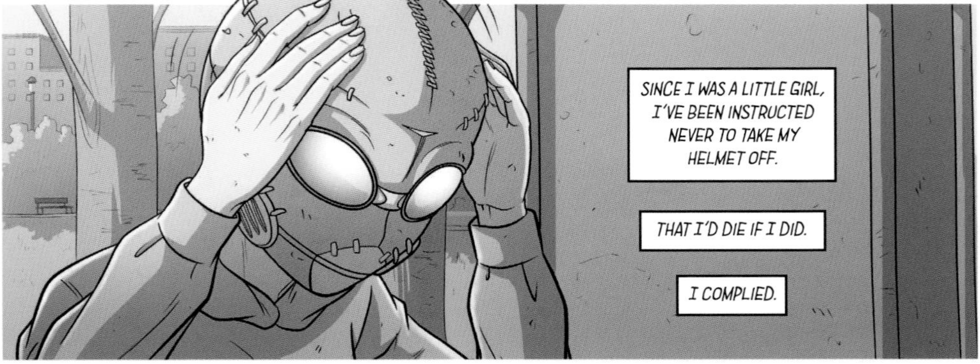
SINCE I WAS A LITTLE GIRL, I'VE BEEN INSTRUCTED NEVER TO TAKE MY HELMET OFF.
THAT I'D DIE IF I DID.
I COMPLIED.

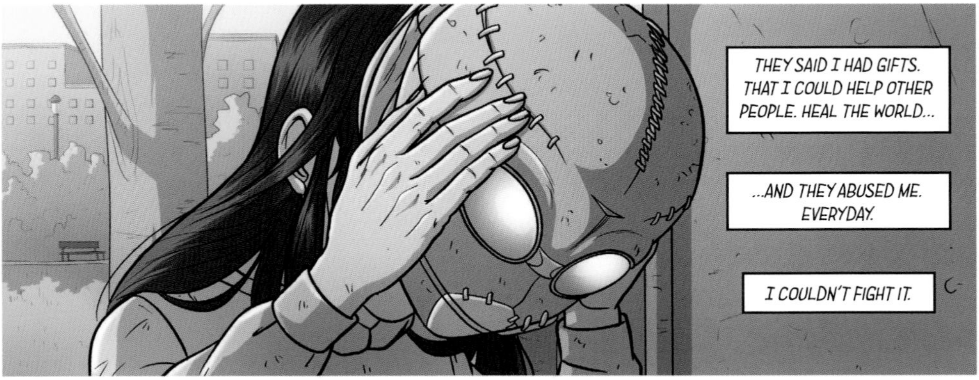
THEY SAID I HAD GIFTS. THAT I COULD HELP OTHER PEOPLE. HEAL THE WORLD...
...AND THEY ABUSED ME. EVERYDAY.
I COULDN'T FIGHT IT.

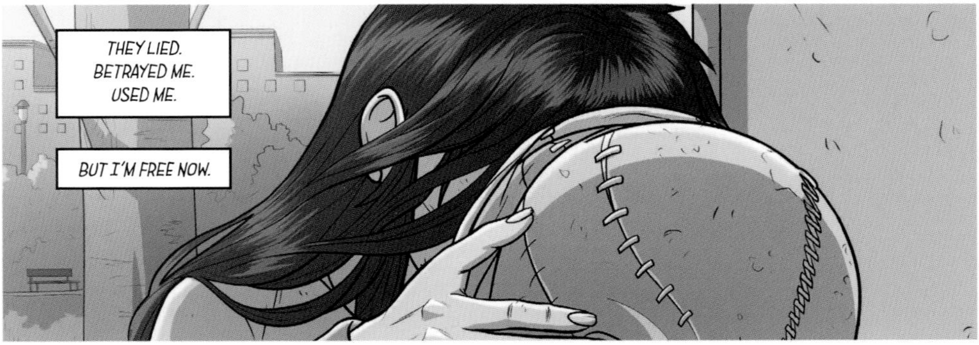
THEY LIED. BETRAYED ME. USED ME.
BUT I'M FREE NOW.

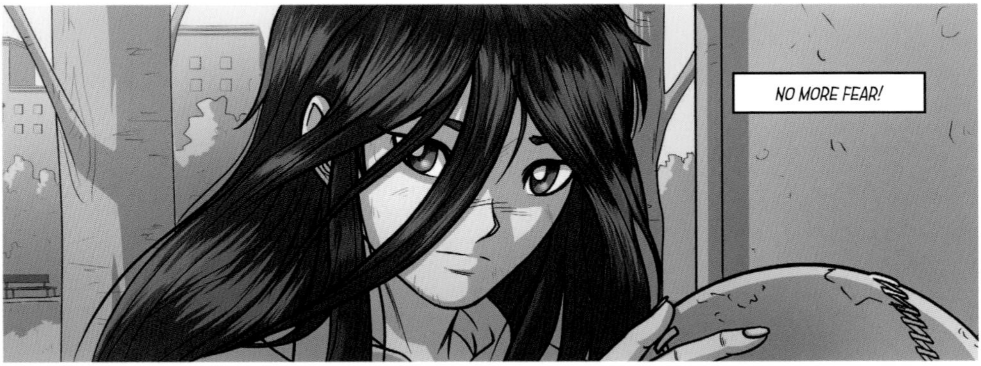
NO MORE FEAR!

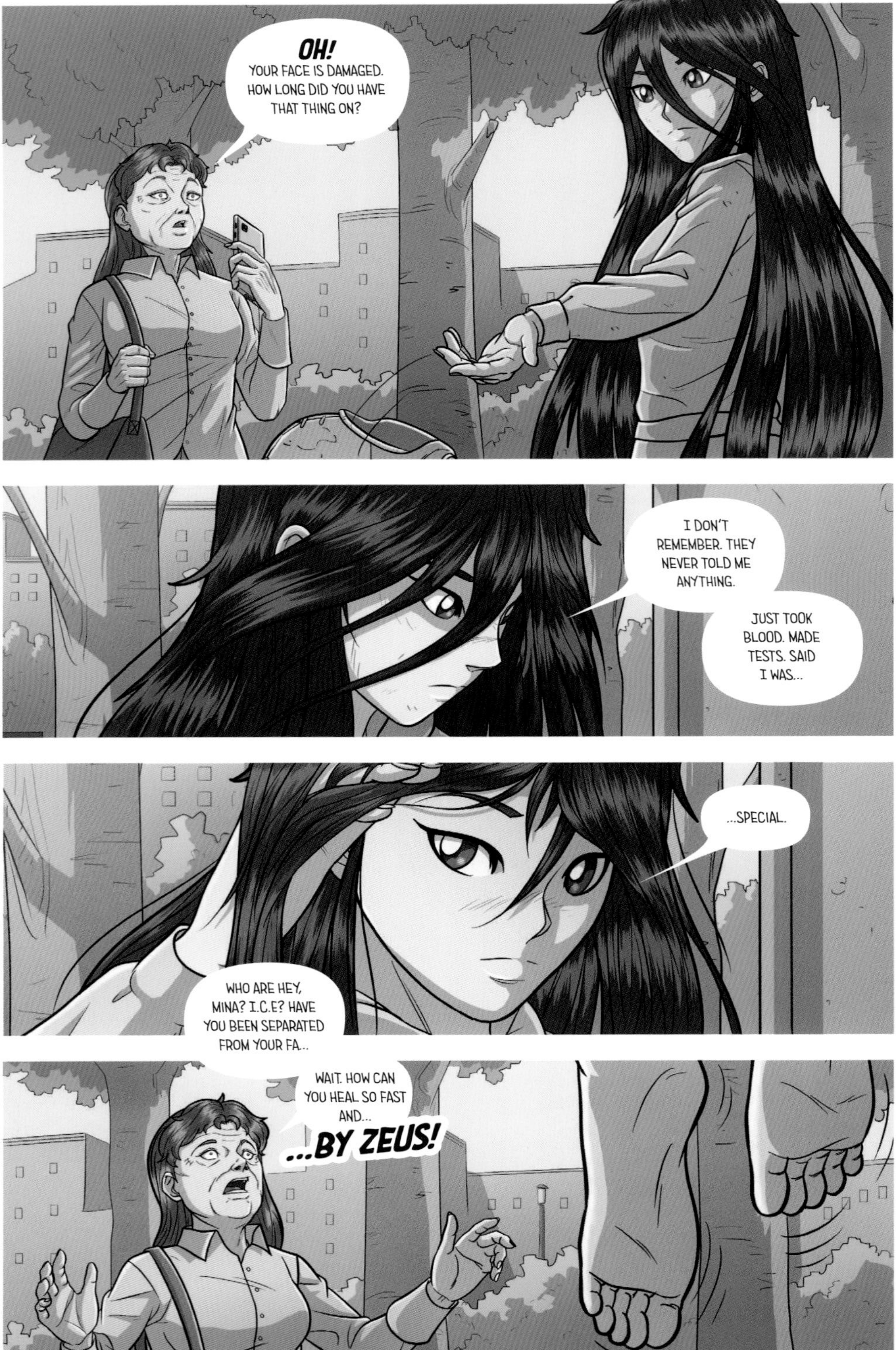
OH! YOUR FACE IS DAMAGED. HOW LONG DID YOU HAVE THAT THING ON?
I DON'T REMEMBER. THEY NEVER TOLD ME ANYTHING.
JUST TOOK BLOOD. MADE TESTS. SAID I WAS...
...SPECIAL.
WHO ARE HEY, MINA? I.C.E? HAVE YOU BEEN SEPARATED FROM YOUR FA...
WAIT. HOW CAN YOU HEAL SO FAST AND...
...BY ZEUS!

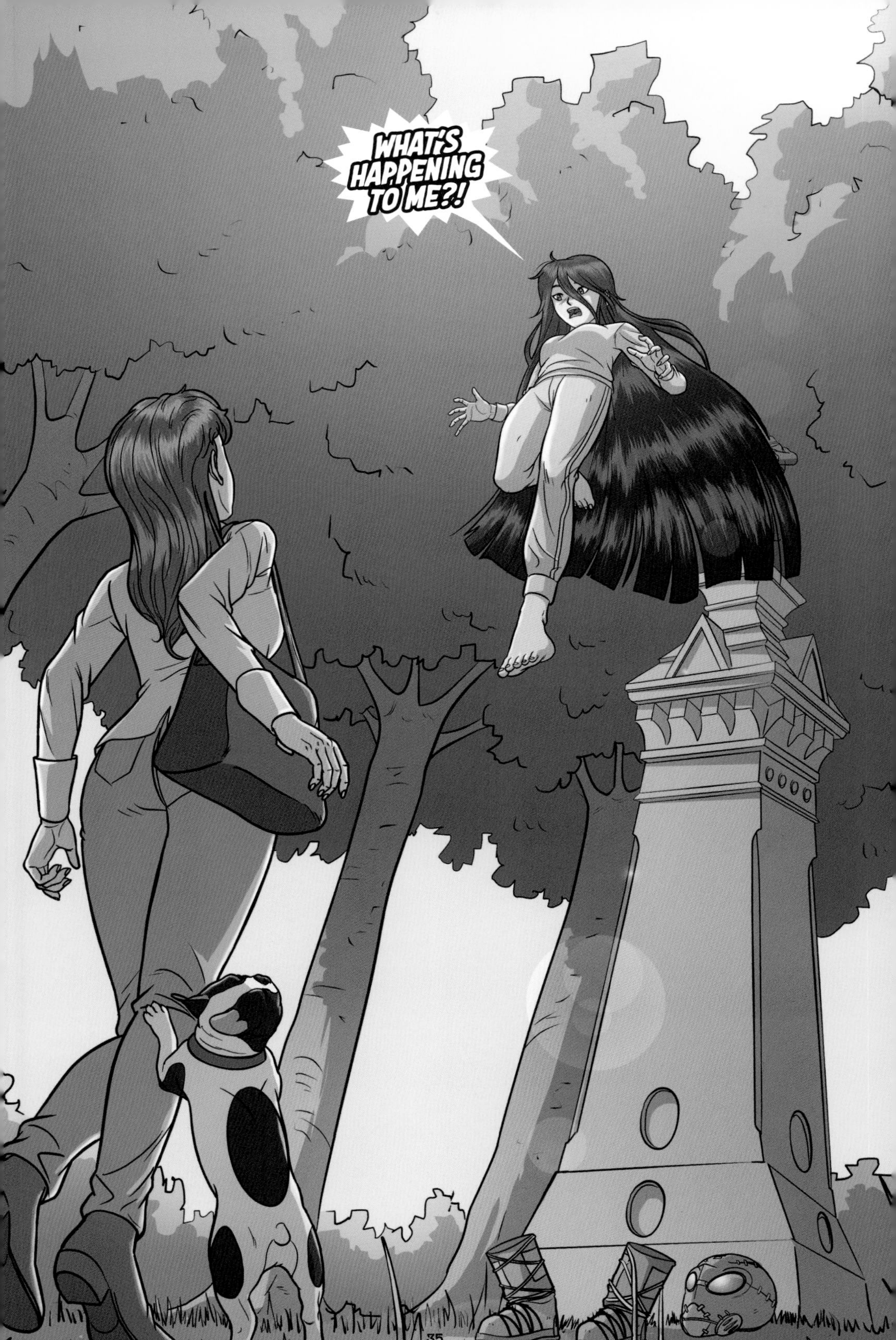
WHAT'S HAPPENING TO ME?!

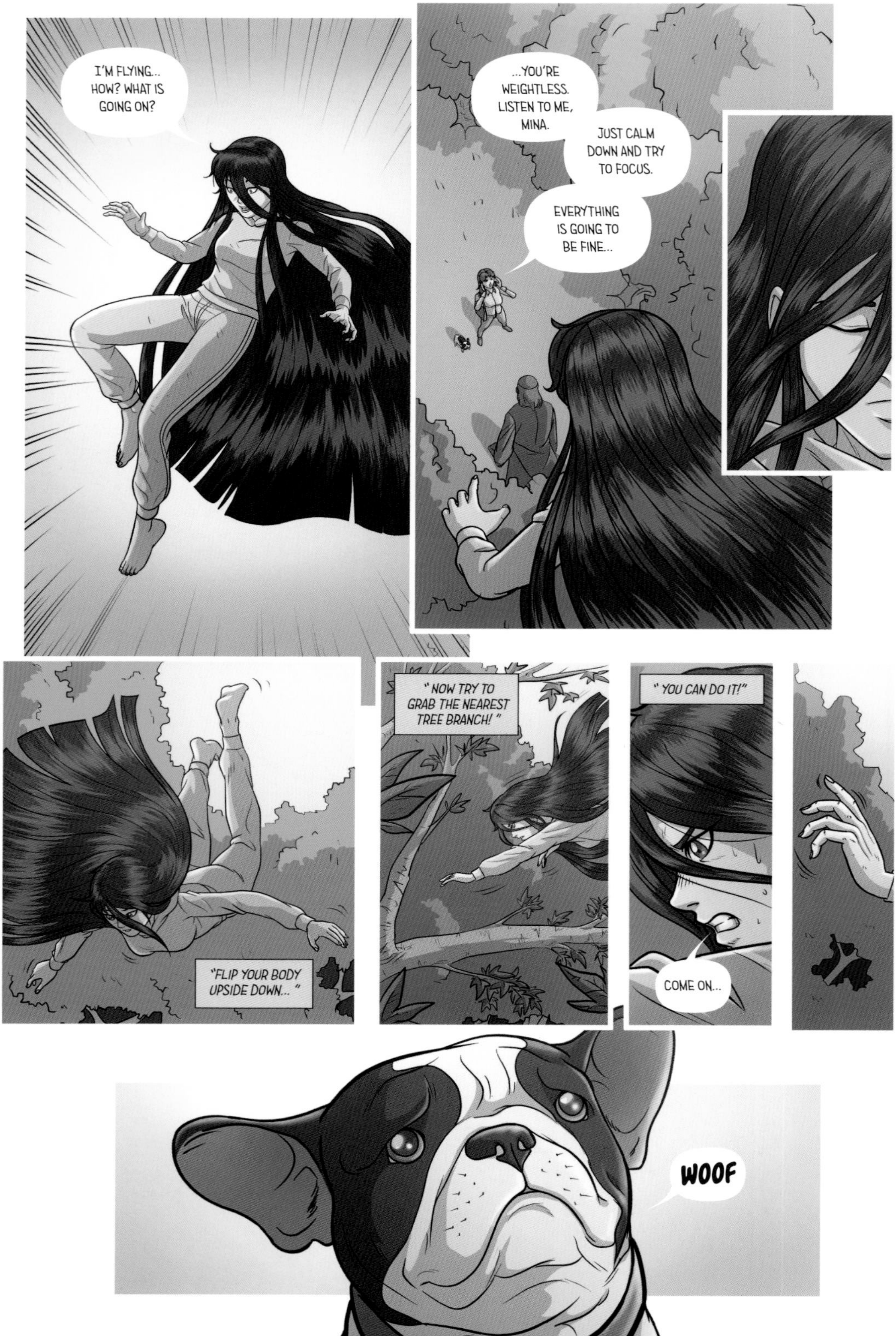
I'M FLYING... HOW? WHAT IS GOING ON?
...YOU'RE WEIGHTLESS. LISTEN TO ME, MINA.
JUST CALM DOWN AND TRY TO FOCUS.
EVERYTHING IS GOING TO BE FINE...
"FLIP YOUR BODY UPSIDE DOWN..."
"NOW TRY TO GRAB THE NEAREST TREE BRANCH!"
"YOU CAN DO IT!"
COME ON...
WOOF

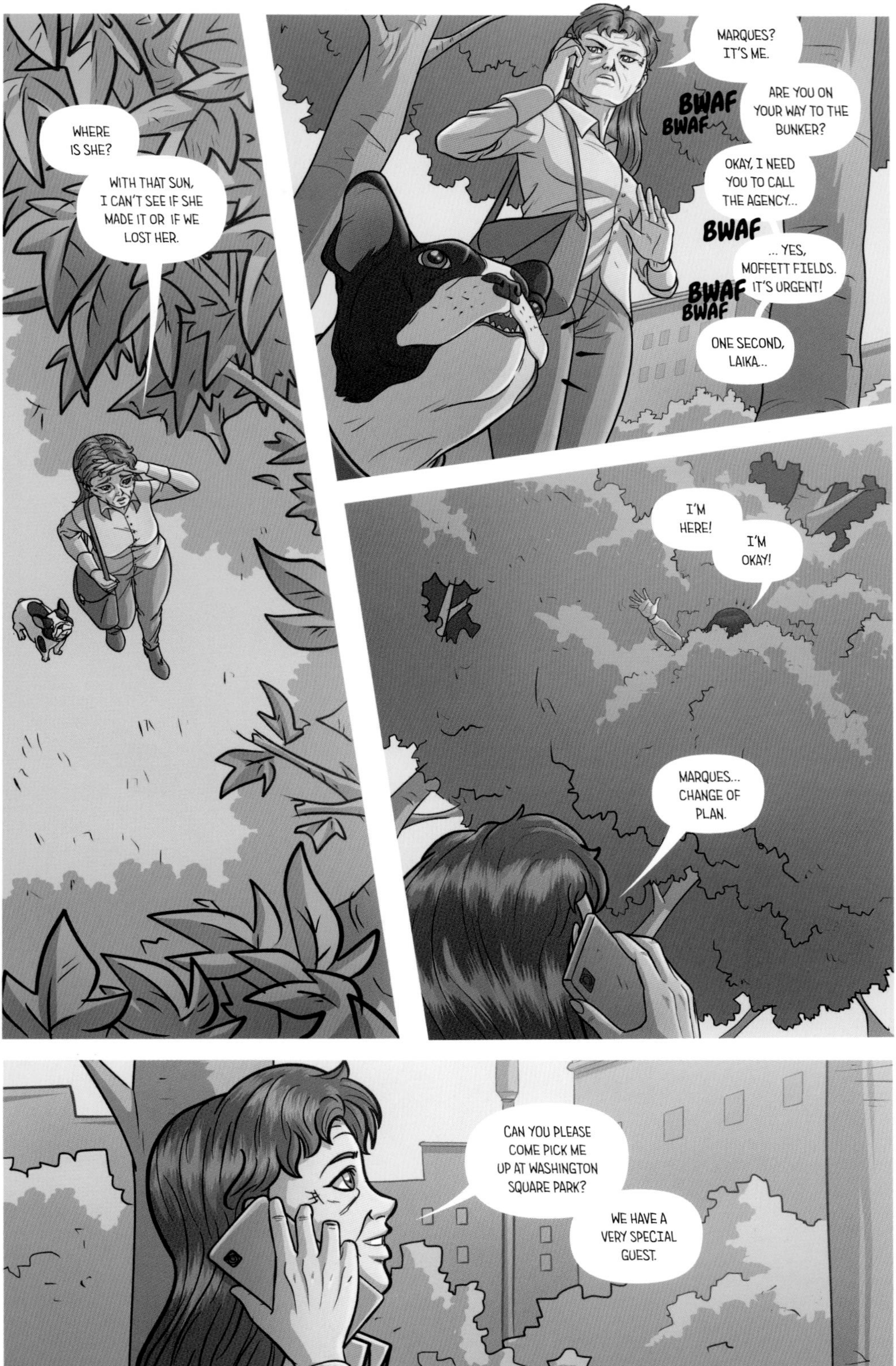
WHERE IS SHE?
WITH THAT SUN, I CAN'T SEE IF SHE MADE IT OR IF WE LOST HER.
MARQUES? IT'S ME.
BWAF BWAF
ARE YOU ON YOUR WAY TO THE BUNKER?
OKAY, I NEED YOU TO CALL THE AGENCY...
BWAF
... YES, MOFFETT FIELDS. IT'S URGENT!
BWAF BWAF
ONE SECOND, LAIKA...
I'M HERE!
I'M OKAY!
MARQUES... CHANGE OF PLAN.
CAN YOU PLEASE COME PICK ME UP AT WASHINGTON SQUARE PARK?
WE HAVE A VERY SPECIAL GUEST.

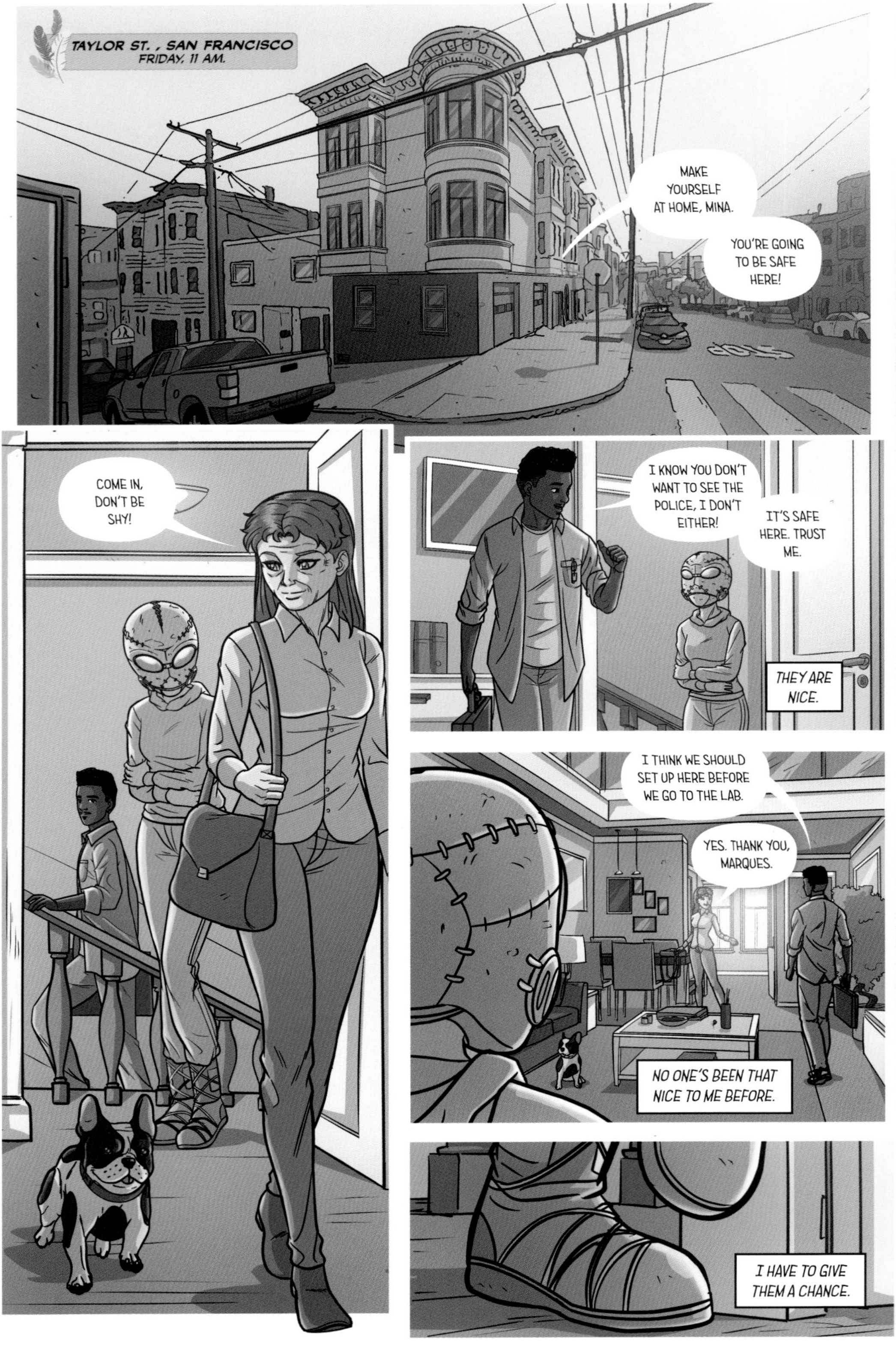
TAYLOR ST., SAN FRANCISCO
FRIDAY, 11 AM.
MAKE YOURSELF AT HOME, MINA.
YOU'RE GOING TO BE SAFE HERE!
COME IN, DON'T BE SHY!
I KNOW YOU DON'T WANT TO SEE THE POLICE, I DON'T EITHER!
IT'S SAFE HERE. TRUST ME.
THEY ARE NICE.
I THINK WE SHOULD SET UP HERE BEFORE WE GO TO THE LAB.
YES. THANK YOU, MARQUES.
NO ONE'S BEEN THAT NICE TO ME BEFORE.
I HAVE TO GIVE THEM A CHANCE.

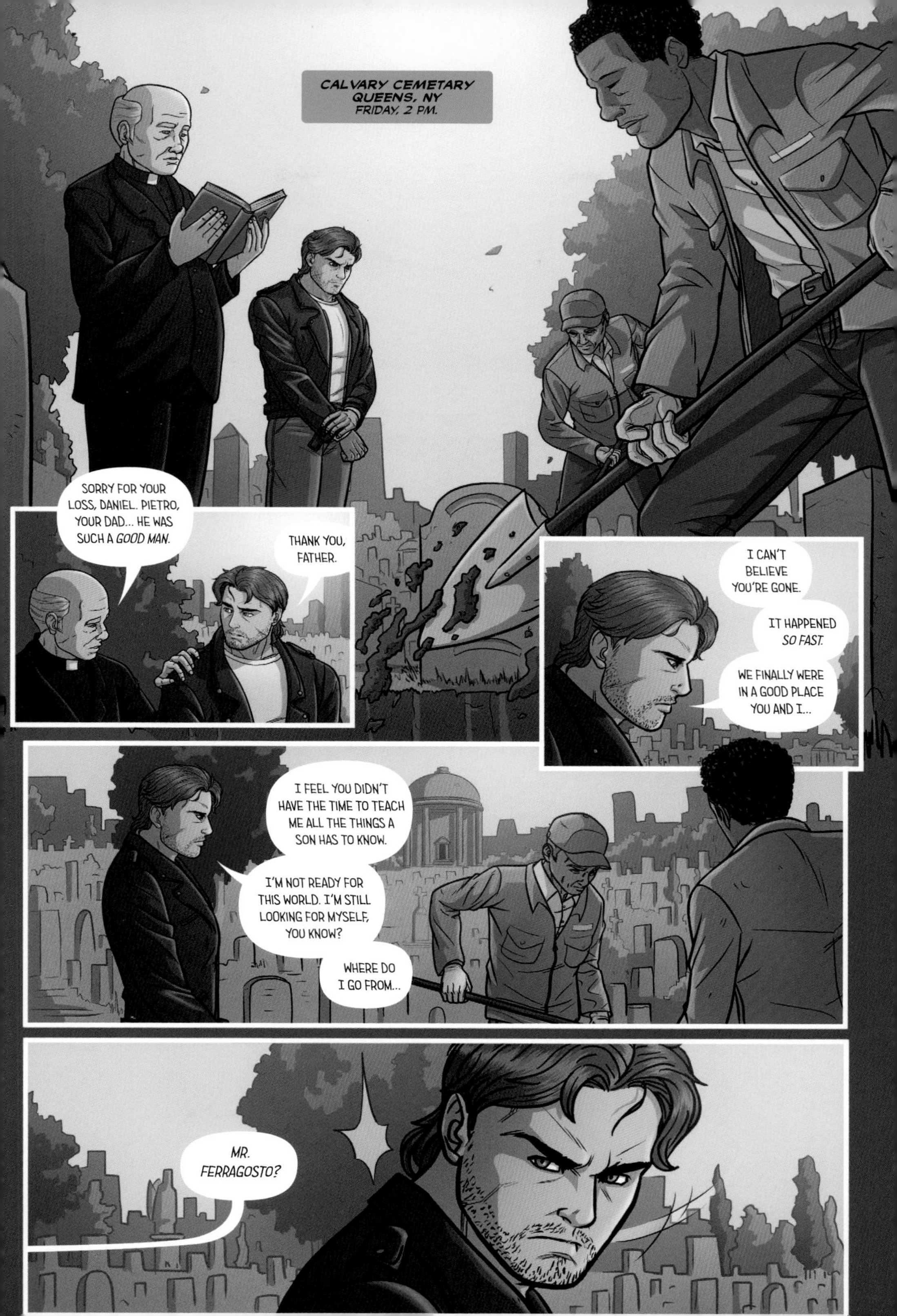
CALVARY CEMETARY
QUEENS, NY
FRIDAY, 2 PM.
SORRY FOR YOUR LOSS, DANIEL. PIETRO, YOUR DAD... HE WAS SUCH A *GOOD MAN.*
THANK YOU, FATHER.
I CAN'T BELIEVE YOU'RE GONE.
IT HAPPENED *SO FAST.*
WE FINALLY WERE IN A GOOD PLACE YOU AND I...
I FEEL YOU DIDN'T HAVE THE TIME TO TEACH ME ALL THE THINGS A SON HAS TO KNOW.
I'M NOT READY FOR THIS WORLD. I'M STILL LOOKING FOR MYSELF, YOU KNOW?
WHERE DO I GO FROM...
MR. FERRAGOSTO?

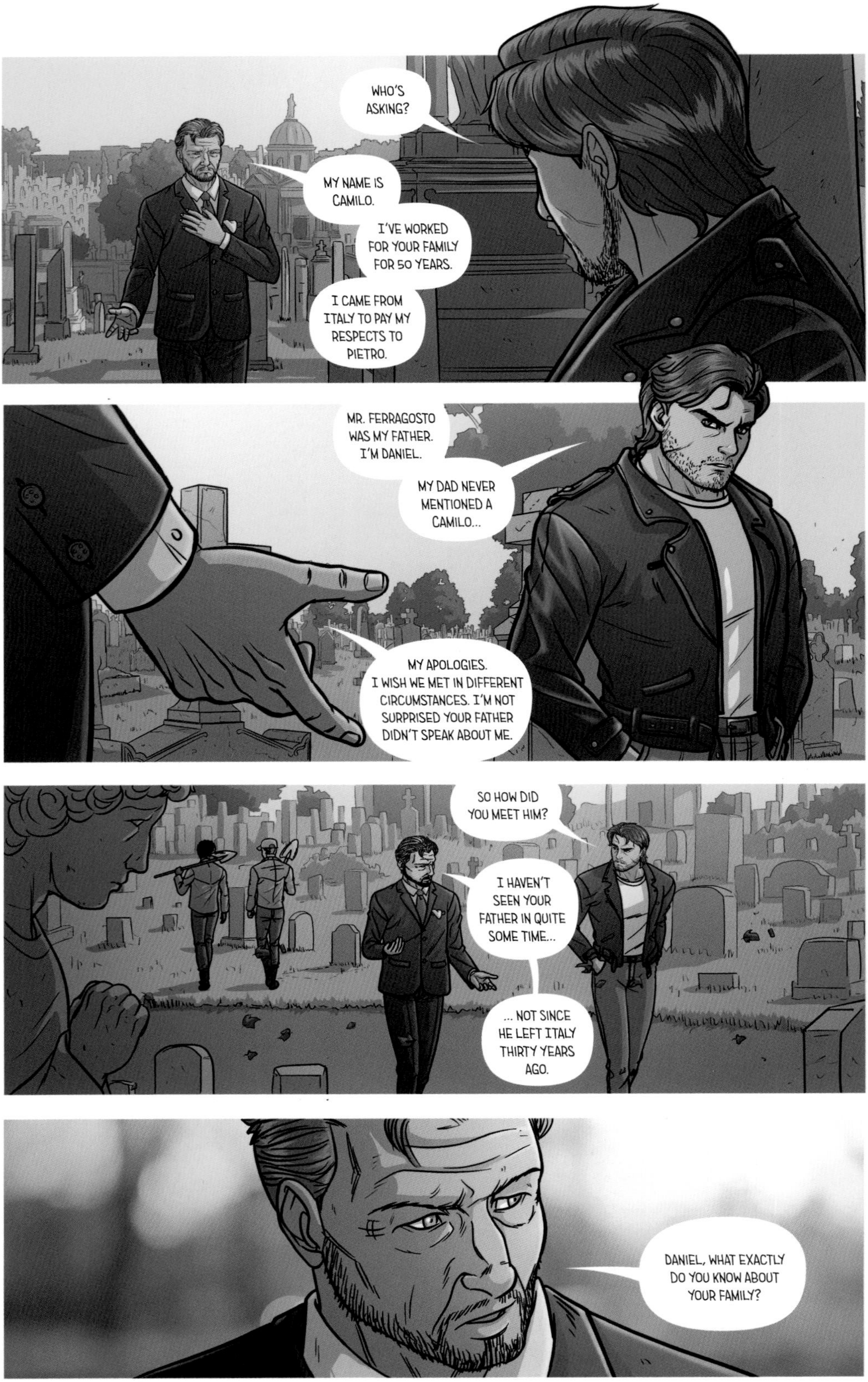
WHO'S ASKING?
MY NAME IS CAMILO.
I'VE WORKED FOR YOUR FAMILY FOR 50 YEARS.
I CAME FROM ITALY TO PAY MY RESPECTS TO PIETRO.
MR. FERRAGOSTO WAS MY FATHER. I'M DANIEL.
MY DAD NEVER MENTIONED A CAMILO...
MY APOLOGIES. I WISH WE MET IN DIFFERENT CIRCUMSTANCES. I'M NOT SURPRISED YOUR FATHER DIDN'T SPEAK ABOUT ME.
SO HOW DID YOU MEET HIM?
I HAVEN'T SEEN YOUR FATHER IN QUITE SOME TIME...
... NOT SINCE HE LEFT ITALY THIRTY YEARS AGO.
DANIEL, WHAT EXACTLY DO YOU KNOW ABOUT YOUR FAMILY?

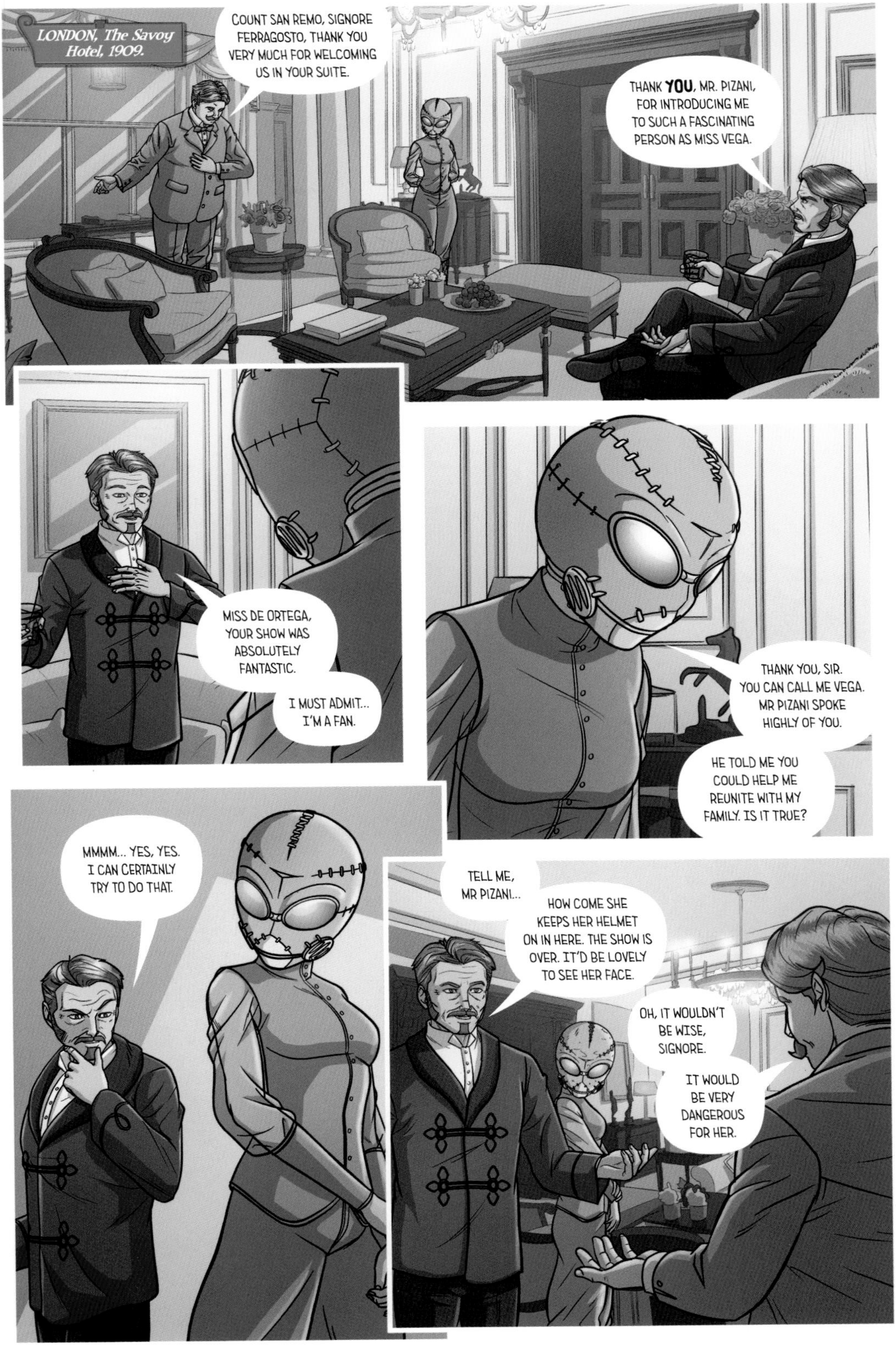
LONDON, The Savoy Hotel, 1909.
COUNT SAN REMO, SIGNORE FERRAGOSTO, THANK YOU VERY MUCH FOR WELCOMING US IN YOUR SUITE.
THANK YOU, MR. PIZANI, FOR INTRODUCING ME TO SUCH A FASCINATING PERSON AS MISS VEGA.
MISS DE ORTEGA, YOUR SHOW WAS ABSOLUTELY FANTASTIC.
I MUST ADMIT... I'M A FAN.
THANK YOU, SIR. YOU CAN CALL ME VEGA. MR PIZANI SPOKE HIGHLY OF YOU.
HE TOLD ME YOU COULD HELP ME REUNITE WITH MY FAMILY. IS IT TRUE?
MMMM... YES, YES. I CAN CERTAINLY TRY TO DO THAT.
TELL ME, MR PIZANI...
HOW COME SHE KEEPS HER HELMET ON IN HERE. THE SHOW IS OVER. IT'D BE LOVELY TO SEE HER FACE.
OH, IT WOULDN'T BE WISE, SIGNORE.
IT WOULD BE VERY DANGEROUS FOR HER.

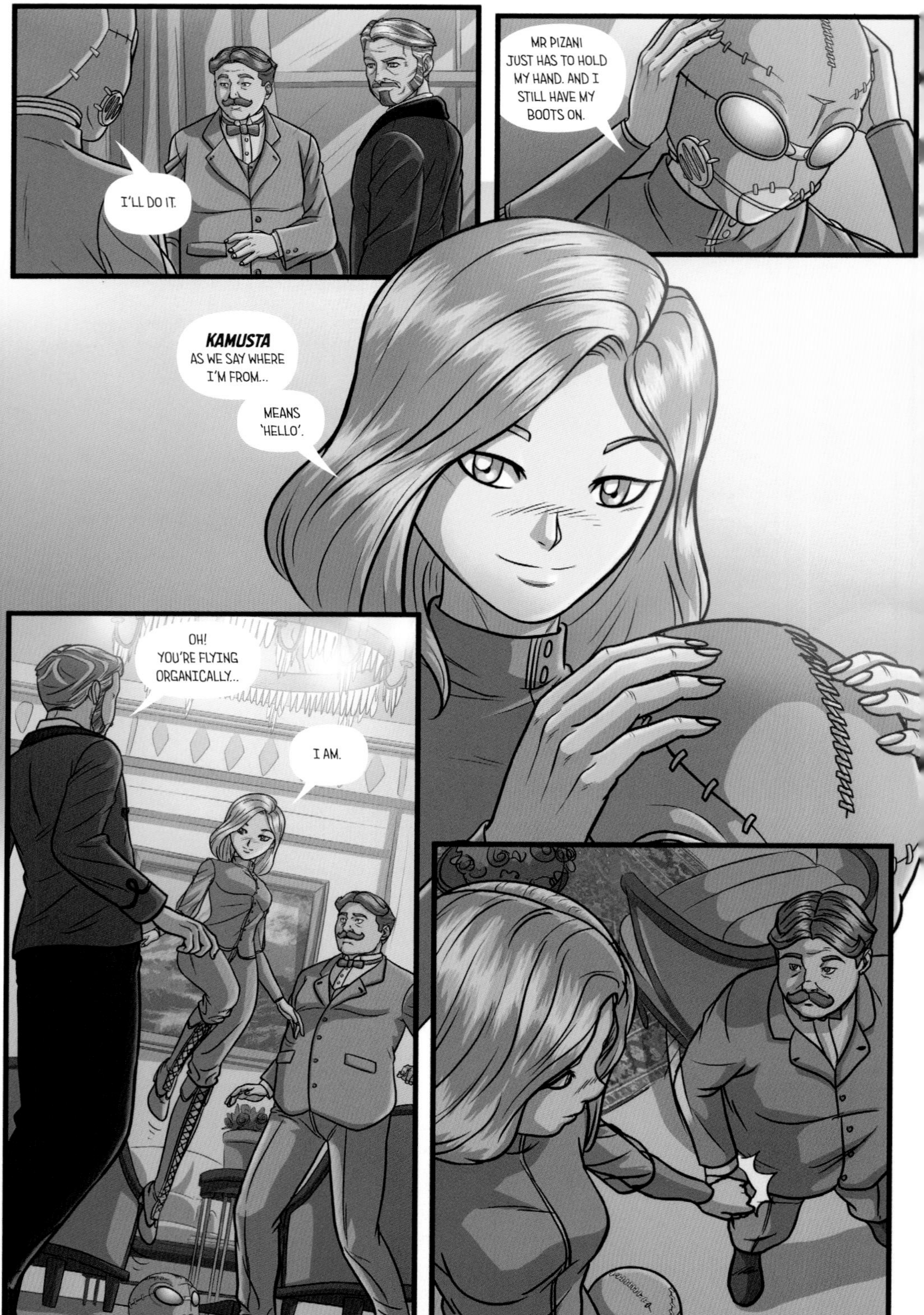
I'LL DO IT.
MR PIZANI JUST HAS TO HOLD MY HAND. AND I STILL HAVE MY BOOTS ON.
KAMUSTA AS WE SAY WHERE I'M FROM...
MEANS 'HELLO'.
OH! YOU'RE FLYING ORGANICALLY...
I AM.

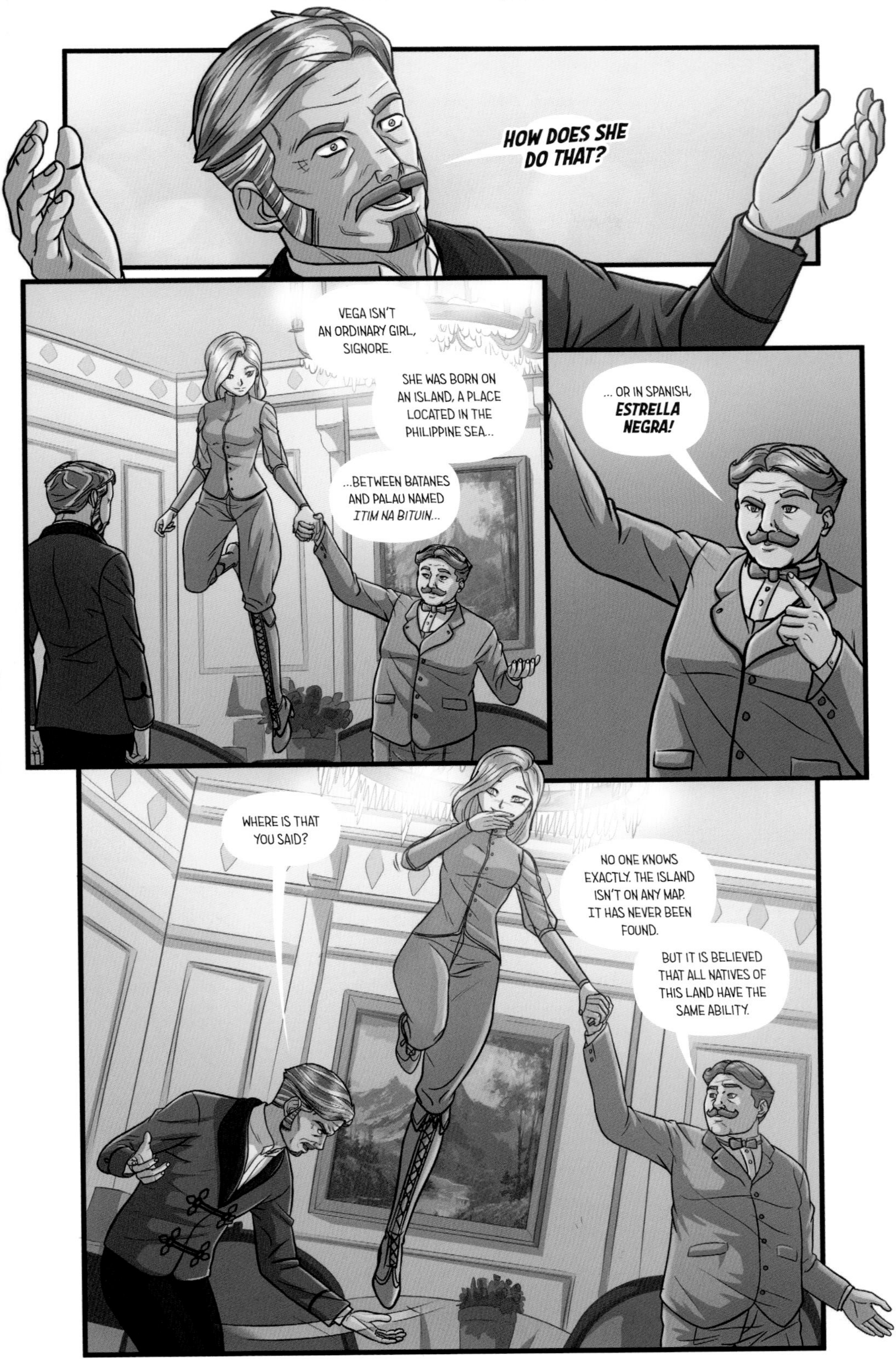
HOW DOES SHE DO THAT?
VEGA ISN'T AN ORDINARY GIRL, SIGNORE.
SHE WAS BORN ON AN ISLAND, A PLACE LOCATED IN THE PHILIPPINE SEA...
...BETWEEN BATANES AND PALAU NAMED *ITIM NA BITUIN*...
... OR IN SPANISH, **ESTRELLA NEGRA!**
WHERE IS THAT YOU SAID?
NO ONE KNOWS EXACTLY. THE ISLAND ISN'T ON ANY MAP. IT HAS NEVER BEEN FOUND.
BUT IT IS BELIEVED THAT ALL NATIVES OF THIS LAND HAVE THE SAME ABILITY.

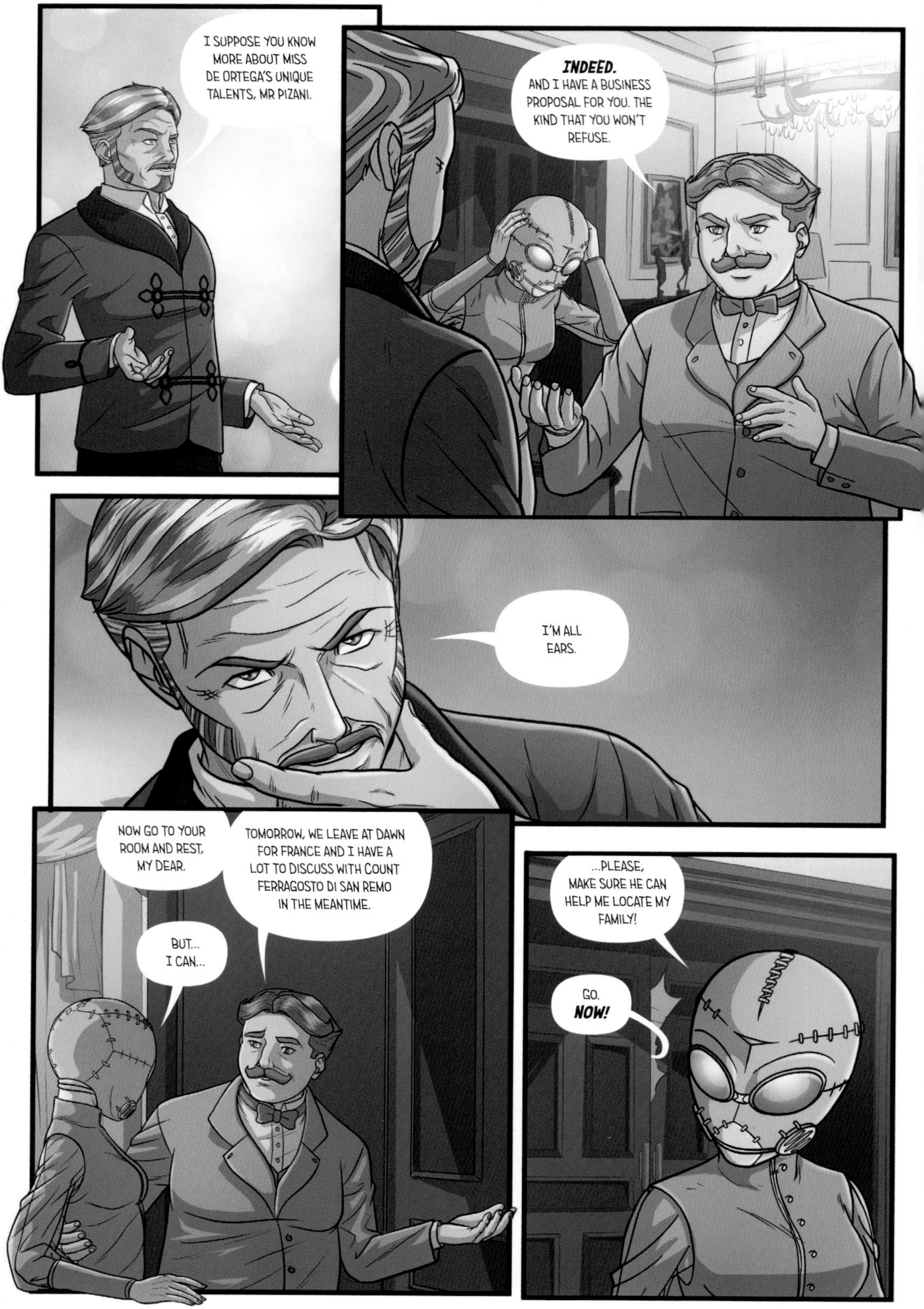
I SUPPOSE YOU KNOW MORE ABOUT MISS DE ORTEGA'S UNIQUE TALENTS, MR PIZANI.
INDEED. AND I HAVE A BUSINESS PROPOSAL FOR YOU. THE KIND THAT YOU WON'T REFUSE.
I'M ALL EARS.
NOW GO TO YOUR ROOM AND REST, MY DEAR.
TOMORROW, WE LEAVE AT DAWN FOR FRANCE AND I HAVE A LOT TO DISCUSS WITH COUNT FERRAGOSTO DI SAN REMO IN THE MEANTIME.
BUT... I CAN...
...PLEASE, MAKE SURE HE CAN HELP ME LOCATE MY FAMILY!
GO. NOW!

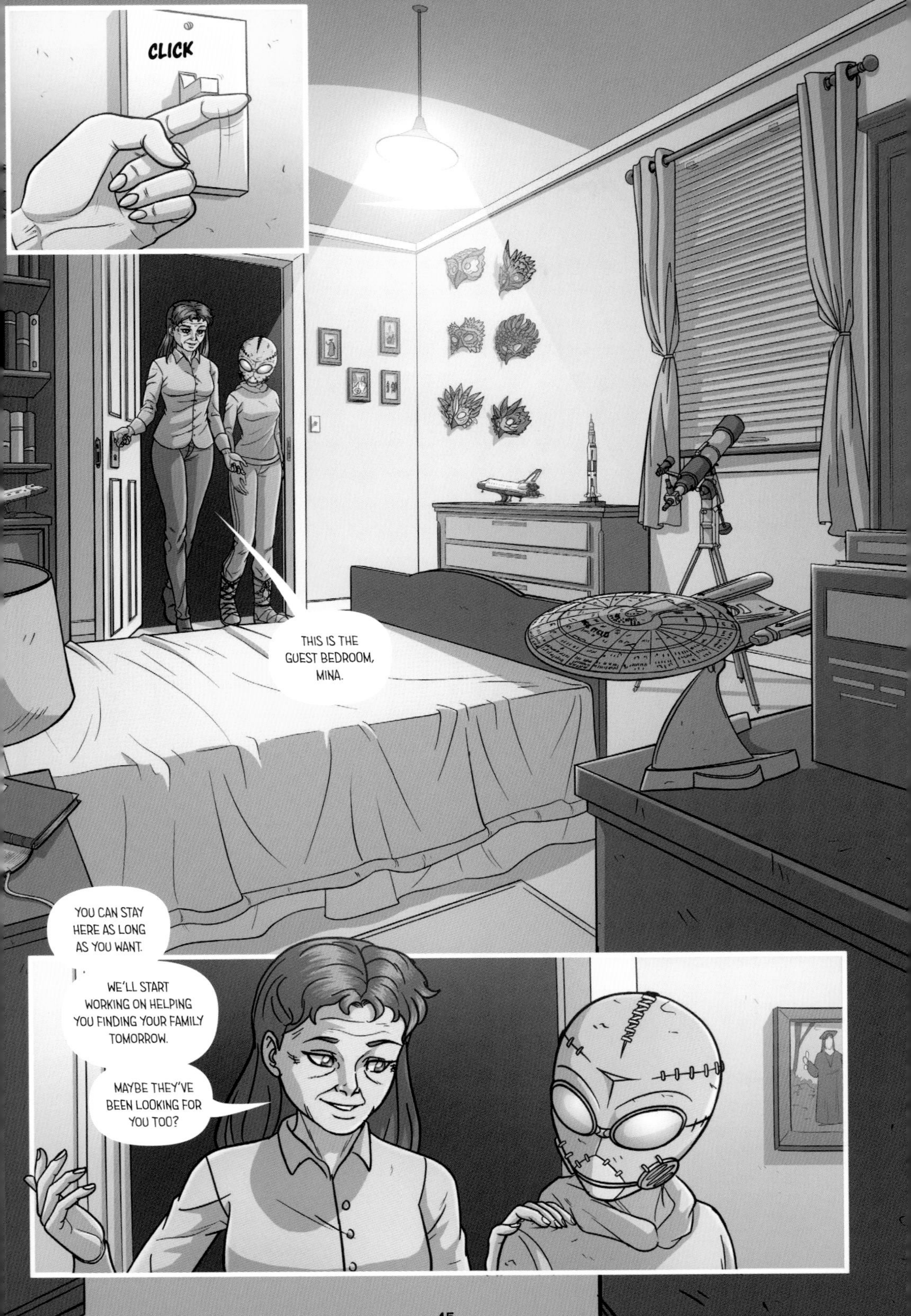
CLICK
THIS IS THE GUEST BEDROOM, MINA.
YOU CAN STAY HERE AS LONG AS YOU WANT.
WE'LL START WORKING ON HELPING YOU FINDING YOUR FAMILY TOMORROW.
MAYBE THEY'VE BEEN LOOKING FOR YOU TOO?

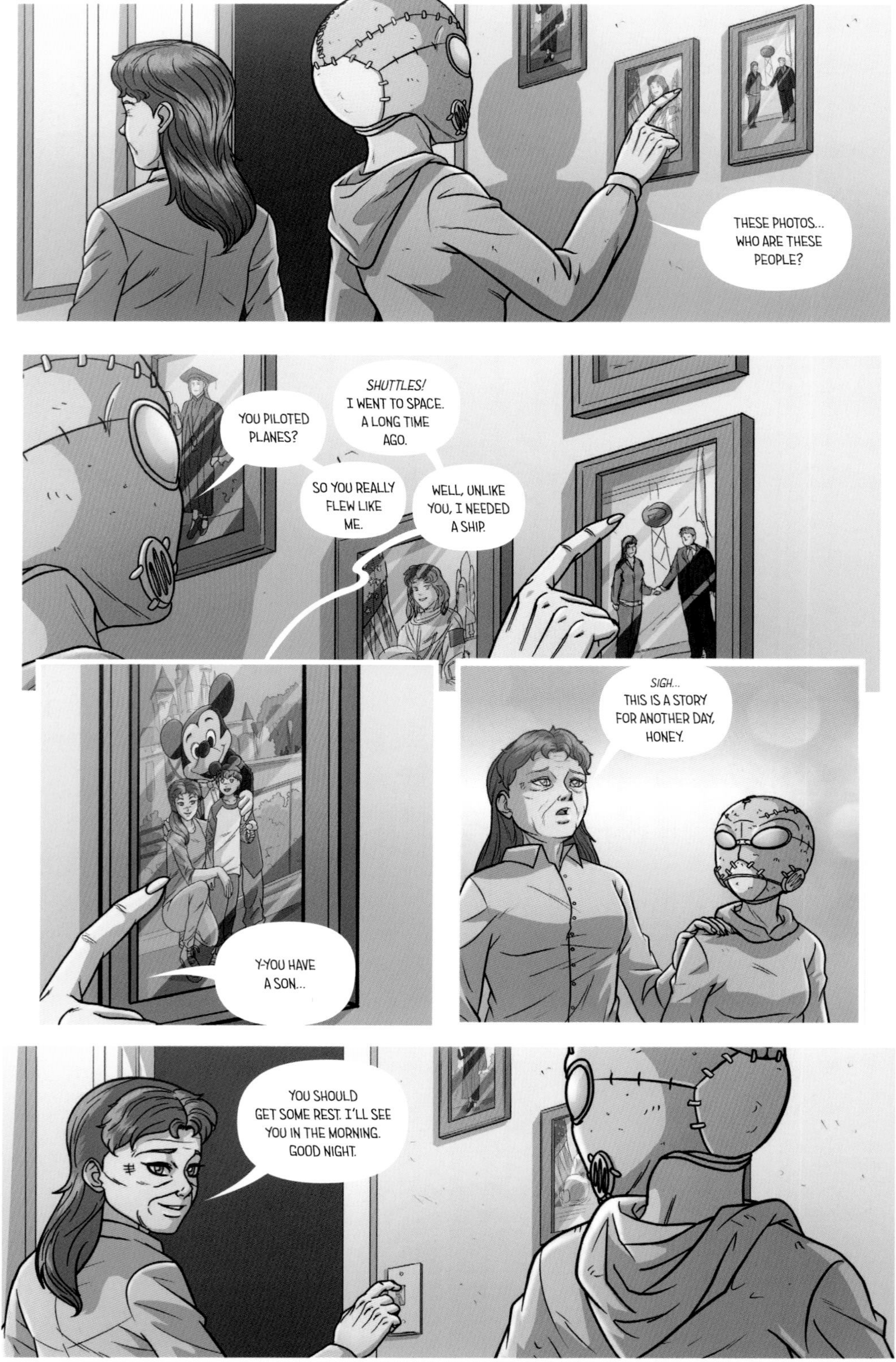
THESE PHOTOS... WHO ARE THESE PEOPLE?
YOU PILOTED PLANES?
SHUTTLES! I WENT TO SPACE. A LONG TIME AGO.
SO YOU REALLY FLEW LIKE ME.
WELL, UNLIKE YOU, I NEEDED A SHIP.
Y-YOU HAVE A SON...
SIGH... THIS IS A STORY FOR ANOTHER DAY, HONEY.
YOU SHOULD GET SOME REST. I'LL SEE YOU IN THE MORNING. GOOD NIGHT.

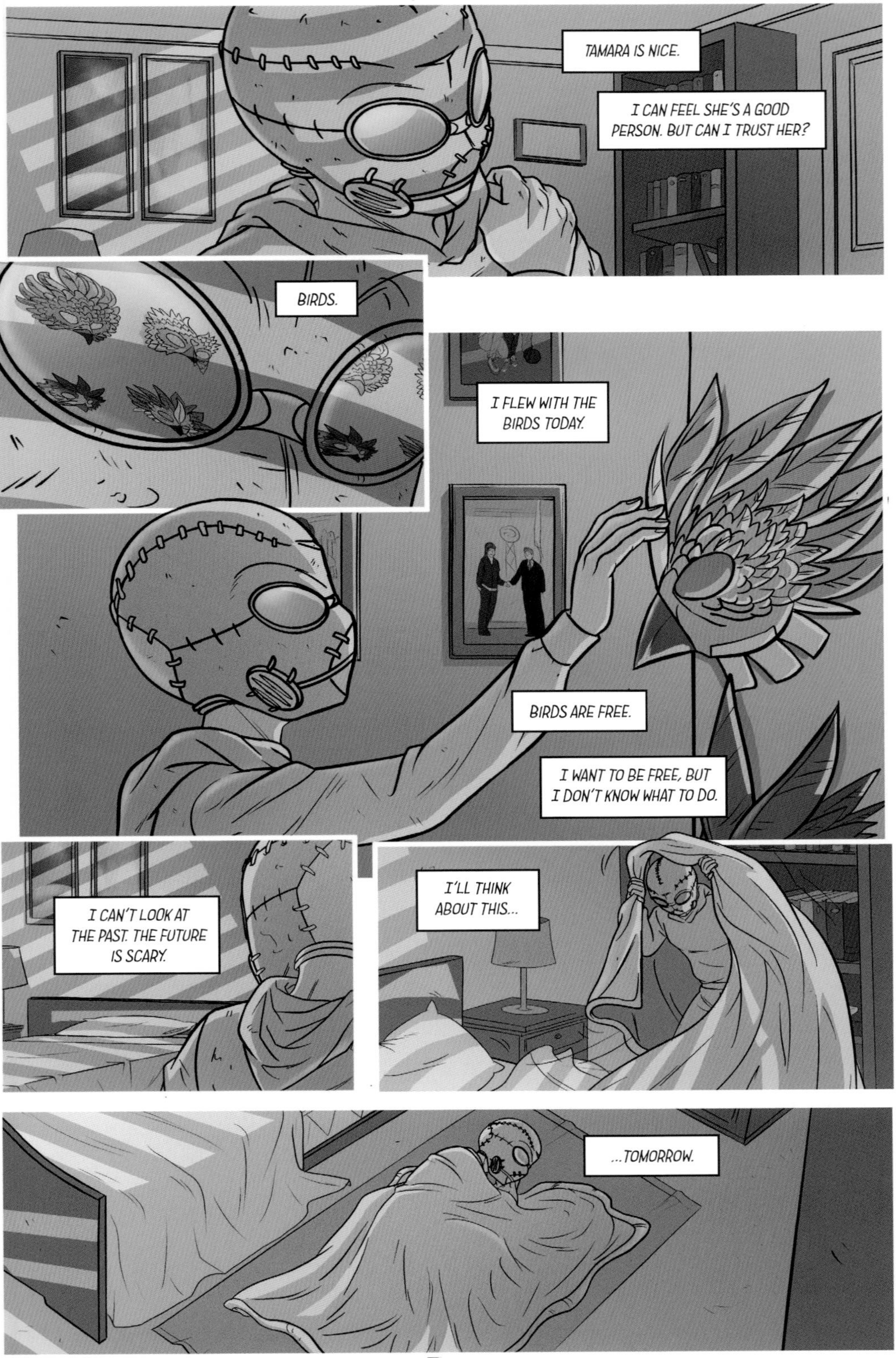
TAMARA IS NICE.
I CAN FEEL SHE'S A GOOD PERSON. BUT CAN I TRUST HER?
BIRDS.
I FLEW WITH THE BIRDS TODAY.
BIRDS ARE FREE.
I WANT TO BE FREE, BUT I DON'T KNOW WHAT TO DO.
I CAN'T LOOK AT THE PAST. THE FUTURE IS SCARY.
I'LL THINK ABOUT THIS...
...TOMORROW.

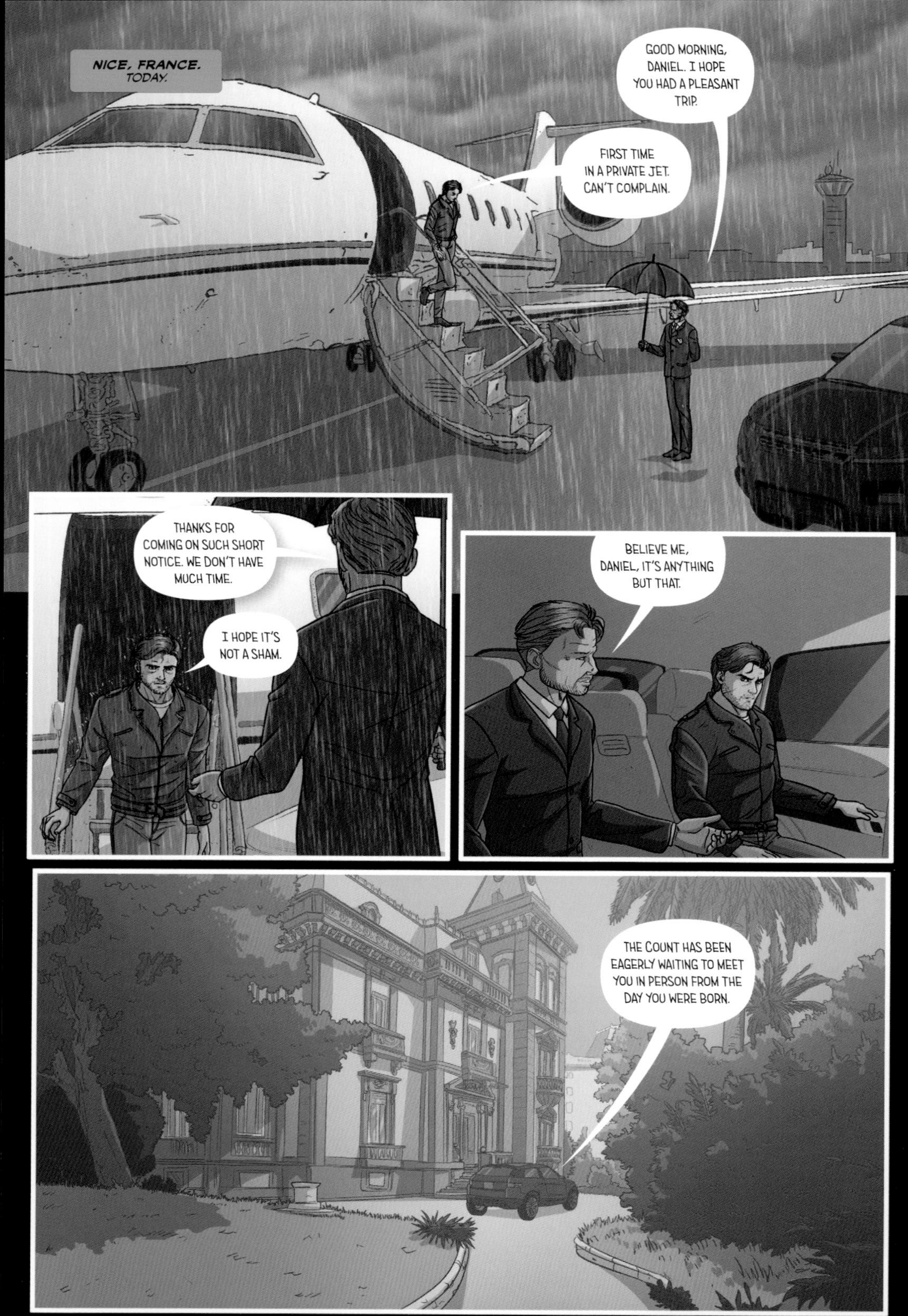
NICE, FRANCE. TODAY.
GOOD MORNING, DANIEL. I HOPE YOU HAD A PLEASANT TRIP.
FIRST TIME IN A PRIVATE JET. CAN'T COMPLAIN.
THANKS FOR COMING ON SUCH SHORT NOTICE. WE DON'T HAVE MUCH TIME.
I HOPE IT'S NOT A SHAM.
BELIEVE ME, DANIEL, IT'S ANYTHING BUT THAT.
THE COUNT HAS BEEN EAGERLY WAITING TO MEET YOU IN PERSON FROM THE DAY YOU WERE BORN.

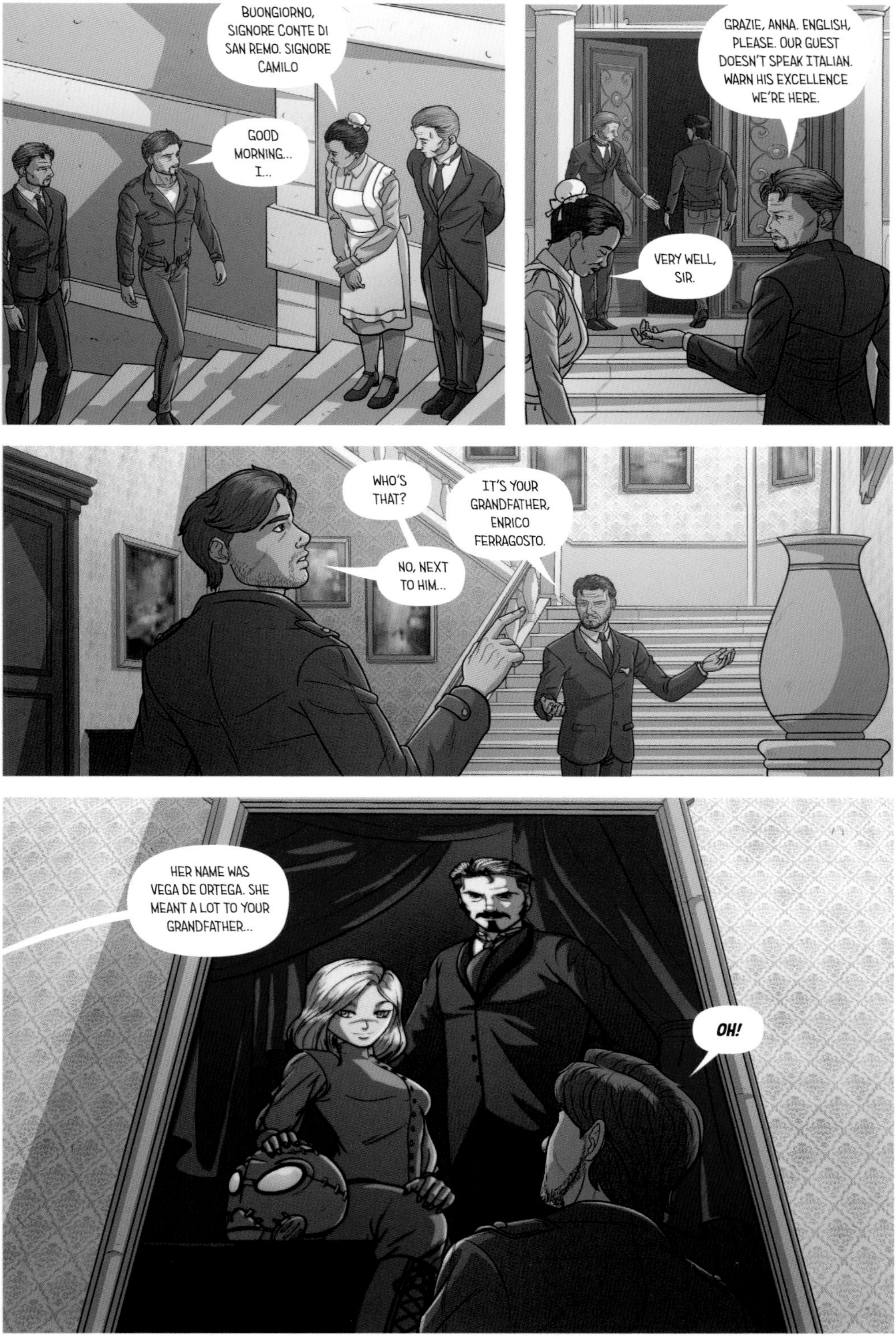
BUONGIORNO, SIGNORE CONTE DI SAN REMO. SIGNORE CAMILO
GOOD MORNING... I...
GRAZIE, ANNA. ENGLISH, PLEASE. OUR GUEST DOESN'T SPEAK ITALIAN. WARN HIS EXCELLENCE WE'RE HERE.
VERY WELL, SIR.
WHO'S THAT?
IT'S YOUR GRANDFATHER, ENRICO FERRAGOSTO.
NO, NEXT TO HIM...
HER NAME WAS VEGA DE ORTEGA. SHE MEANT A LOT TO YOUR GRANDFATHER...
OH!

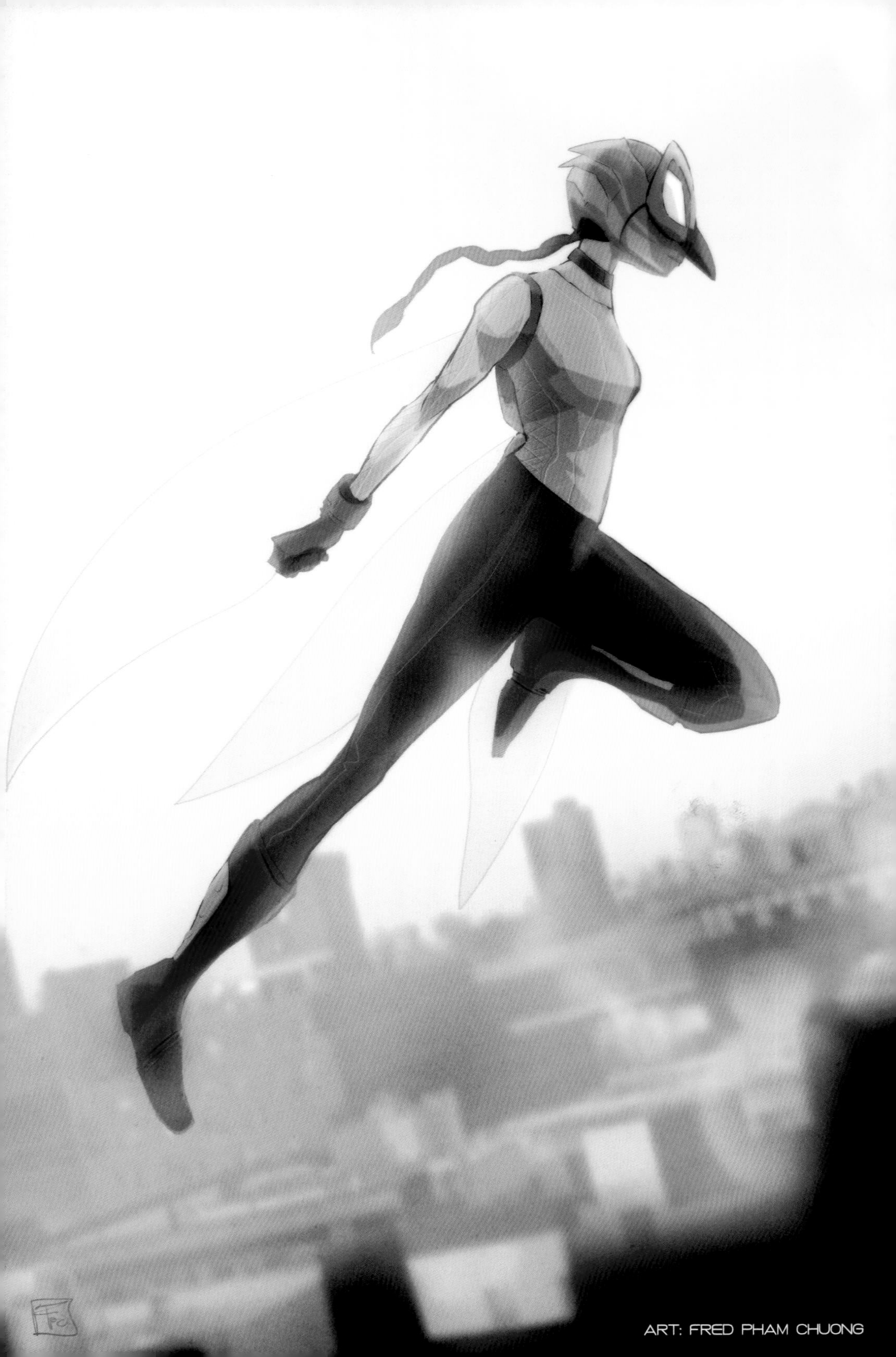

ART: FRED PHAM CHUONG

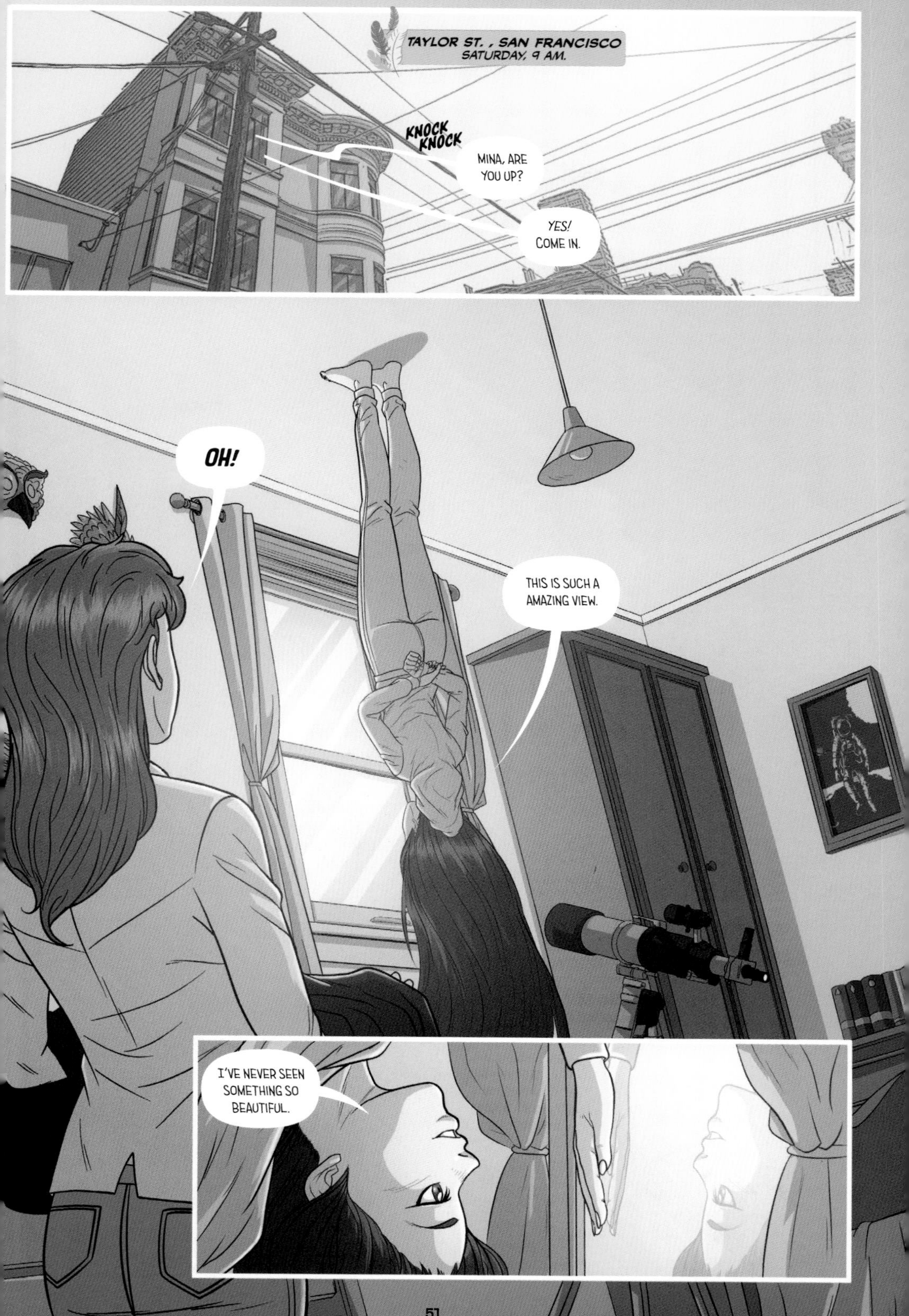
TAYLOR ST. , SAN FRANCISCO
SATURDAY, 9 AM.
KNOCK KNOCK
MINA, ARE YOU UP?
YES! COME IN.
OH!
THIS IS SUCH A AMAZING VIEW.
I'VE NEVER SEEN SOMETHING SO BEAUTIFUL.

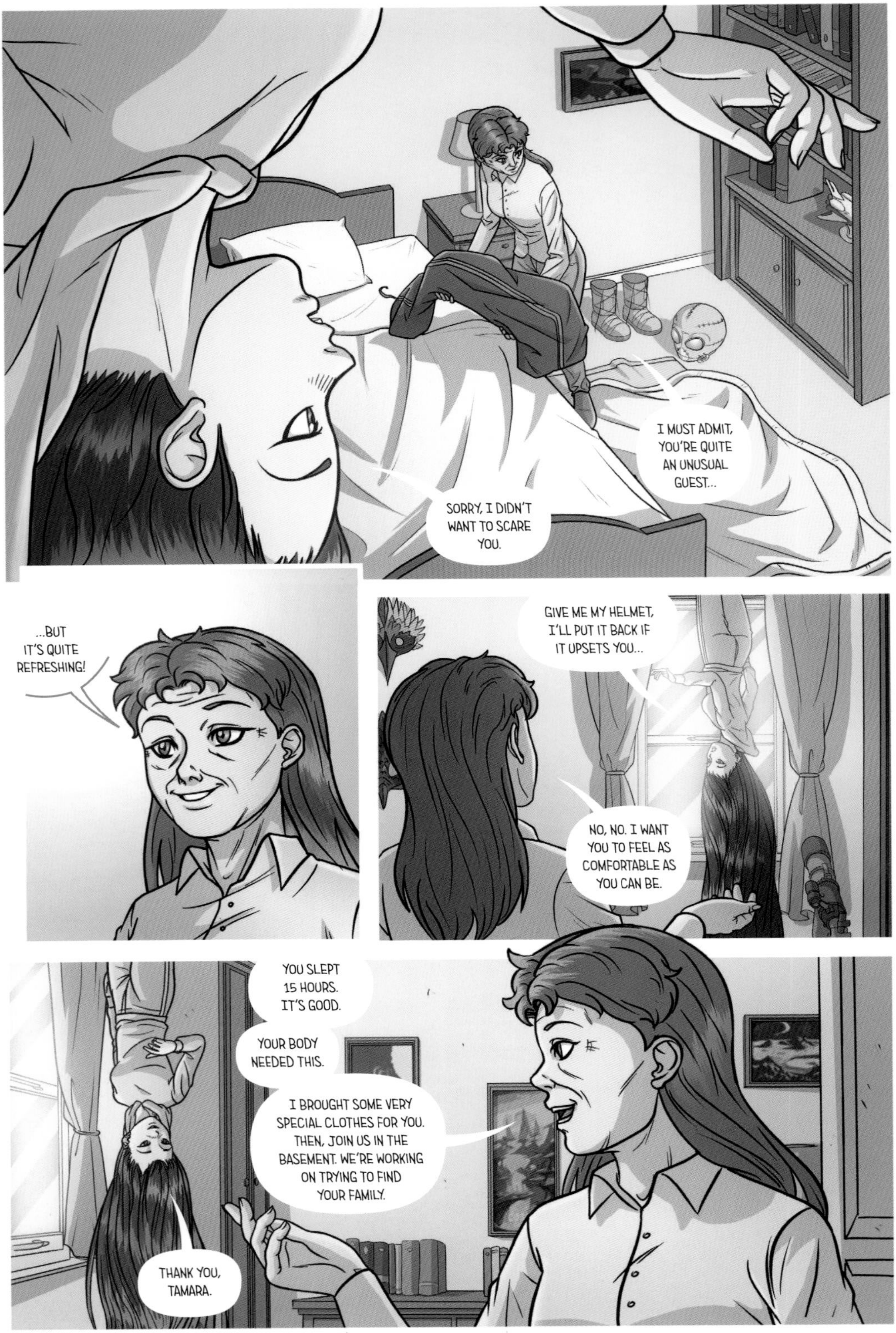
SORRY, I DIDN'T WANT TO SCARE YOU.
I MUST ADMIT, YOU'RE QUITE AN UNUSUAL GUEST...
...BUT IT'S QUITE REFRESHING!
GIVE ME MY HELMET, I'LL PUT IT BACK IF IT UPSETS YOU...
NO, NO. I WANT YOU TO FEEL AS COMFORTABLE AS YOU CAN BE.
YOU SLEPT 15 HOURS. IT'S GOOD.
YOUR BODY NEEDED THIS.
I BROUGHT SOME VERY SPECIAL CLOTHES FOR YOU. THEN, JOIN US IN THE BASEMENT. WE'RE WORKING ON TRYING TO FIND YOUR FAMILY.
THANK YOU, TAMARA.

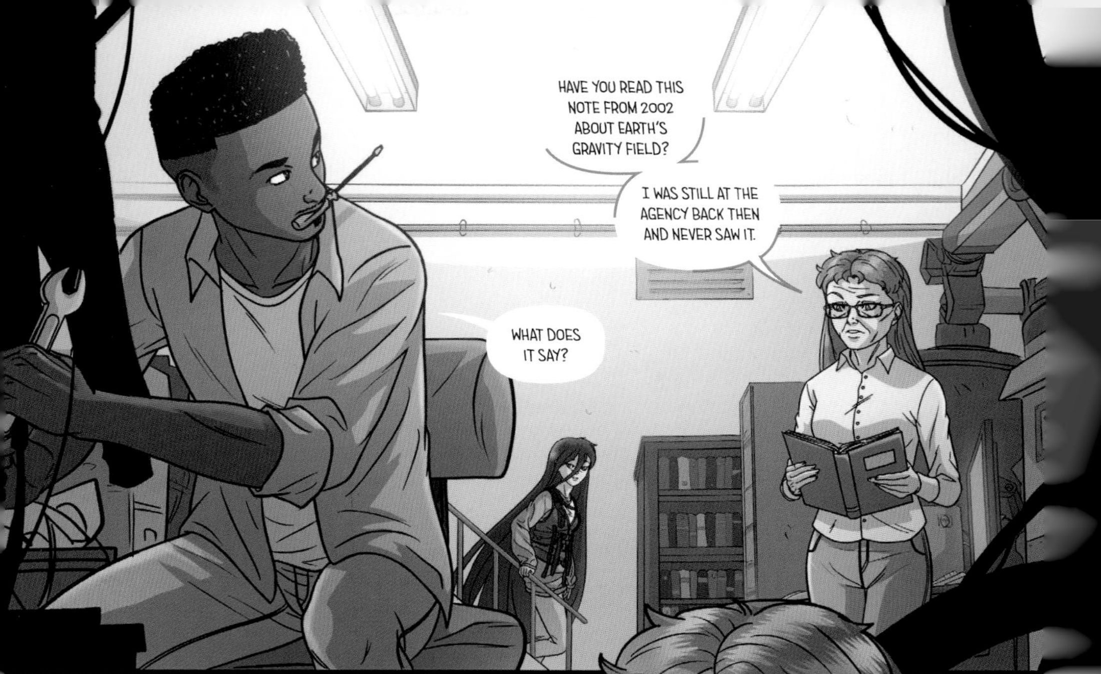
HAVE YOU READ THIS NOTE FROM 2002 ABOUT EARTH'S GRAVITY FIELD?
I WAS STILL AT THE AGENCY BACK THEN AND NEVER SAW IT.
WHAT DOES IT SAY?

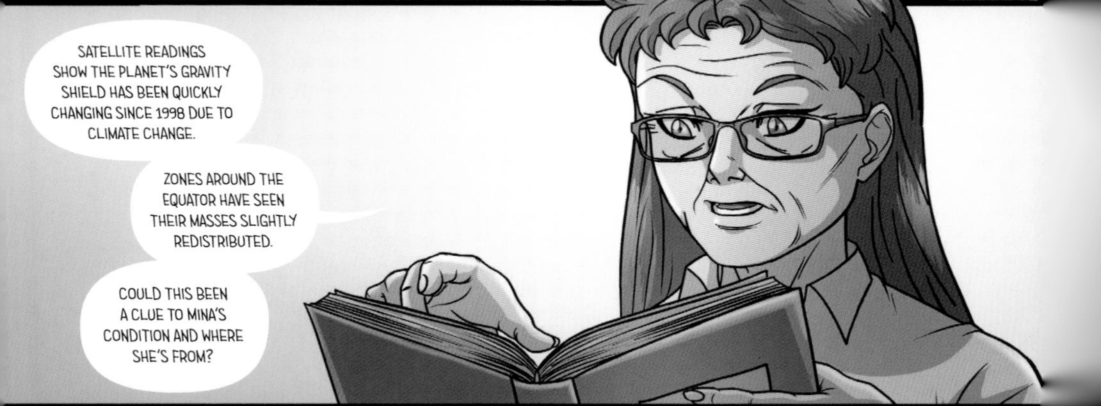
SATELLITE READINGS SHOW THE PLANET'S GRAVITY SHIELD HAS BEEN QUICKLY CHANGING SINCE 1998 DUE TO CLIMATE CHANGE.
ZONES AROUND THE EQUATOR HAVE SEEN THEIR MASSES SLIGHTLY REDISTRIBUTED.
COULD THIS BEEN A CLUE TO MINA'S CONDITION AND WHERE SHE'S FROM?

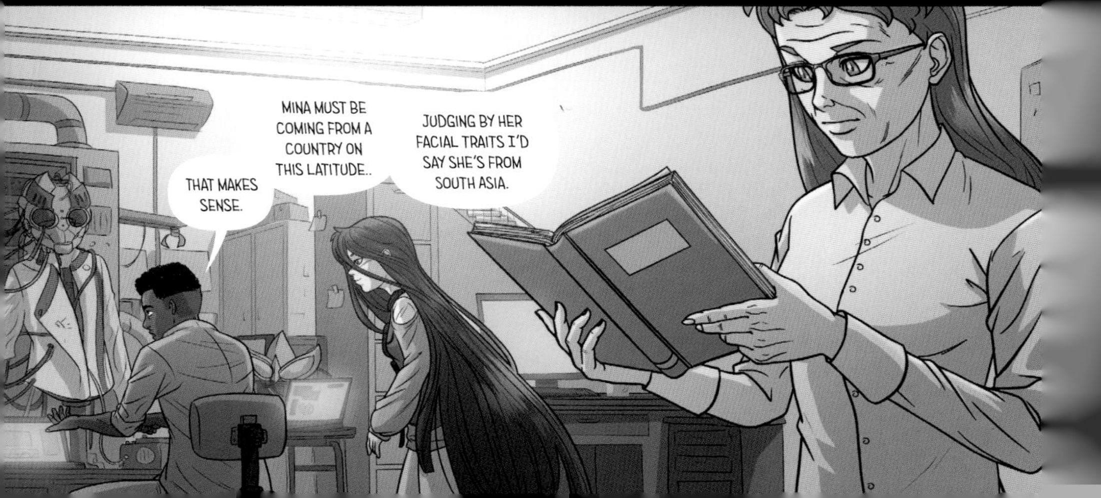
THAT MAKES SENSE.
MINA MUST BE COMING FROM A COUNTRY ON THIS LATITUDE..
JUDGING BY HER FACIAL TRAITS I'D SAY SHE'S FROM SOUTH ASIA.

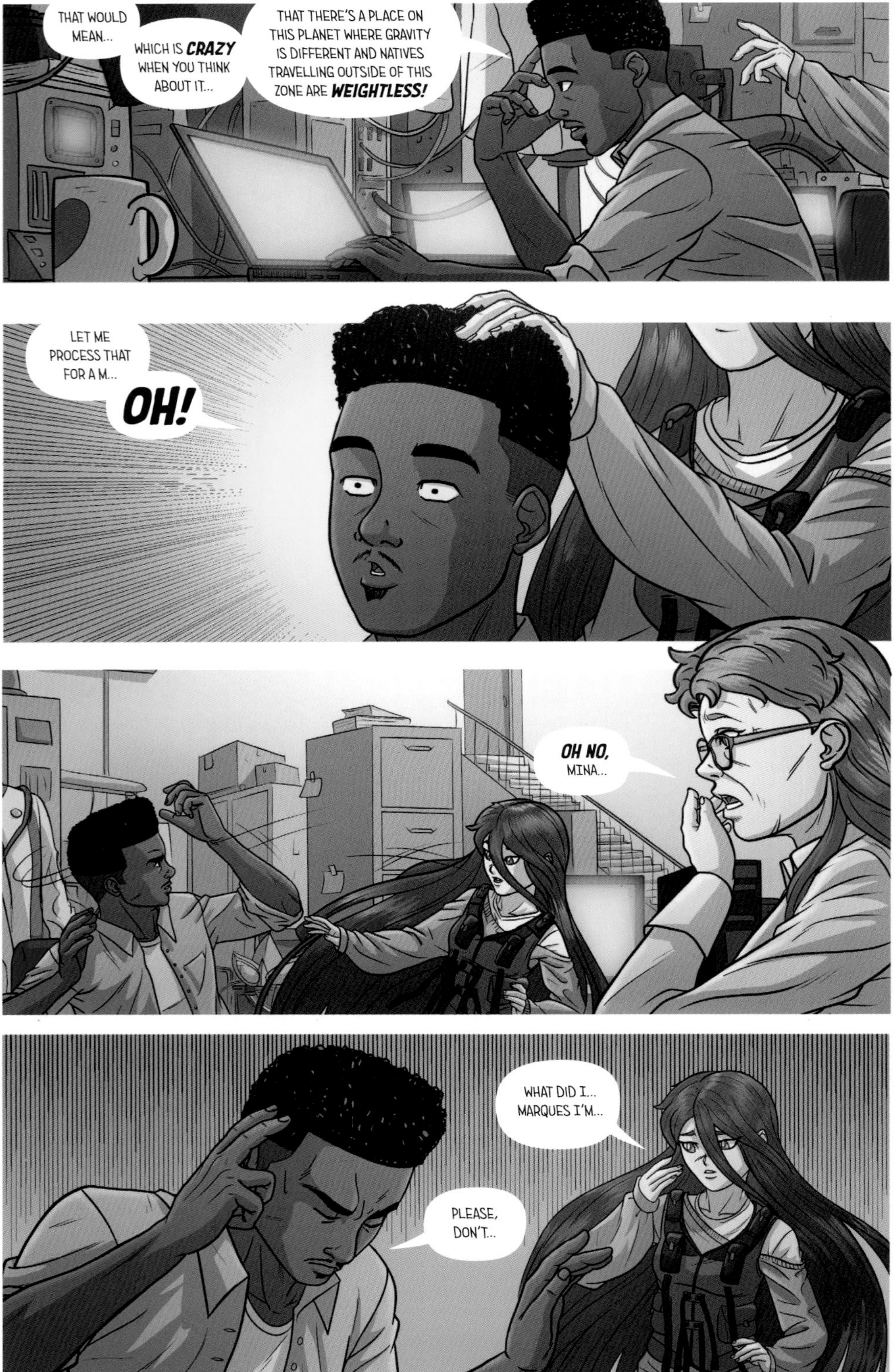
THAT WOULD MEAN...
WHICH IS CRAZY WHEN YOU THINK ABOUT IT...
THAT THERE'S A PLACE ON THIS PLANET WHERE GRAVITY IS DIFFERENT AND NATIVES TRAVELLING OUTSIDE OF THIS ZONE ARE WEIGHTLESS!
LET ME PROCESS THAT FOR A M...
OH!
OH NO, MINA...
WHAT DID I... MARQUES I'M...
PLEASE, DON'T...

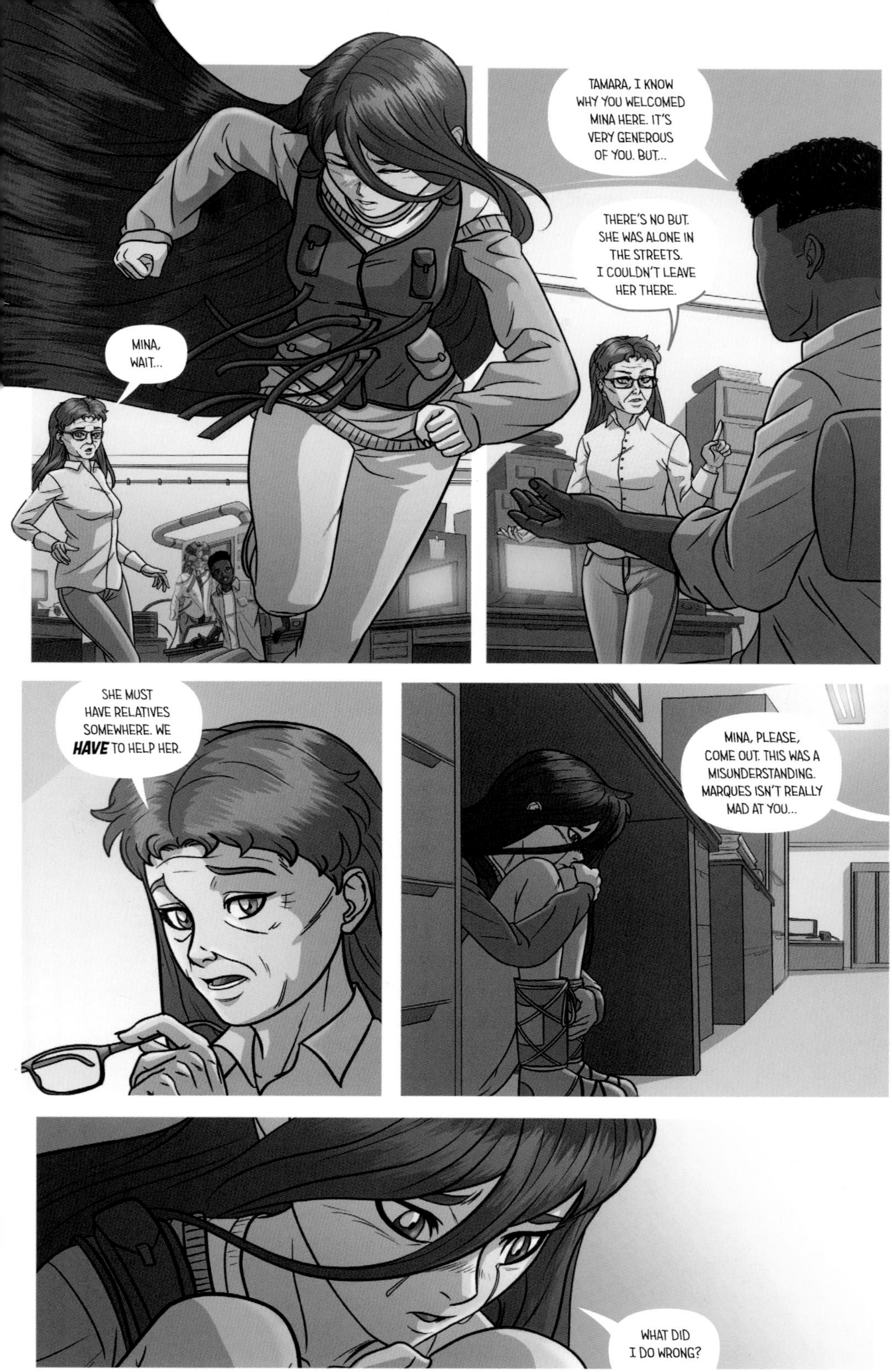
MINA, WAIT...
TAMARA, I KNOW WHY YOU WELCOMED MINA HERE. IT'S VERY GENEROUS OF YOU. BUT...
THERE'S NO BUT. SHE WAS ALONE IN THE STREETS. I COULDN'T LEAVE HER THERE.
SHE MUST HAVE RELATIVES SOMEWHERE. WE ***HAVE*** TO HELP HER.
MINA, PLEASE, COME OUT. THIS WAS A MISUNDERSTANDING. MARQUES ISN'T REALLY MAD AT YOU...
WHAT DID I DO WRONG?

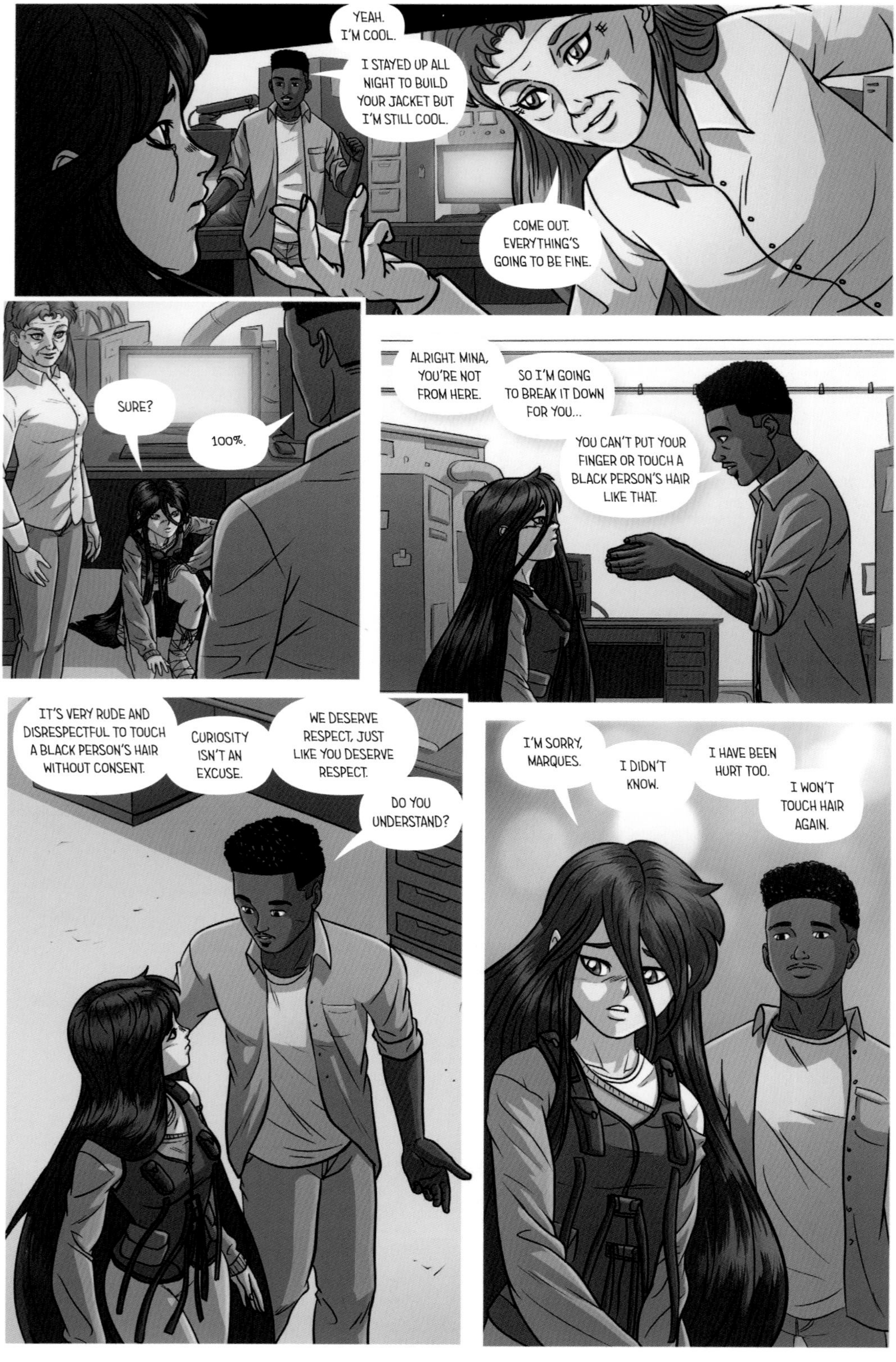
YEAH. I'M COOL.
I STAYED UP ALL NIGHT TO BUILD YOUR JACKET BUT I'M STILL COOL.
COME OUT. EVERYTHING'S GOING TO BE FINE.
SURE?
100%.
ALRIGHT. MINA, YOU'RE NOT FROM HERE.
SO I'M GOING TO BREAK IT DOWN FOR YOU...
YOU CAN'T PUT YOUR FINGER OR TOUCH A BLACK PERSON'S HAIR LIKE THAT.
IT'S VERY RUDE AND DISRESPECTFUL TO TOUCH A BLACK PERSON'S HAIR WITHOUT CONSENT.
CURIOSITY ISN'T AN EXCUSE.
WE DESERVE RESPECT, JUST LIKE YOU DESERVE RESPECT.
DO YOU UNDERSTAND?
I'M SORRY, MARQUES.
I DIDN'T KNOW.
I HAVE BEEN HURT TOO.
I WON'T TOUCH HAIR AGAIN.

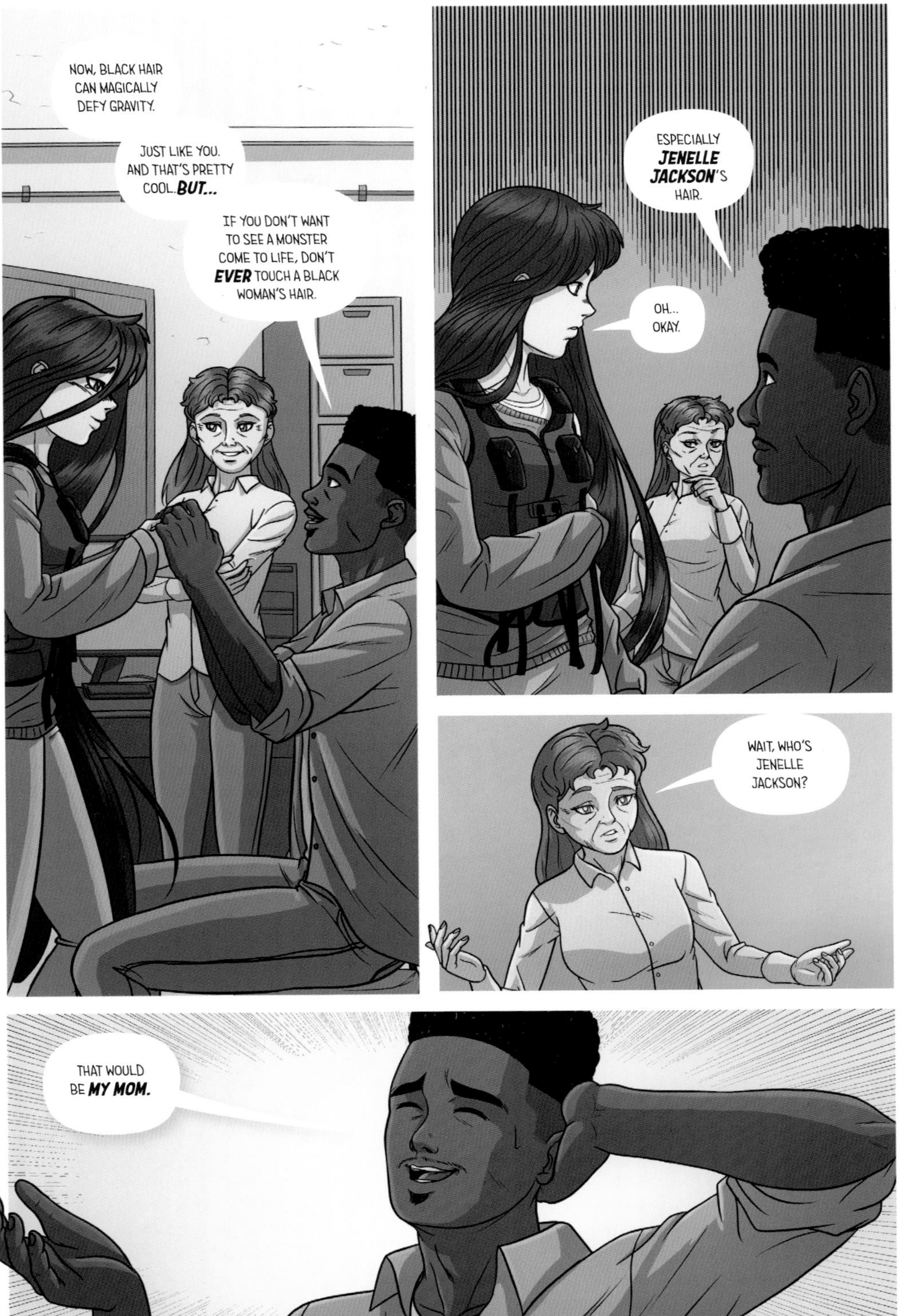
NOW, BLACK HAIR CAN MAGICALLY DEFY GRAVITY.
JUST LIKE YOU. AND THAT'S PRETTY COOL. **BUT...**
IF YOU DON'T WANT TO SEE A MONSTER COME TO LIFE, DON'T **EVER** TOUCH A BLACK WOMAN'S HAIR.
ESPECIALLY **JENELLE JACKSON**'S HAIR.
OH... OKAY.
WAIT, WHO'S JENELLE JACKSON?
THAT WOULD BE **MY MOM.**

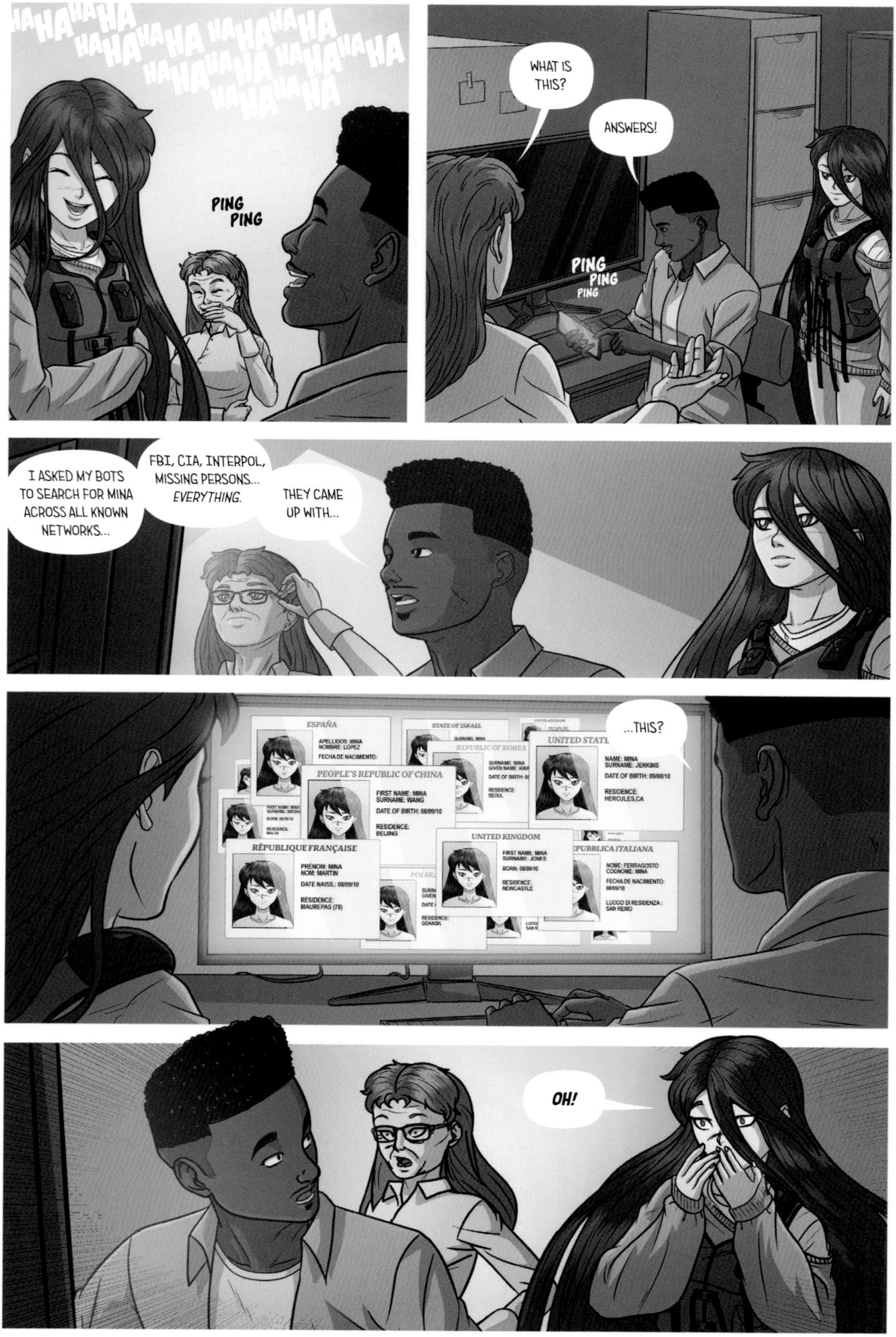
HAHAHAHA HAHAHAHA HAHAHAHA HAHAHAHAHAHA HAHAHAHA
PING PING
WHAT IS THIS?
ANSWERS!
PING PING PING
I ASKED MY BOTS TO SEARCH FOR MINA ACROSS ALL KNOWN NETWORKS...
FBI, CIA, INTERPOL, MISSING PERSONS... *EVERYTHING.*
THEY CAME UP WITH...
ESPAÑA
APELLIDOS: MINA
NOMBRE: LOPEZ
FECHA DE NACIMIENTO:
STATE OF ISRAEL
REPUBLIC OF KOREA
RESIDENCE: SEOUL
UNITED STATE
NAME: MINA
SURNAME: JENKINS
DATE OF BIRTH: 09/08/10
RESIDENCE: HERCULES,CA
...THIS?
PEOPLE'S REPUBLIC OF CHINA
FIRST NAME: MINA
SURNAME: WANG
DATE OF BIRTH: 08/09/10
RESIDENCE: BEIJING
RÉPUBLIQUE FRANÇAISE
PRÉNOM: MINA
NOM: MARTIN
DATE NAISS.: 08/09/10
RÉSIDENCE: MAUREPAS (78)
UNITED KINGDOM
FIRST NAME: MINA
SURNAME: JONES
BORN: 08/09/10
RESIDENCE: NEWCASTLE
RESIDENCE: GDANSK
EPUBBLICA ITALIANA
NOME: FERRAGOSTO
COGNOME: MINA
FECHA DE NACIMIENTO: 08/09/10
LUOGO DI RESIDENZA : SAN REMO
OH!

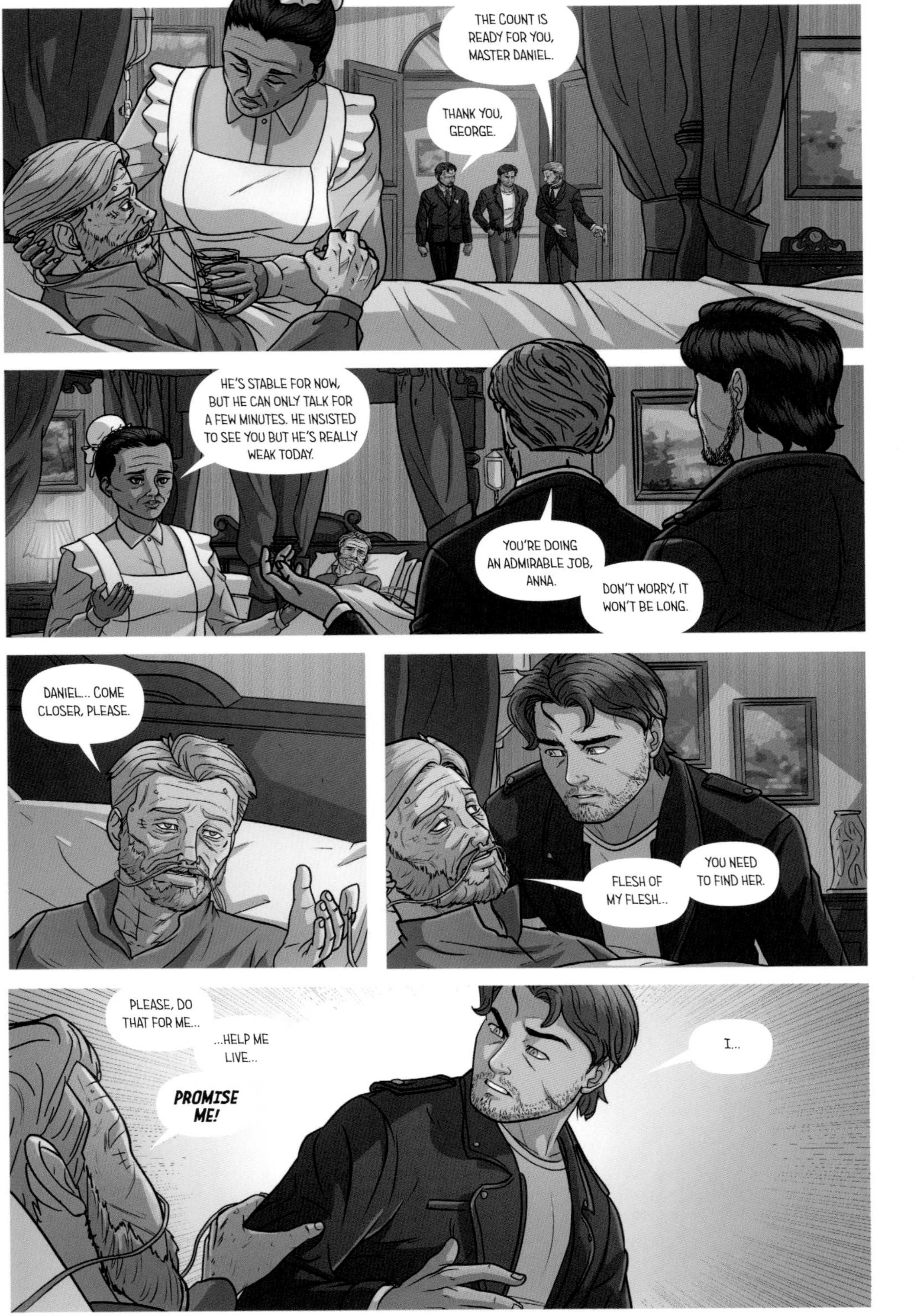
THE COUNT IS READY FOR YOU, MASTER DANIEL.
THANK YOU, GEORGE.
HE'S STABLE FOR NOW, BUT HE CAN ONLY TALK FOR A FEW MINUTES. HE INSISTED TO SEE YOU BUT HE'S REALLY WEAK TODAY.
YOU'RE DOING AN ADMIRABLE JOB, ANNA.
DON'T WORRY, IT WON'T BE LONG.
DANIEL... COME CLOSER, PLEASE.
FLESH OF MY FLESH...
YOU NEED TO FIND HER.
PLEASE, DO THAT FOR ME...
...HELP ME LIVE...
PROMISE ME!
I...

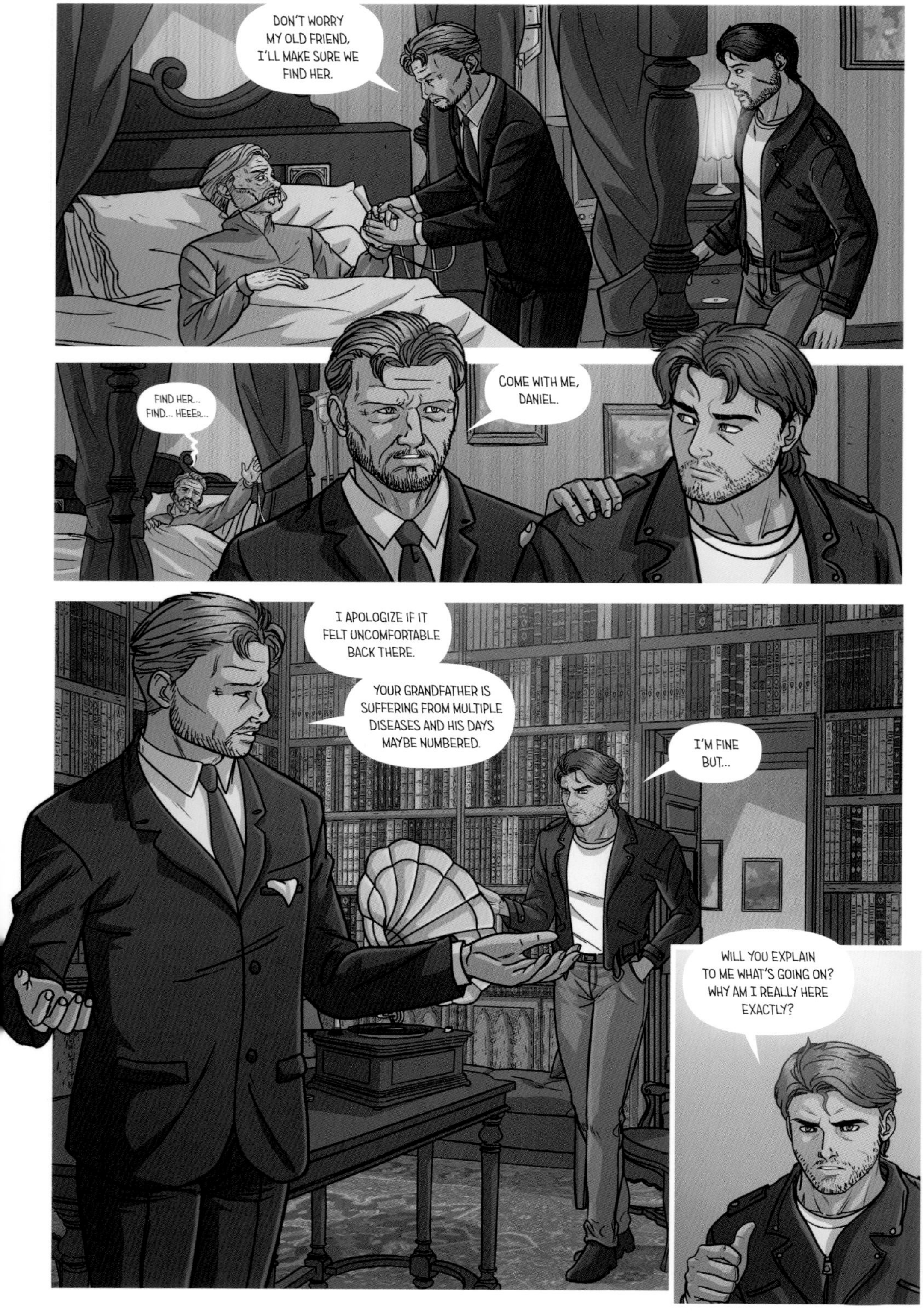
DON'T WORRY MY OLD FRIEND, I'LL MAKE SURE WE FIND HER.
FIND HER... FIND... HEEER...
COME WITH ME, DANIEL.
I APOLOGIZE IF IT FELT UNCOMFORTABLE BACK THERE.
YOUR GRANDFATHER IS SUFFERING FROM MULTIPLE DISEASES AND HIS DAYS MAYBE NUMBERED.
I'M FINE BUT...
WILL YOU EXPLAIN TO ME WHAT'S GOING ON? WHY AM I REALLY HERE EXACTLY?

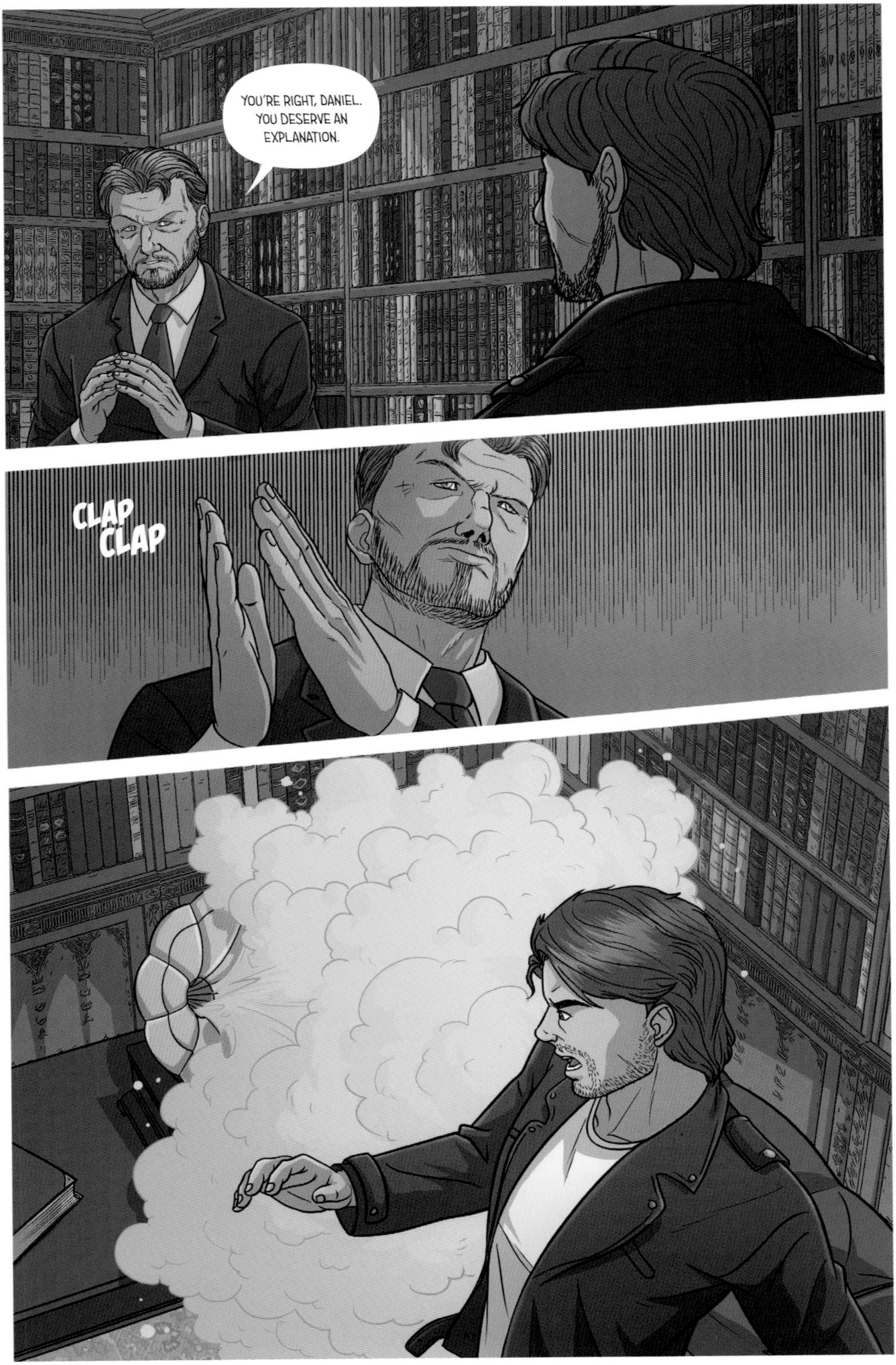
YOU'RE RIGHT, DANIEL. YOU DESERVE AN EXPLANATION.
CLAP CLAP

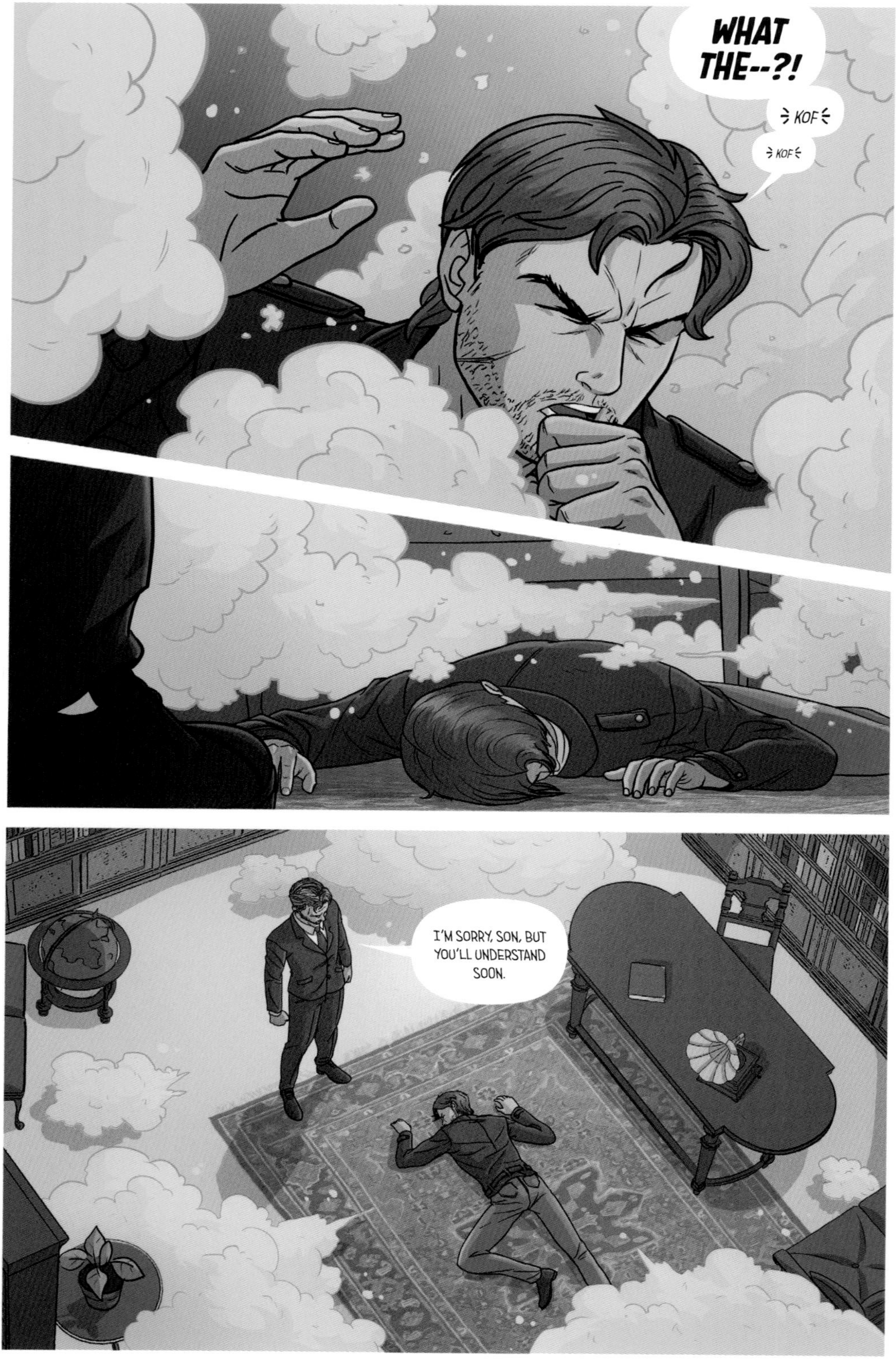
WHAT THE--?!
KOF
KOF
I'M SORRY, SON, BUT YOU'LL UNDERSTAND SOON.

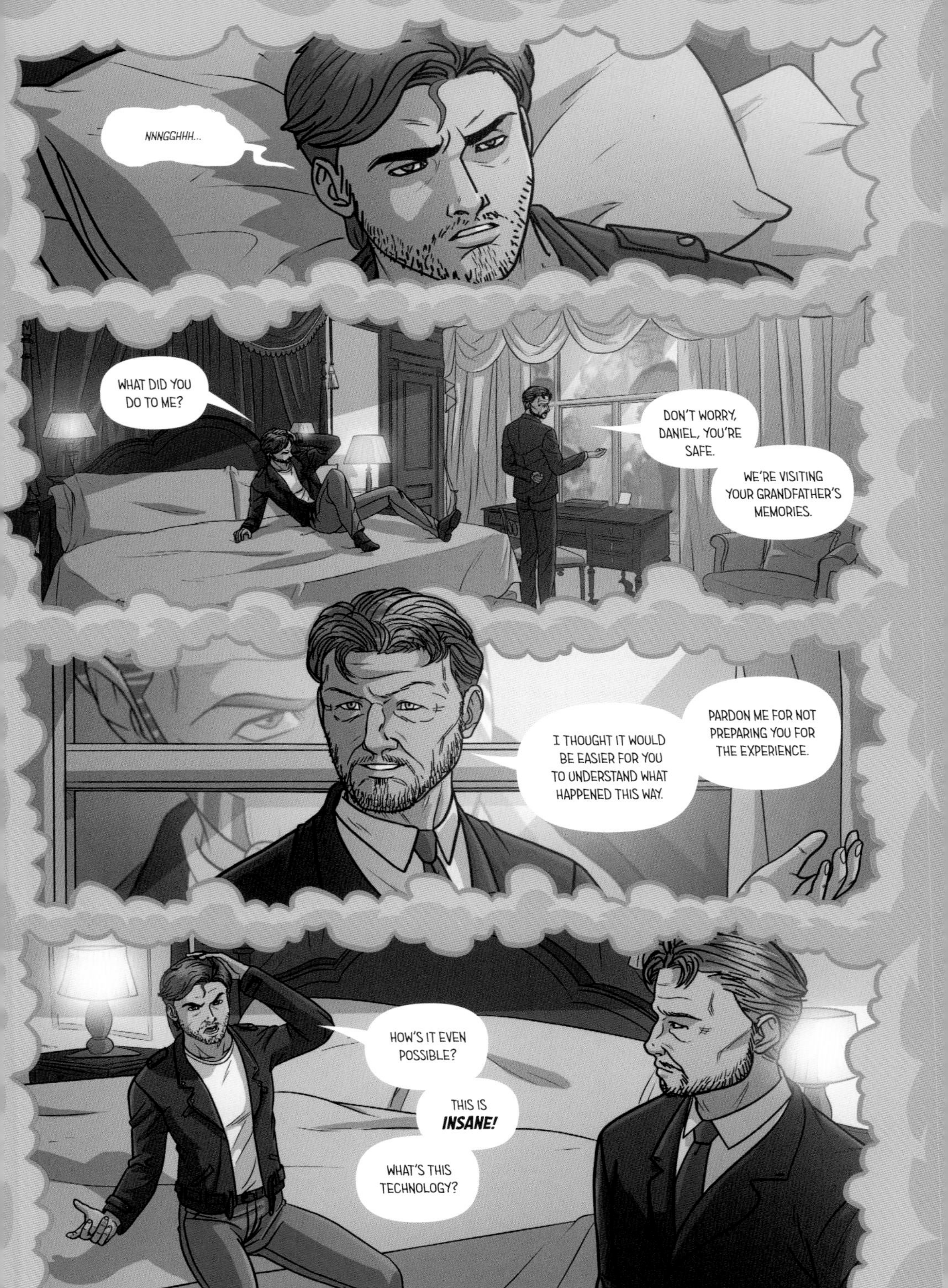
NNNGGHHH...
WHAT DID YOU DO TO ME?
DON'T WORRY, DANIEL, YOU'RE SAFE.
WE'RE VISITING YOUR GRANDFATHER'S MEMORIES.
PARDON ME FOR NOT PREPARING YOU FOR THE EXPERIENCE.
I THOUGHT IT WOULD BE EASIER FOR YOU TO UNDERSTAND WHAT HAPPENED THIS WAY.
HOW'S IT EVEN POSSIBLE?
THIS IS ***INSANE!***
WHAT'S THIS TECHNOLOGY?

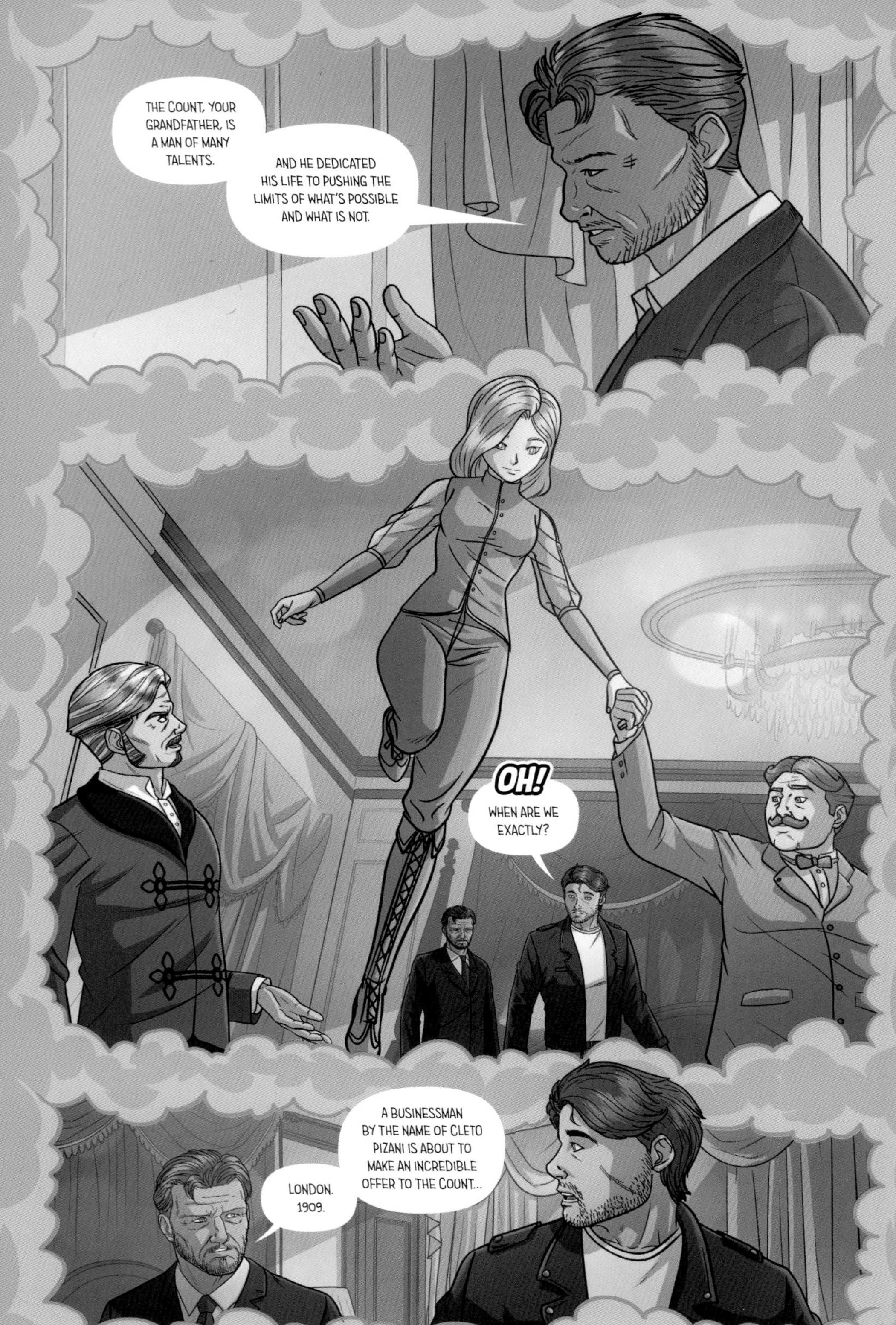
THE COUNT, YOUR GRANDFATHER, IS A MAN OF MANY TALENTS.
AND HE DEDICATED HIS LIFE TO PUSHING THE LIMITS OF WHAT'S POSSIBLE AND WHAT IS NOT.
OH!
WHEN ARE WE EXACTLY?
LONDON. 1909.
A BUSINESSMAN BY THE NAME OF CLETO PIZANI IS ABOUT TO MAKE AN INCREDIBLE OFFER TO THE COUNT...

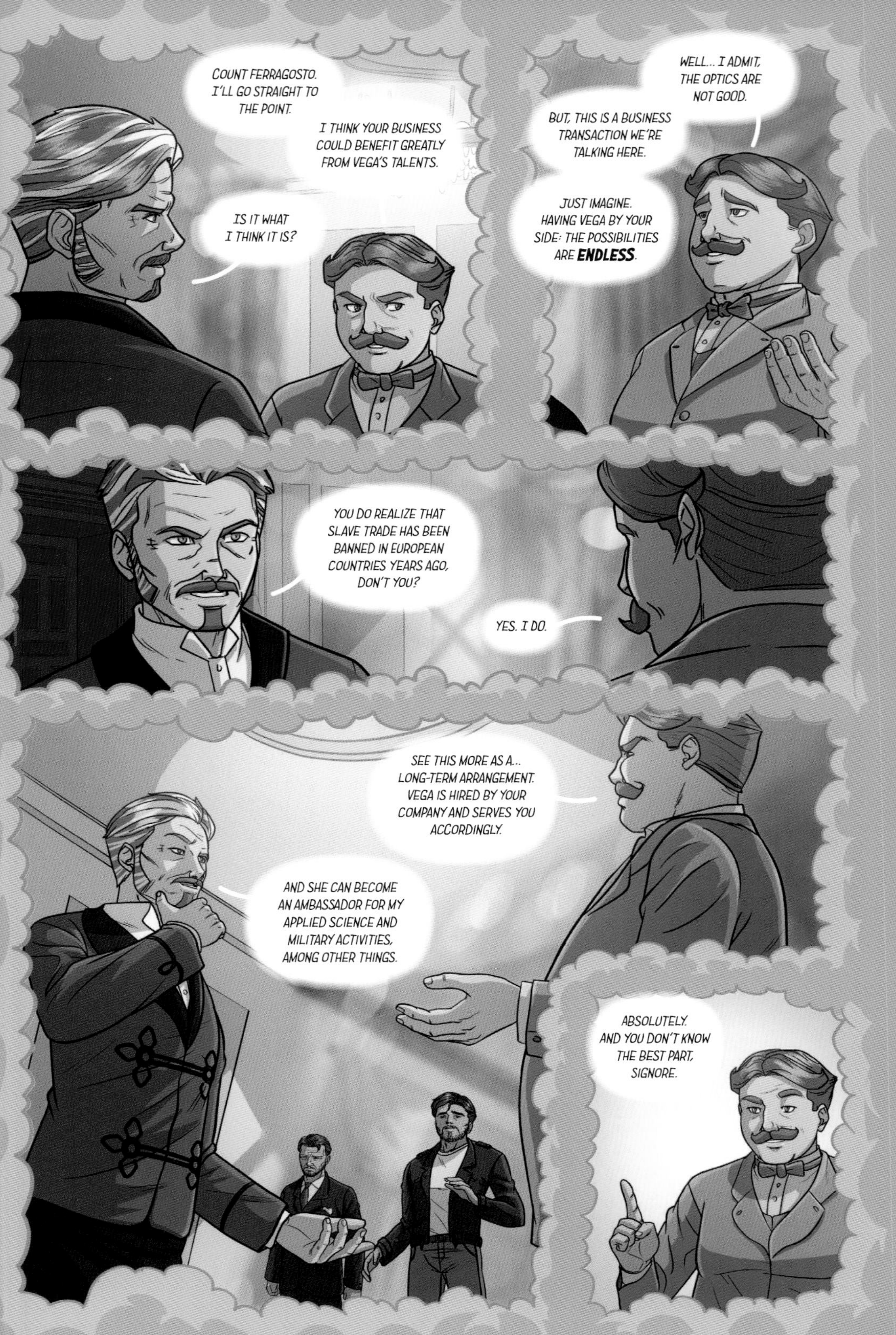
COUNT FERRAGOSTO. I'LL GO STRAIGHT TO THE POINT.
I THINK YOUR BUSINESS COULD BENEFIT GREATLY FROM VEGA'S TALENTS.
IS IT WHAT I THINK IT IS?
WELL... I ADMIT, THE OPTICS ARE NOT GOOD.
BUT, THIS IS A BUSINESS TRANSACTION WE'RE TALKING HERE.
JUST IMAGINE. HAVING VEGA BY YOUR SIDE: THE POSSIBILITIES ARE **ENDLESS**.
YOU DO REALIZE THAT SLAVE TRADE HAS BEEN BANNED IN EUROPEAN COUNTRIES YEARS AGO, DON'T YOU?
YES. I DO.
SEE THIS MORE AS A... LONG-TERM ARRANGEMENT. VEGA IS HIRED BY YOUR COMPANY AND SERVES YOU ACCORDINGLY.
AND SHE CAN BECOME AN AMBASSADOR FOR MY APPLIED SCIENCE AND MILITARY ACTIVITIES, AMONG OTHER THINGS.
ABSOLUTELY. AND YOU DON'T KNOW THE BEST PART, SIGNORE.

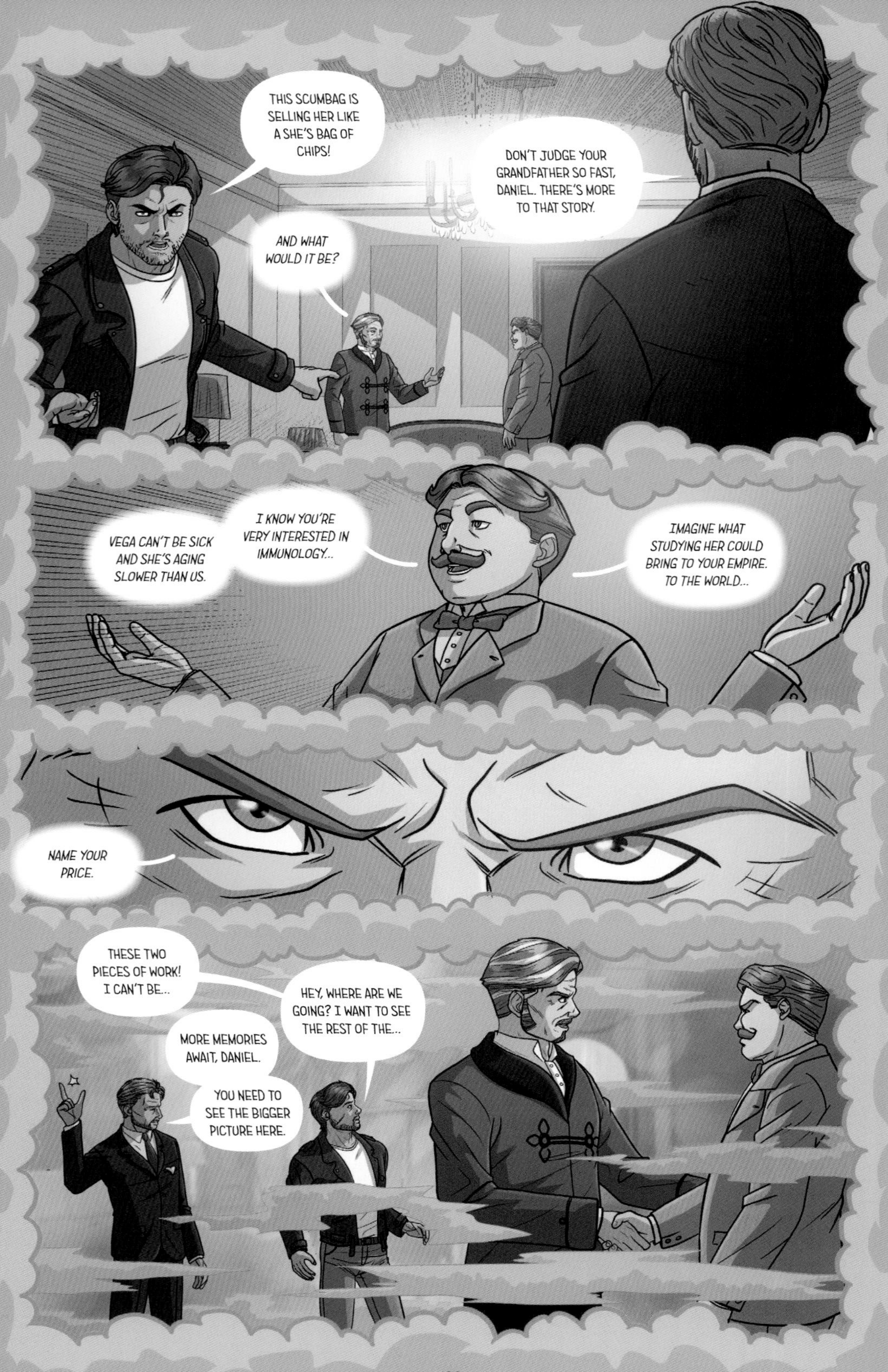
THIS SCUMBAG IS SELLING HER LIKE A SHE'S BAG OF CHIPS!
DON'T JUDGE YOUR GRANDFATHER SO FAST, DANIEL. THERE'S MORE TO THAT STORY.
AND WHAT WOULD IT BE?
VEGA CAN'T BE SICK AND SHE'S AGING SLOWER THAN US.
I KNOW YOU'RE VERY INTERESTED IN IMMUNOLOGY...
IMAGINE WHAT STUDYING HER COULD BRING TO YOUR EMPIRE. TO THE WORLD...
NAME YOUR PRICE.
THESE TWO PIECES OF WORK! I CAN'T BE...
HEY, WHERE ARE WE GOING? I WANT TO SEE THE REST OF THE...
MORE MEMORIES AWAIT, DANIEL.
YOU NEED TO SEE THE BIGGER PICTURE HERE.

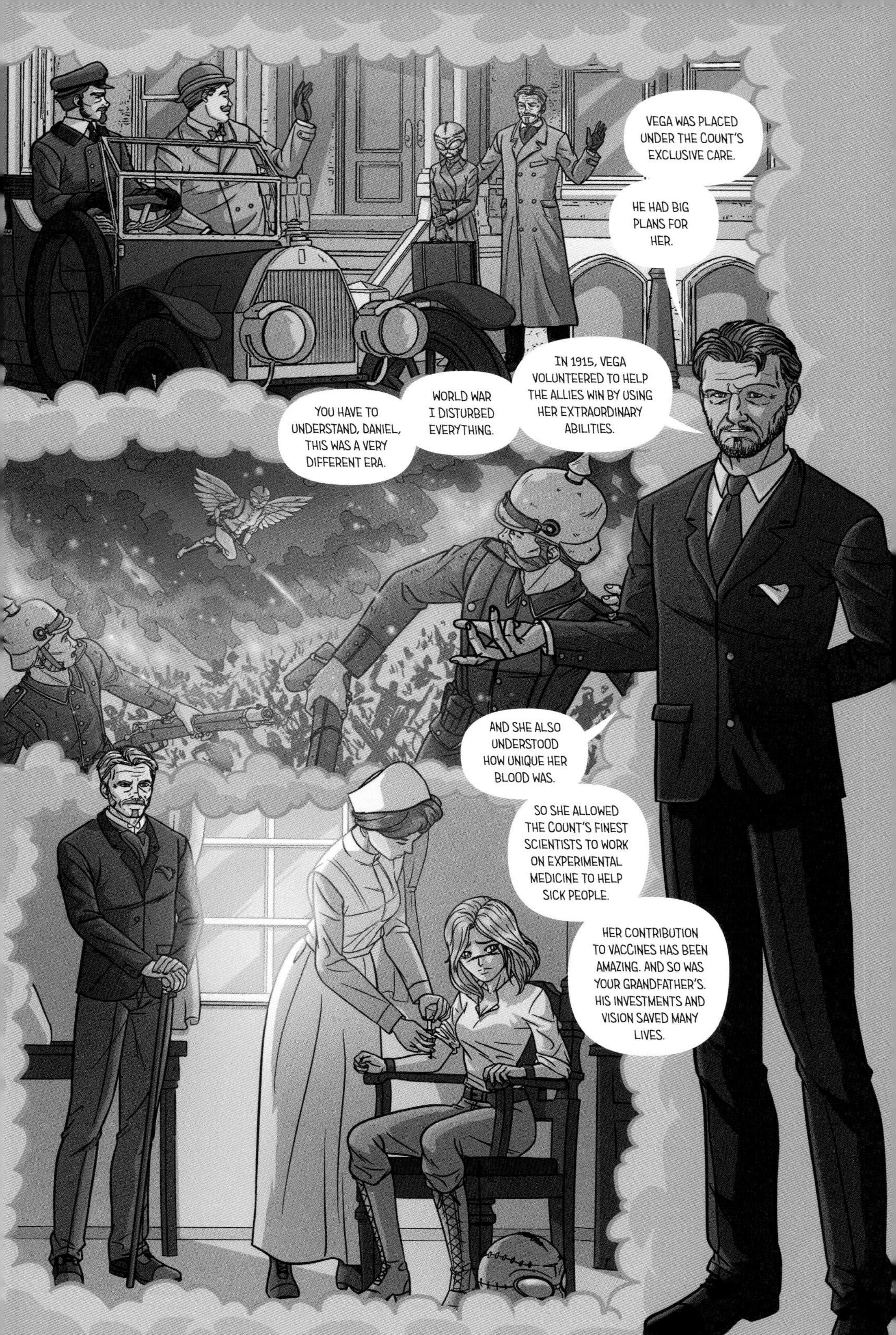
VEGA WAS PLACED UNDER THE COUNT'S EXCLUSIVE CARE.
HE HAD BIG PLANS FOR HER.
YOU HAVE TO UNDERSTAND, DANIEL, THIS WAS A VERY DIFFERENT ERA.
WORLD WAR I DISTURBED EVERYTHING.
IN 1915, VEGA VOLUNTEERED TO HELP THE ALLIES WIN BY USING HER EXTRAORDINARY ABILITIES.
AND SHE ALSO UNDERSTOOD HOW UNIQUE HER BLOOD WAS.
SO SHE ALLOWED THE COUNT'S FINEST SCIENTISTS TO WORK ON EXPERIMENTAL MEDICINE TO HELP SICK PEOPLE.
HER CONTRIBUTION TO VACCINES HAS BEEN AMAZING. AND SO WAS YOUR GRANDFATHER'S. HIS INVESTMENTS AND VISION SAVED MANY LIVES.

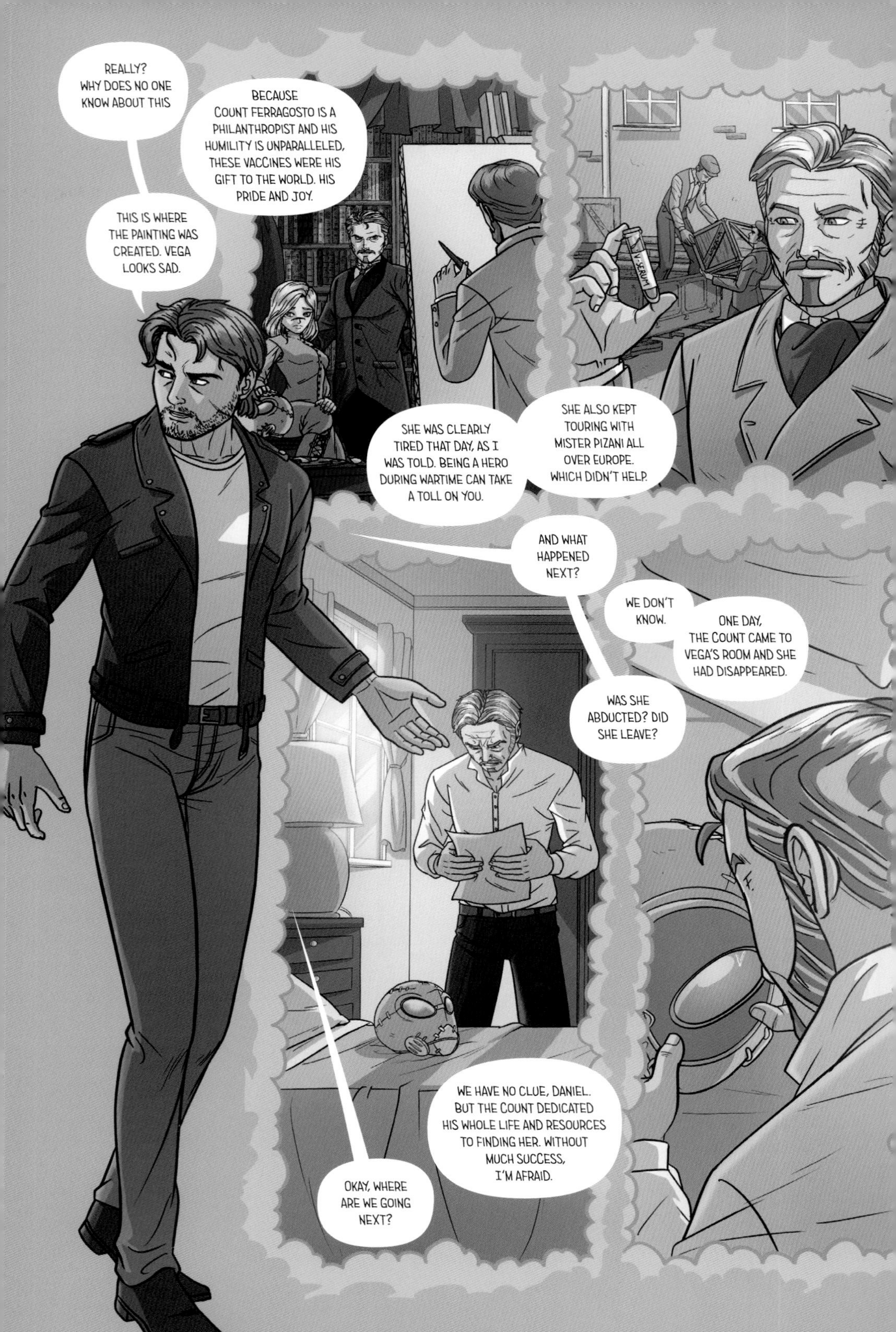
REALLY? WHY DOES NO ONE KNOW ABOUT THIS
BECAUSE COUNT FERRAGOSTO IS A PHILANTHROPIST AND HIS HUMILITY IS UNPARALLELED, THESE VACCINES WERE HIS GIFT TO THE WORLD. HIS PRIDE AND JOY.
THIS IS WHERE THE PAINTING WAS CREATED. VEGA LOOKS SAD.
V-SERUM
SHE WAS CLEARLY TIRED THAT DAY, AS I WAS TOLD. BEING A HERO DURING WARTIME CAN TAKE A TOLL ON YOU.
SHE ALSO KEPT TOURING WITH MISTER PIZANI ALL OVER EUROPE. WHICH DIDN'T HELP.
AND WHAT HAPPENED NEXT?
WE DON'T KNOW.
ONE DAY, THE COUNT CAME TO VEGA'S ROOM AND SHE HAD DISAPPEARED.
WAS SHE ABDUCTED? DID SHE LEAVE?
WE HAVE NO CLUE, DANIEL. BUT THE COUNT DEDICATED HIS WHOLE LIFE AND RESOURCES TO FINDING HER. WITHOUT MUCH SUCCESS, I'M AFRAID.
OKAY, WHERE ARE WE GOING NEXT?

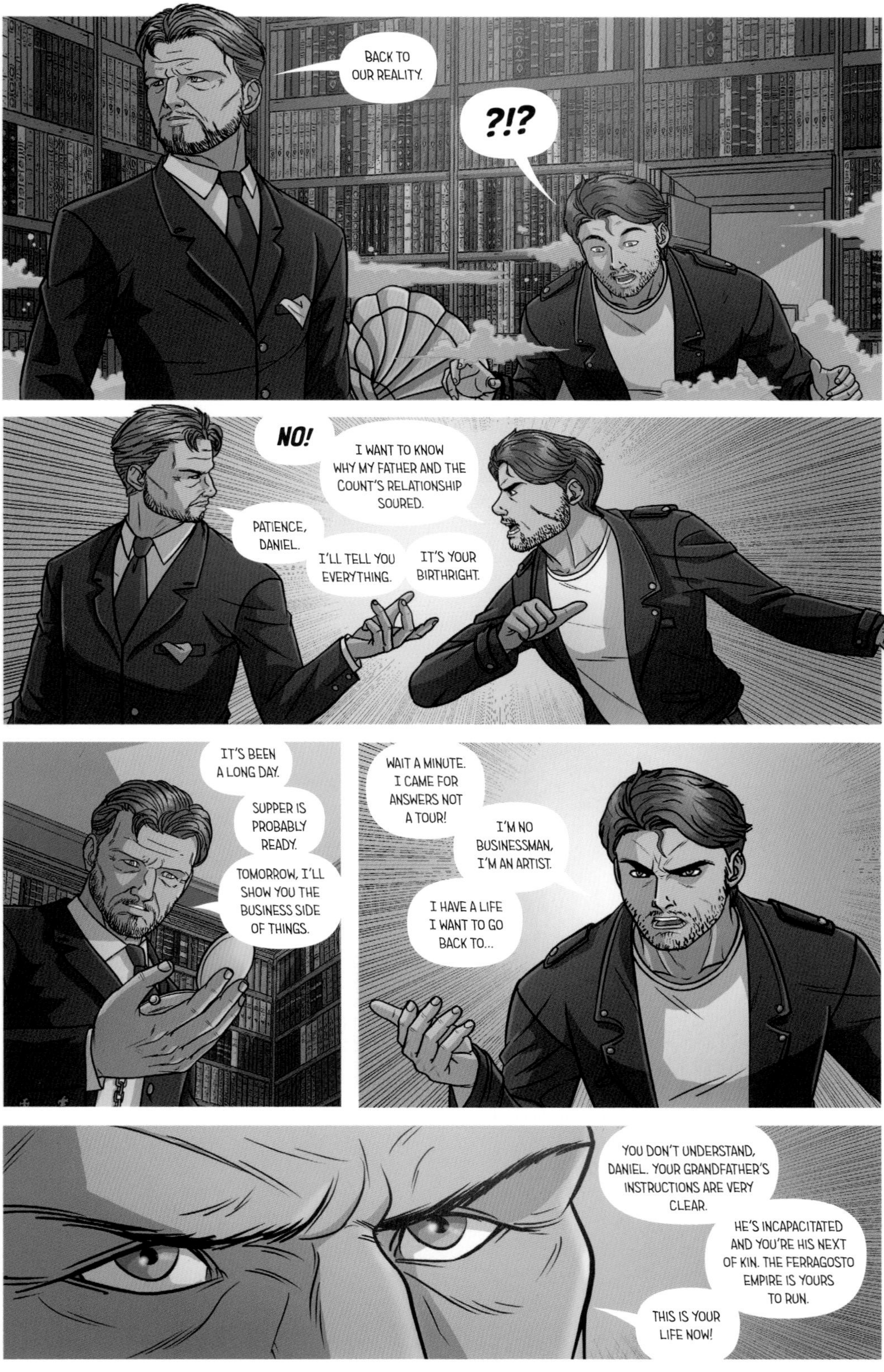
BACK TO OUR REALITY.
?!?
NO!
I WANT TO KNOW WHY MY FATHER AND THE COUNT'S RELATIONSHIP SOURED.
PATIENCE, DANIEL.
I'LL TELL YOU EVERYTHING.
IT'S YOUR BIRTHRIGHT.
IT'S BEEN A LONG DAY.
SUPPER IS PROBABLY READY.
TOMORROW, I'LL SHOW YOU THE BUSINESS SIDE OF THINGS.
WAIT A MINUTE. I CAME FOR ANSWERS NOT A TOUR!
I'M NO BUSINESSMAN, I'M AN ARTIST.
I HAVE A LIFE I WANT TO GO BACK TO...
YOU DON'T UNDERSTAND, DANIEL. YOUR GRANDFATHER'S INSTRUCTIONS ARE VERY CLEAR.
HE'S INCAPACITATED AND YOU'RE HIS NEXT OF KIN. THE FERRAGOSTO EMPIRE IS YOURS TO RUN.
THIS IS YOUR LIFE NOW!

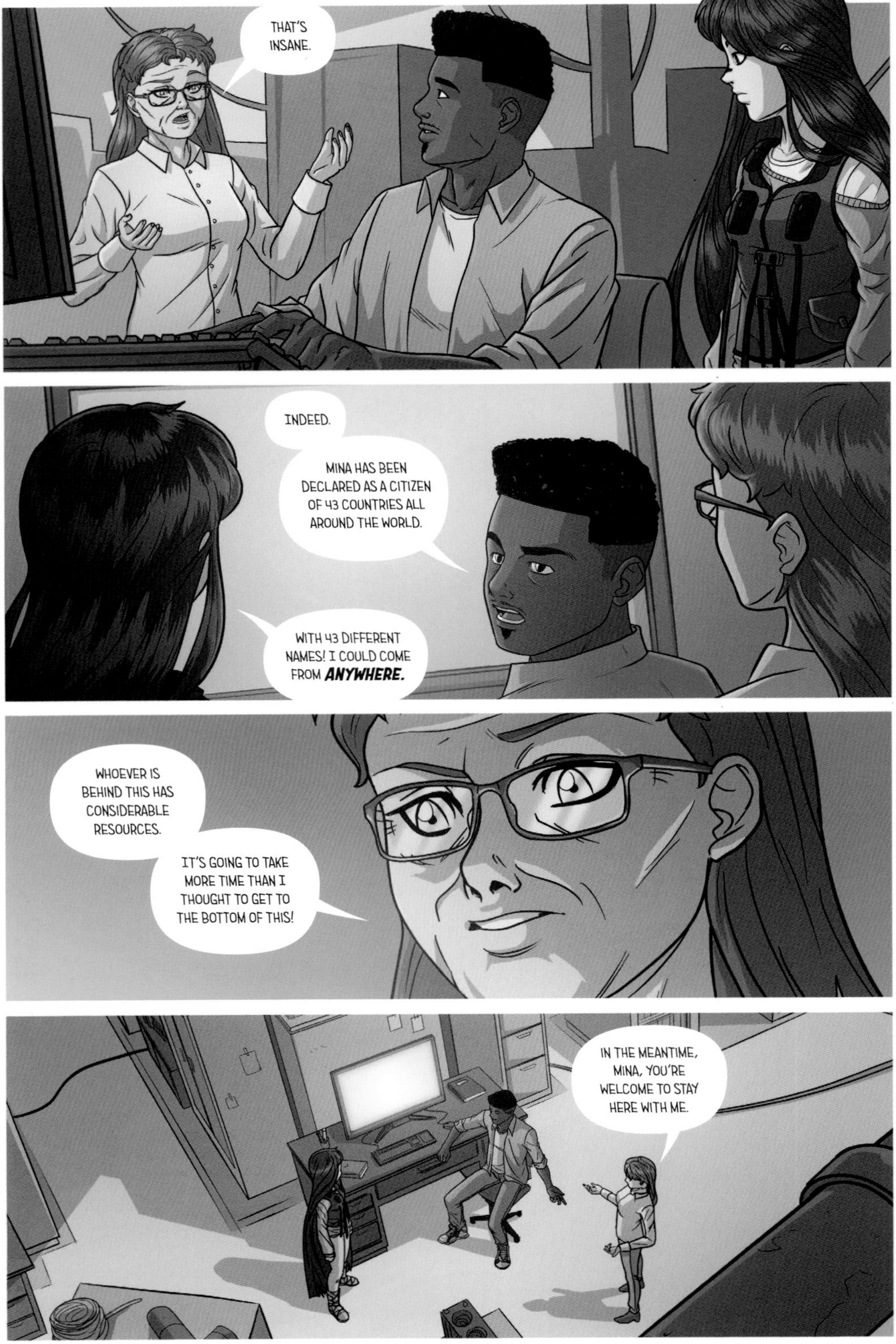
THAT'S INSANE.
INDEED.
MINA HAS BEEN DECLARED AS A CITIZEN OF 43 COUNTRIES ALL AROUND THE WORLD.
WITH 43 DIFFERENT NAMES! I COULD COME FROM ANYWHERE.
WHOEVER IS BEHIND THIS HAS CONSIDERABLE RESOURCES.
IT'S GOING TO TAKE MORE TIME THAN I THOUGHT TO GET TO THE BOTTOM OF THIS!
IN THE MEANTIME, MINA, YOU'RE WELCOME TO STAY HERE WITH ME.

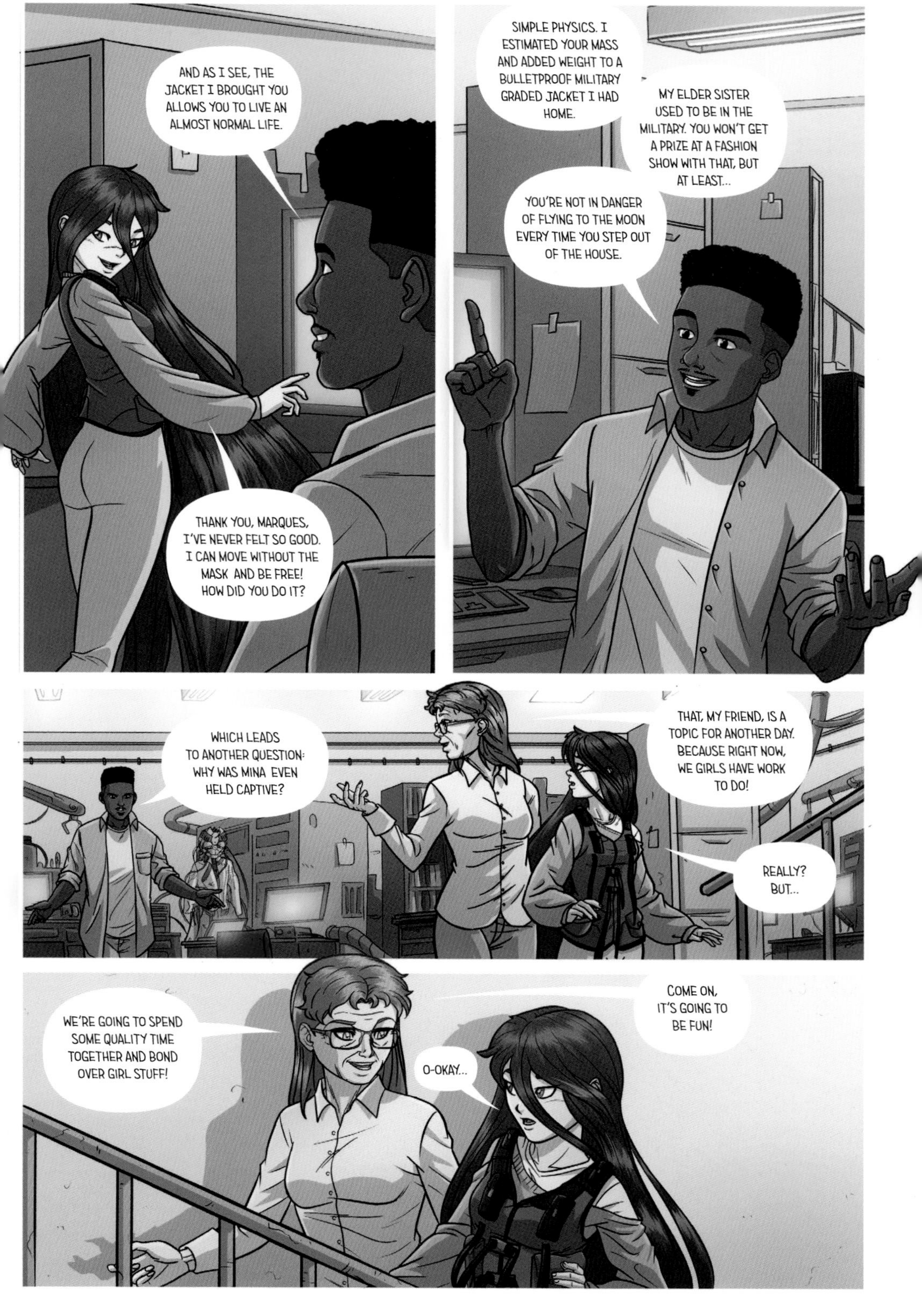
AND AS I SEE, THE JACKET I BROUGHT YOU ALLOWS YOU TO LIVE AN ALMOST NORMAL LIFE.
THANK YOU, MARQUES, I'VE NEVER FELT SO GOOD. I CAN MOVE WITHOUT THE MASK AND BE FREE! HOW DID YOU DO IT?
SIMPLE PHYSICS. I ESTIMATED YOUR MASS AND ADDED WEIGHT TO A BULLETPROOF MILITARY GRADED JACKET I HAD HOME.
MY ELDER SISTER USED TO BE IN THE MILITARY. YOU WON'T GET A PRIZE AT A FASHION SHOW WITH THAT, BUT AT LEAST...
YOU'RE NOT IN DANGER OF FLYING TO THE MOON EVERY TIME YOU STEP OUT OF THE HOUSE.
WHICH LEADS TO ANOTHER QUESTION: WHY WAS MINA EVEN HELD CAPTIVE?
THAT, MY FRIEND, IS A TOPIC FOR ANOTHER DAY. BECAUSE RIGHT NOW, WE GIRLS HAVE WORK TO DO!
REALLY? BUT...
WE'RE GOING TO SPEND SOME QUALITY TIME TOGETHER AND BOND OVER GIRL STUFF!
O-OKAY...
COME ON, IT'S GOING TO BE FUN!

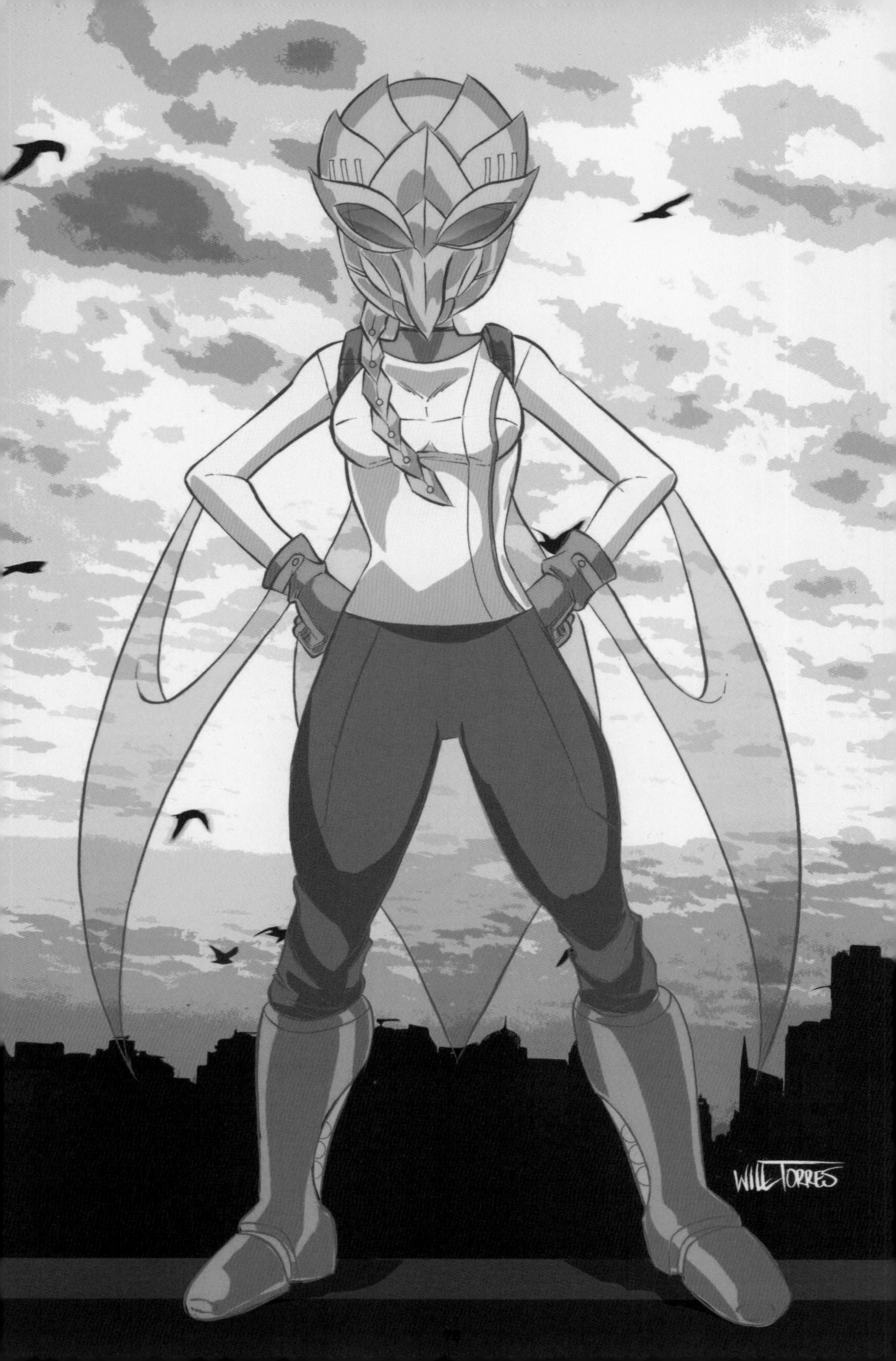
WILL TORRES

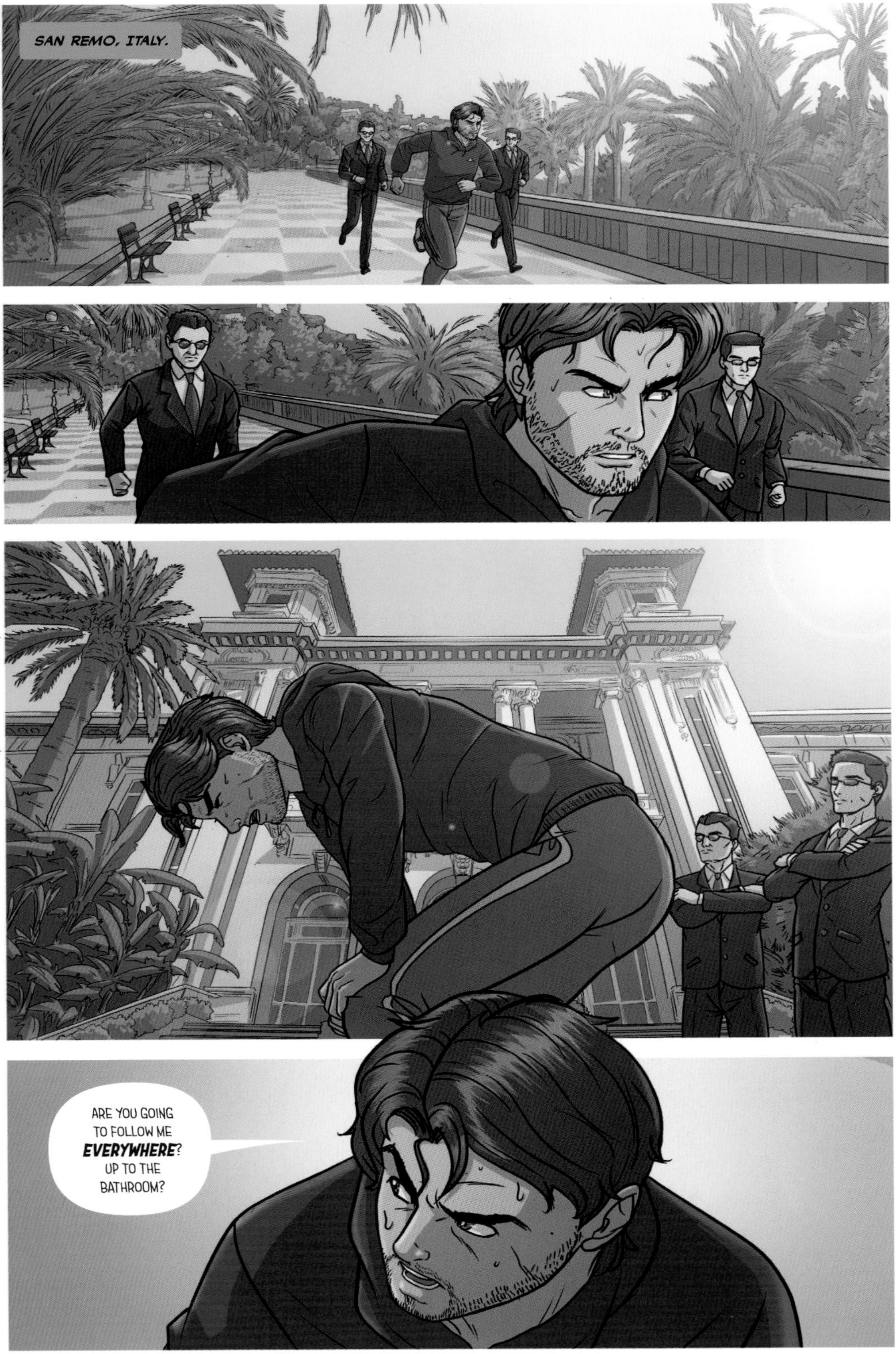
SAN REMO, ITALY.
ARE YOU GOING TO FOLLOW ME **EVERYWHERE**? UP TO THE BATHROOM?

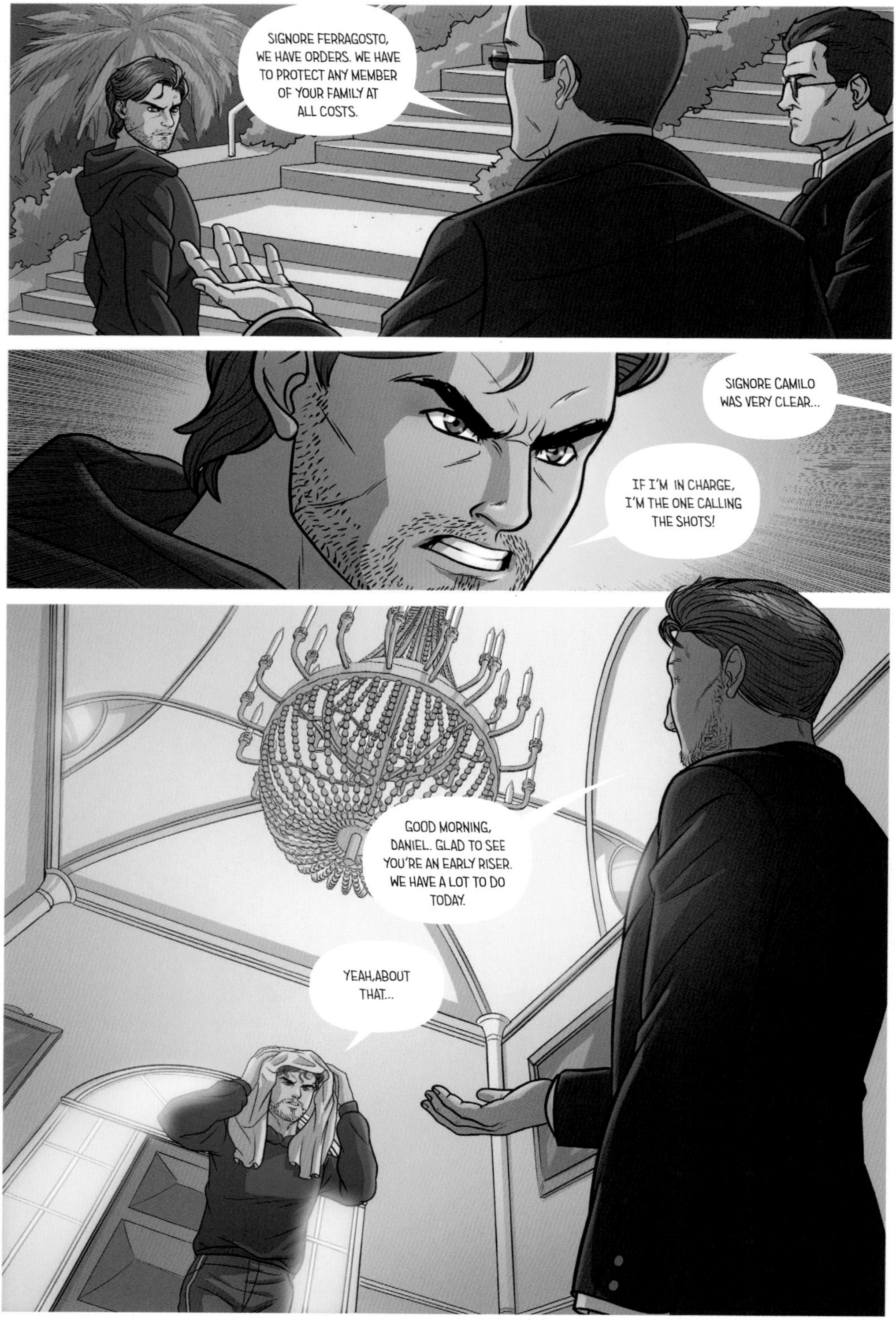
SIGNORE FERRAGOSTO, WE HAVE ORDERS. WE HAVE TO PROTECT ANY MEMBER OF YOUR FAMILY AT ALL COSTS.
SIGNORE CAMILO WAS VERY CLEAR...
IF I'M IN CHARGE, I'M THE ONE CALLING THE SHOTS!
GOOD MORNING, DANIEL. GLAD TO SEE YOU'RE AN EARLY RISER. WE HAVE A LOT TO DO TODAY.
YEAH,ABOUT THAT...

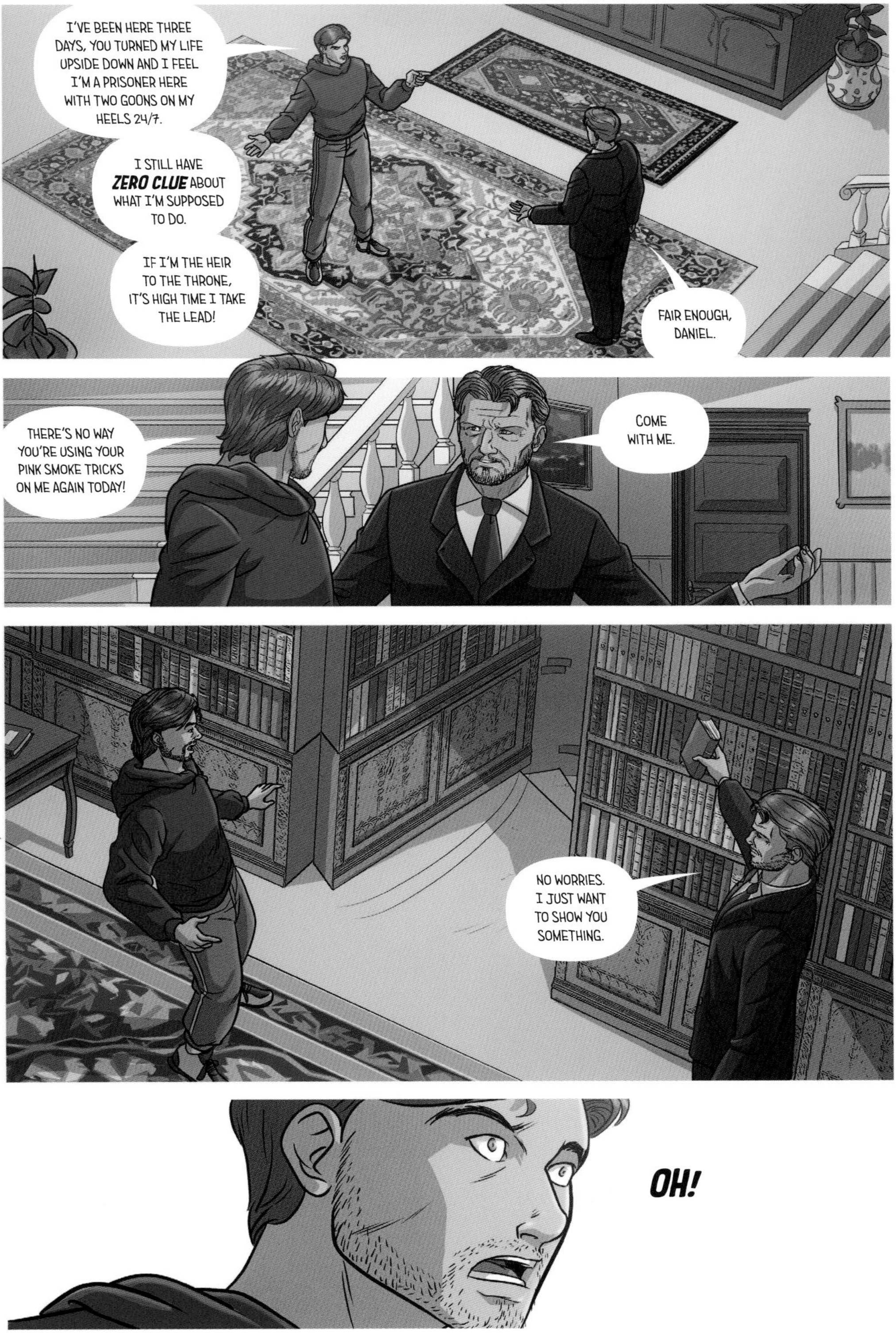
I'VE BEEN HERE THREE DAYS, YOU TURNED MY LIFE UPSIDE DOWN AND I FEEL I'M A PRISONER HERE WITH TWO GOONS ON MY HEELS 24/7.
I STILL HAVE **ZERO CLUE** ABOUT WHAT I'M SUPPOSED TO DO.
IF I'M THE HEIR TO THE THRONE, IT'S HIGH TIME I TAKE THE LEAD!
FAIR ENOUGH, DANIEL.
THERE'S NO WAY YOU'RE USING YOUR PINK SMOKE TRICKS ON ME AGAIN TODAY!
COME WITH ME.
NO WORRIES. I JUST WANT TO SHOW YOU SOMETHING.
OH!

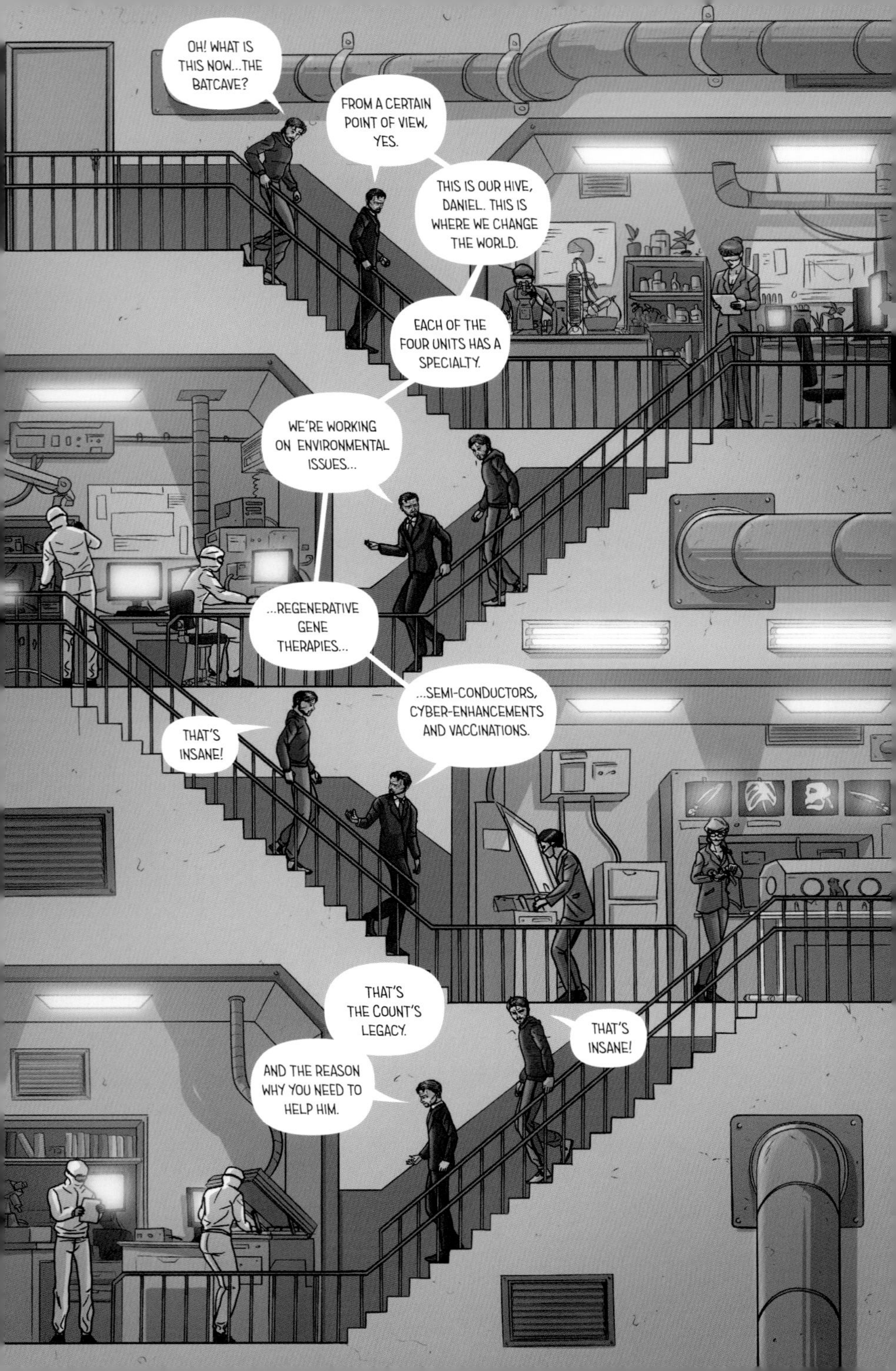
OH! WHAT IS THIS NOW...THE BATCAVE?
FROM A CERTAIN POINT OF VIEW, YES.
THIS IS OUR HIVE, DANIEL. THIS IS WHERE WE CHANGE THE WORLD.
EACH OF THE FOUR UNITS HAS A SPECIALTY.
WE'RE WORKING ON ENVIRONMENTAL ISSUES...
...REGENERATIVE GENE THERAPIES...
...SEMI-CONDUCTORS, CYBER-ENHANCEMENTS AND VACCINATIONS.
THAT'S INSANE!
THAT'S THE COUNT'S LEGACY.
AND THE REASON WHY YOU NEED TO HELP HIM.
THAT'S INSANE!

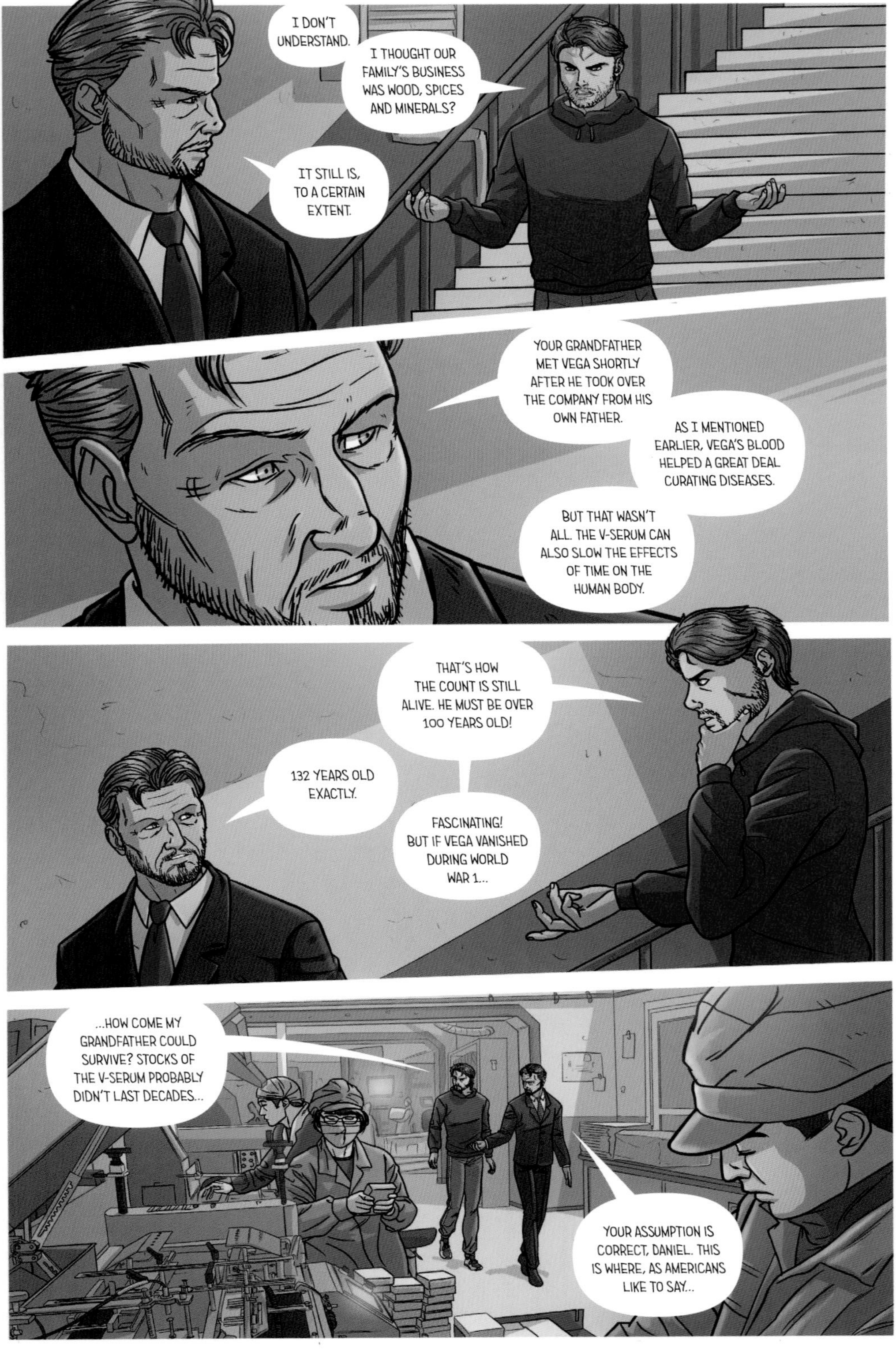
I DON'T UNDERSTAND.
I THOUGHT OUR FAMILY'S BUSINESS WAS WOOD, SPICES AND MINERALS?
IT STILL IS, TO A CERTAIN EXTENT.
YOUR GRANDFATHER MET VEGA SHORTLY AFTER HE TOOK OVER THE COMPANY FROM HIS OWN FATHER.
AS I MENTIONED EARLIER, VEGA'S BLOOD HELPED A GREAT DEAL CURATING DISEASES.
BUT THAT WASN'T ALL. THE V-SERUM CAN ALSO SLOW THE EFFECTS OF TIME ON THE HUMAN BODY.
THAT'S HOW THE COUNT IS STILL ALIVE. HE MUST BE OVER 100 YEARS OLD!
132 YEARS OLD EXACTLY.
FASCINATING! BUT IF VEGA VANISHED DURING WORLD WAR 1...
...HOW COME MY GRANDFATHER COULD SURVIVE? STOCKS OF THE V-SERUM PROBABLY DIDN'T LAST DECADES...
YOUR ASSUMPTION IS CORRECT, DANIEL. THIS IS WHERE, AS AMERICANS LIKE TO SAY...

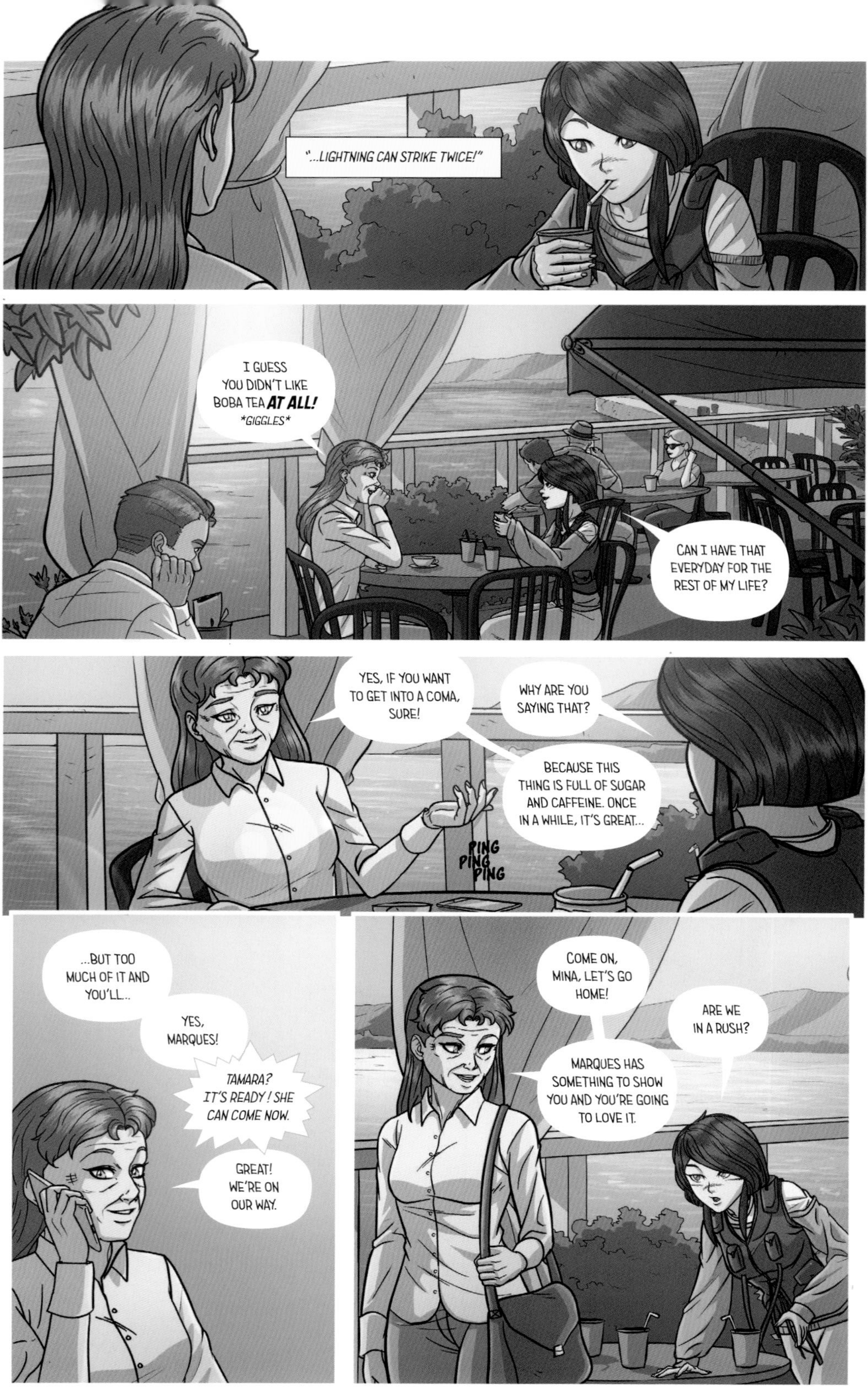
"...LIGHTNING CAN STRIKE TWICE!"
I GUESS YOU DIDN'T LIKE BOBA TEA **AT ALL!** *GIGGLES*
CAN I HAVE THAT EVERYDAY FOR THE REST OF MY LIFE?
YES, IF YOU WANT TO GET INTO A COMA, SURE!
WHY ARE YOU SAYING THAT?
BECAUSE THIS THING IS FULL OF SUGAR AND CAFFEINE. ONCE IN A WHILE, IT'S GREAT...
PING PING PING
...BUT TOO MUCH OF IT AND YOU'LL...
YES, MARQUES!
TAMARA? IT'S READY! SHE CAN COME NOW.
GREAT! WE'RE ON OUR WAY.
COME ON, MINA, LET'S GO HOME!
ARE WE IN A RUSH?
MARQUES HAS SOMETHING TO SHOW YOU AND YOU'RE GOING TO LOVE IT.

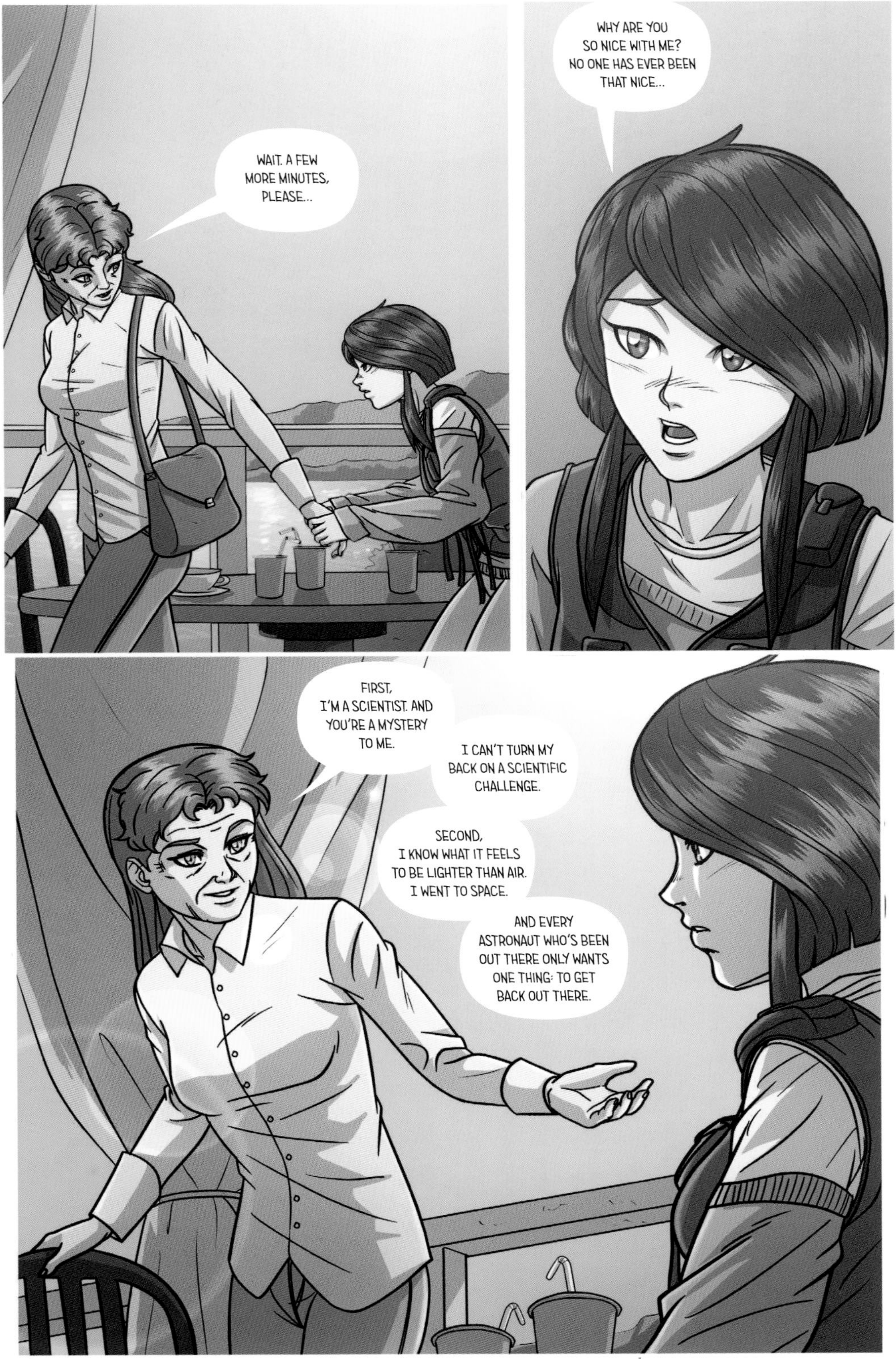
WAIT. A FEW MORE MINUTES, PLEASE...
WHY ARE YOU SO NICE WITH ME? NO ONE HAS EVER BEEN THAT NICE...
FIRST, I'M A SCIENTIST. AND YOU'RE A MYSTERY TO ME.
I CAN'T TURN MY BACK ON A SCIENTIFIC CHALLENGE.
SECOND, I KNOW WHAT IT FEELS TO BE LIGHTER THAN AIR. I WENT TO SPACE.
AND EVERY ASTRONAUT WHO'S BEEN OUT THERE ONLY WANTS ONE THING: TO GET BACK OUT THERE.

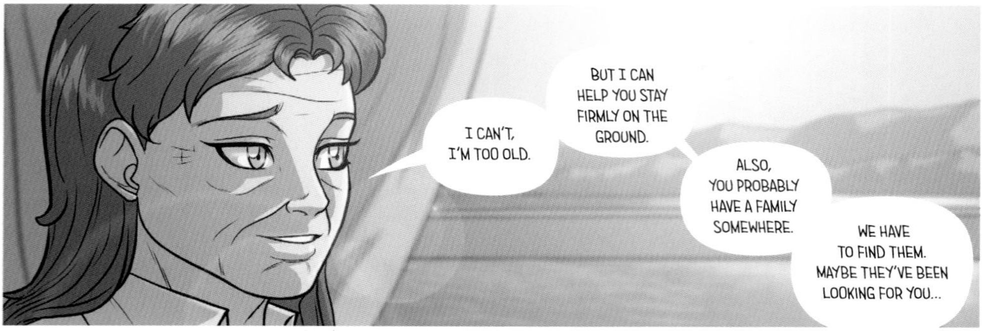
I CAN'T, I'M TOO OLD.
BUT I CAN HELP YOU STAY FIRMLY ON THE GROUND.
ALSO, YOU PROBABLY HAVE A FAMILY SOMEWHERE.
WE HAVE TO FIND THEM. MAYBE THEY'VE BEEN LOOKING FOR YOU...
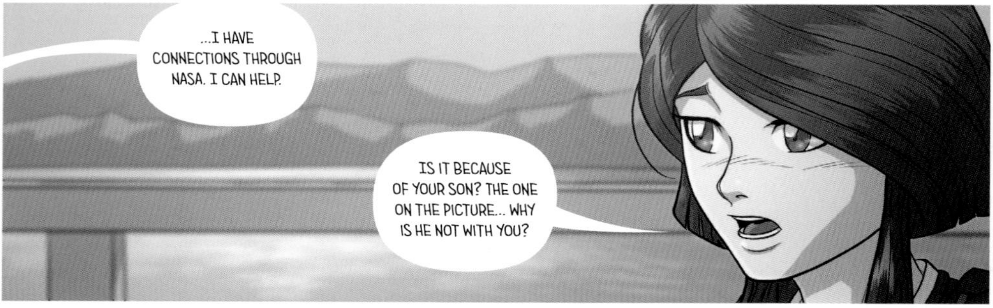
...I HAVE CONNECTIONS THROUGH NASA. I CAN HELP.
IS IT BECAUSE OF YOUR SON? THE ONE ON THE PICTURE... WHY IS HE NOT WITH YOU?
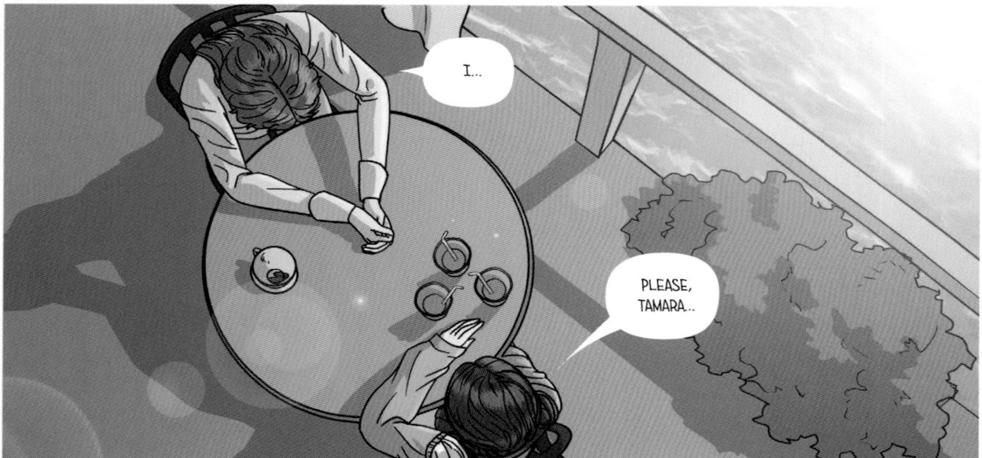
I...
PLEASE, TAMARA...
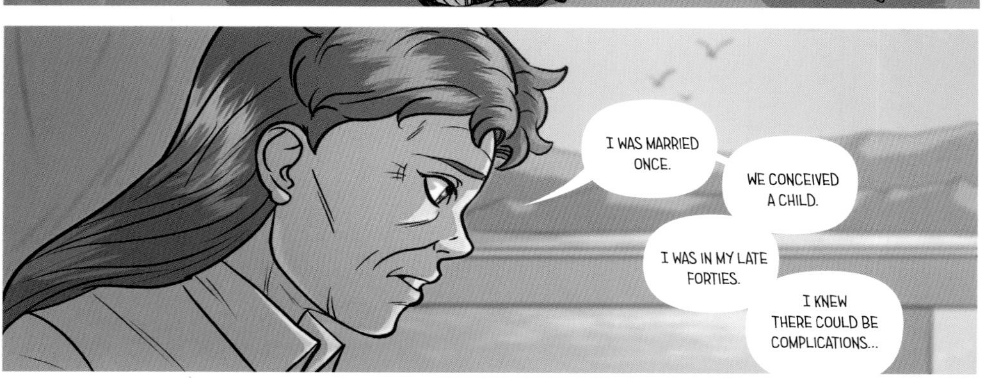
I WAS MARRIED ONCE.
WE CONCEIVED A CHILD.
I WAS IN MY LATE FORTIES.
I KNEW THERE COULD BE COMPLICATIONS...

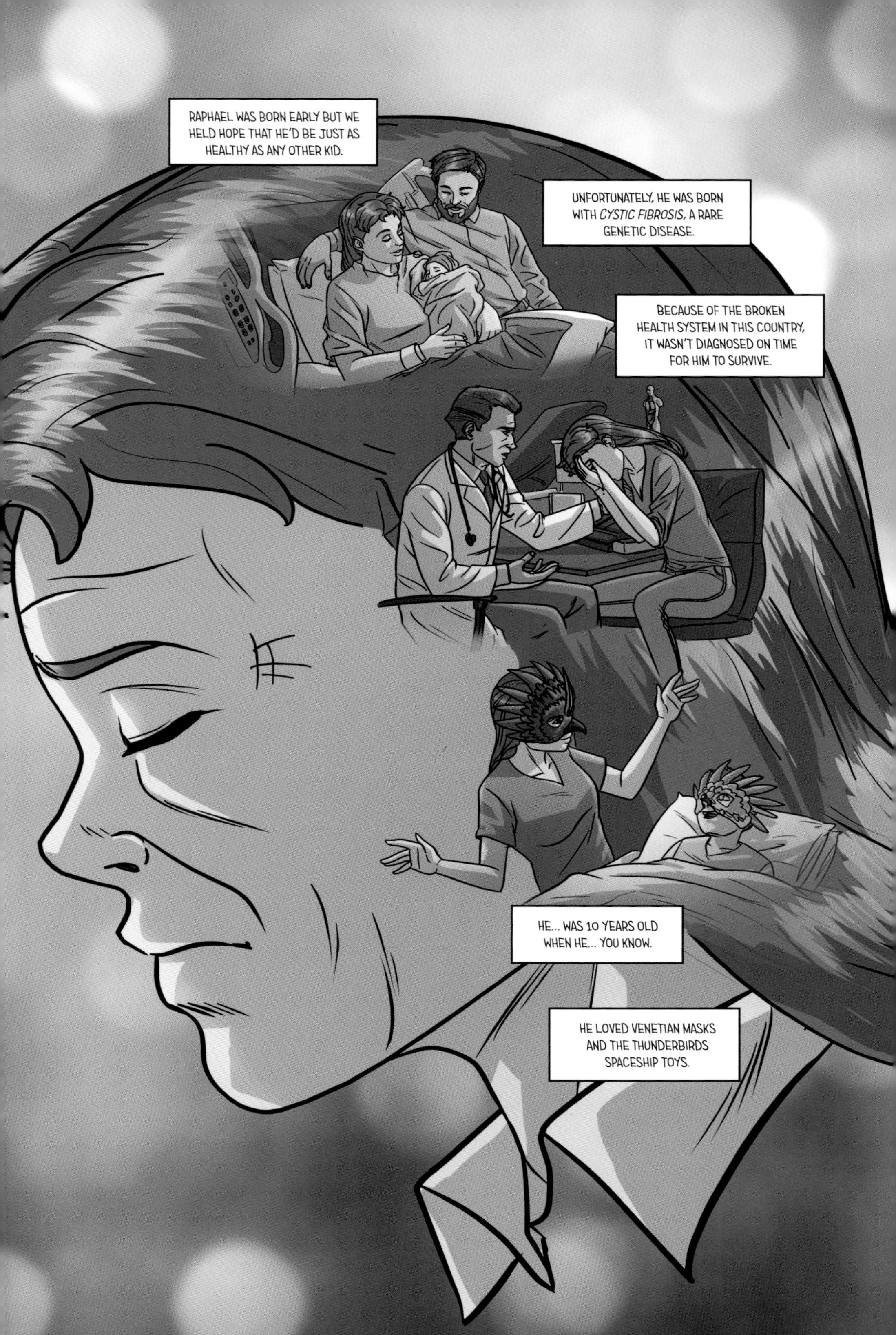
RAPHAEL WAS BORN EARLY BUT WE HELD HOPE THAT HE'D BE JUST AS HEALTHY AS ANY OTHER KID.
UNFORTUNATELY, HE WAS BORN WITH *CYSTIC FIBROSIS*, A RARE GENETIC DISEASE.
BECAUSE OF THE BROKEN HEALTH SYSTEM IN THIS COUNTRY, IT WASN'T DIAGNOSED ON TIME FOR HIM TO SURVIVE.
HE... WAS 10 YEARS OLD WHEN HE... YOU KNOW.
HE LOVED VENETIAN MASKS AND THE THUNDERBIRDS SPACESHIP TOYS.

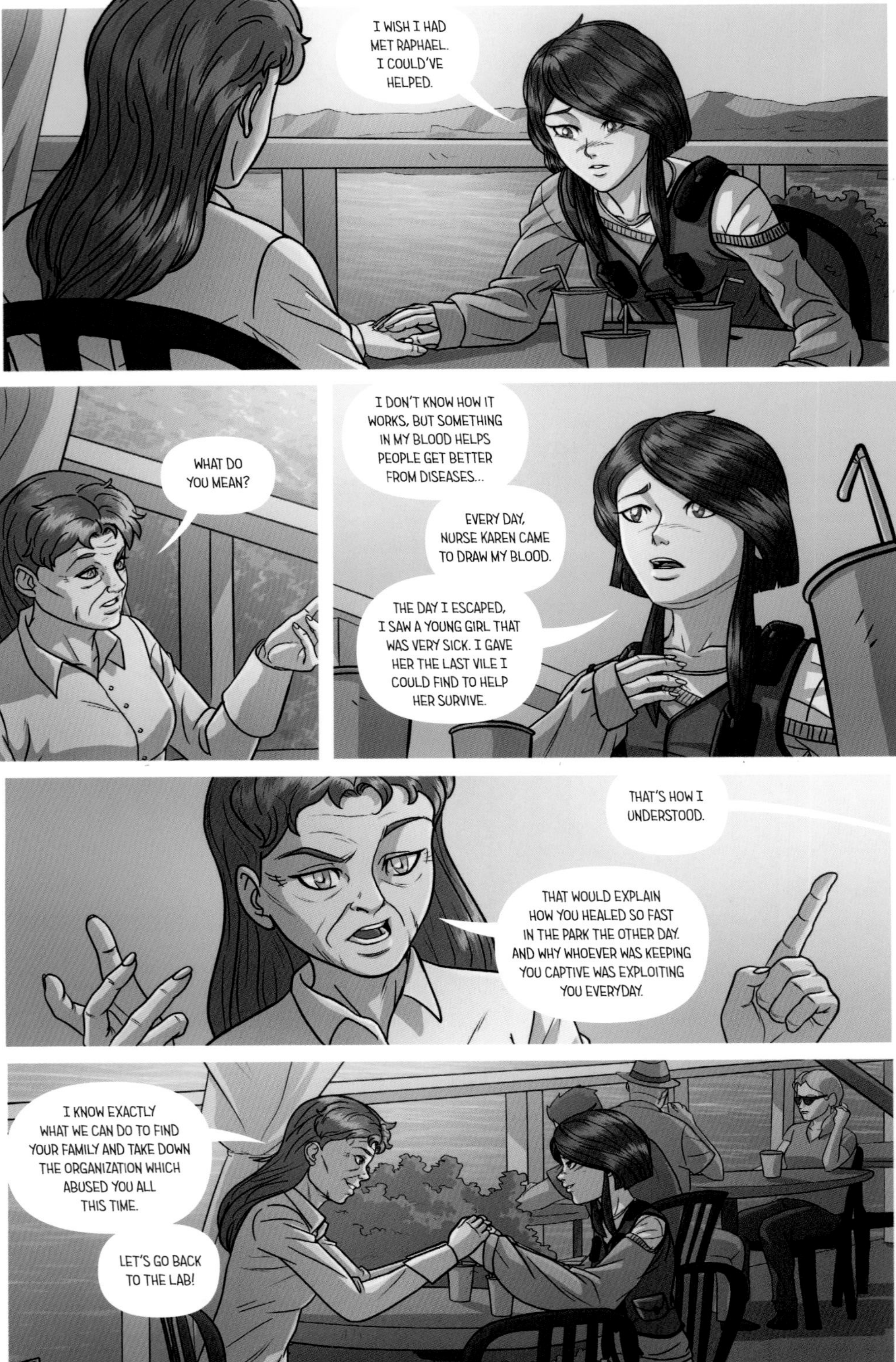
I WISH I HAD MET RAPHAEL. I COULD'VE HELPED.
WHAT DO YOU MEAN?
I DON'T KNOW HOW IT WORKS, BUT SOMETHING IN MY BLOOD HELPS PEOPLE GET BETTER FROM DISEASES...
EVERY DAY, NURSE KAREN CAME TO DRAW MY BLOOD.
THE DAY I ESCAPED, I SAW A YOUNG GIRL THAT WAS VERY SICK. I GAVE HER THE LAST VILE I COULD FIND TO HELP HER SURVIVE.
THAT'S HOW I UNDERSTOOD.
THAT WOULD EXPLAIN HOW YOU HEALED SO FAST IN THE PARK THE OTHER DAY. AND WHY WHOEVER WAS KEEPING YOU CAPTIVE WAS EXPLOITING YOU EVERYDAY.
I KNOW EXACTLY WHAT WE CAN DO TO FIND YOUR FAMILY AND TAKE DOWN THE ORGANIZATION WHICH ABUSED YOU ALL THIS TIME.
LET'S GO BACK TO THE LAB!

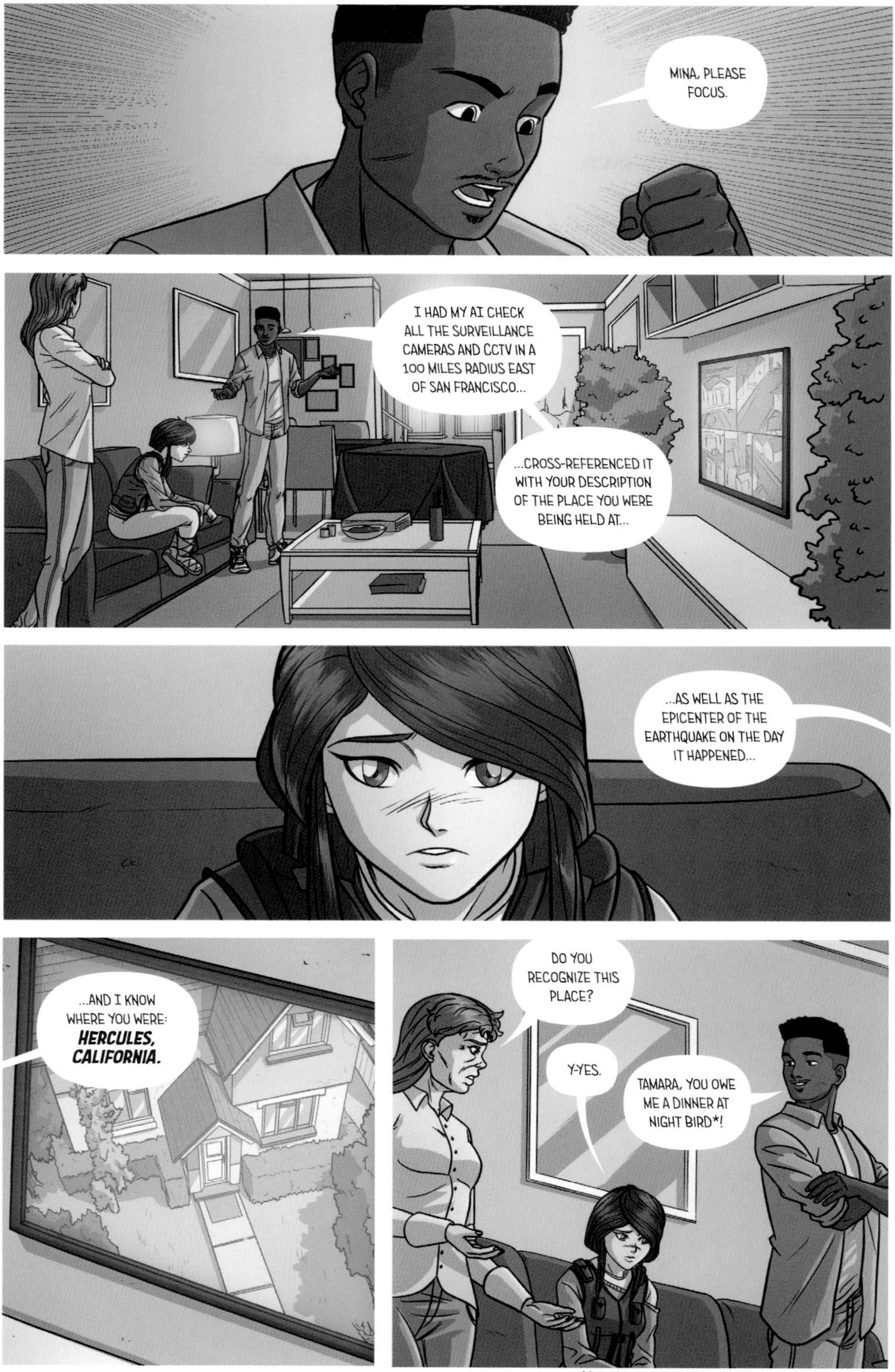
MINA, PLEASE FOCUS.
I HAD MY AI CHECK ALL THE SURVEILLANCE CAMERAS AND CCTV IN A 100 MILES RADIUS EAST OF SAN FRANCISCO...
...CROSS-REFERENCED IT WITH YOUR DESCRIPTION OF THE PLACE YOU WERE BEING HELD AT...
...AS WELL AS THE EPICENTER OF THE EARTHQUAKE ON THE DAY IT HAPPENED...
...AND I KNOW WHERE YOU WERE: **HERCULES, CALIFORNIA.**
DO YOU RECOGNIZE THIS PLACE?
Y-YES.
TAMARA, YOU OWE ME A DINNER AT NIGHT BIRD*!

**ONE OF THE MOST EXPENSIVE RESTAURANTS IN SAN FRANCISCO.*

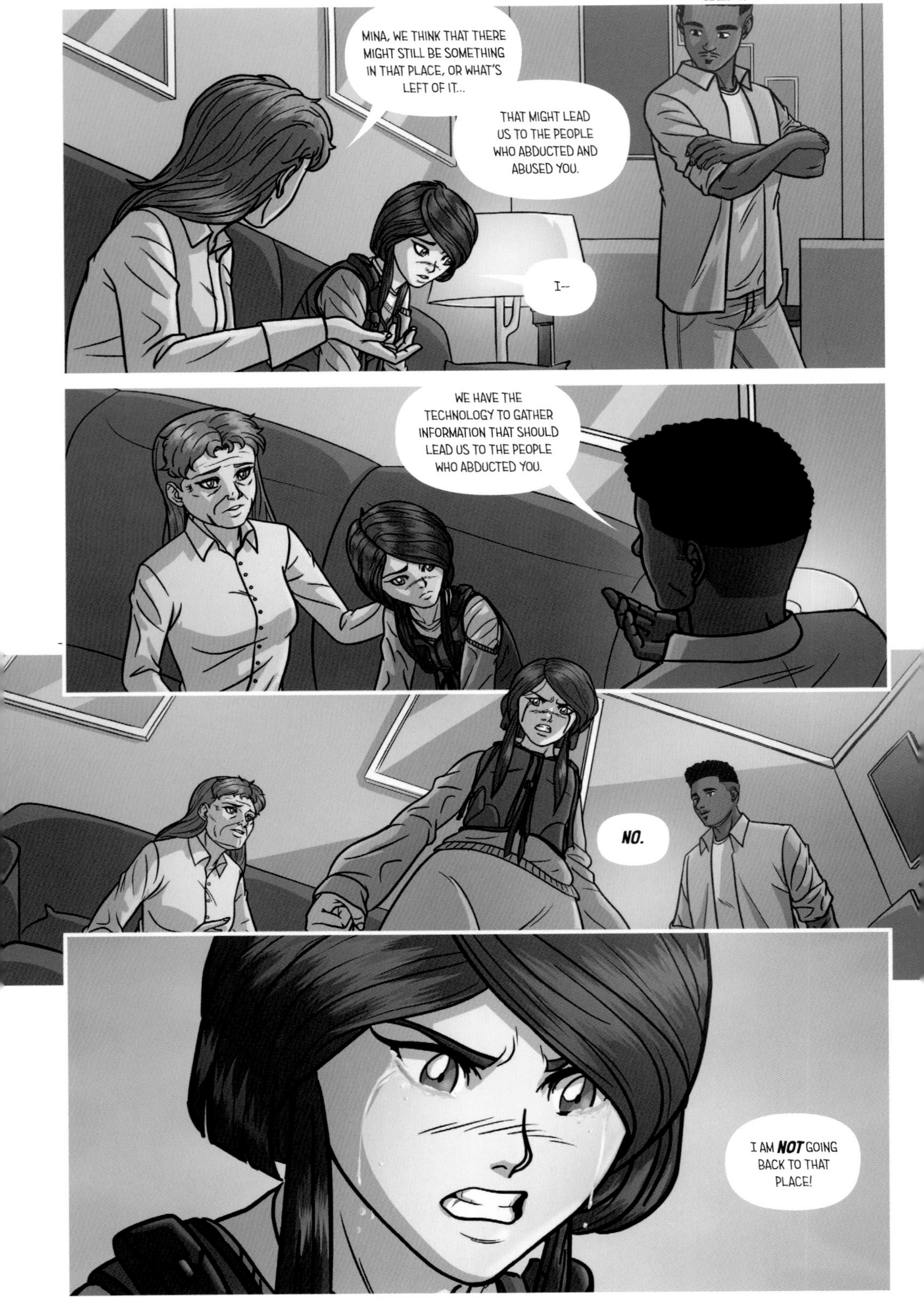
MINA, WE THINK THAT THERE MIGHT STILL BE SOMETHING IN THAT PLACE, OR WHAT'S LEFT OF IT...
THAT MIGHT LEAD US TO THE PEOPLE WHO ABDUCTED AND ABUSED YOU.
I--
WE HAVE THE TECHNOLOGY TO GATHER INFORMATION THAT SHOULD LEAD US TO THE PEOPLE WHO ABDUCTED YOU.
NO.
I AM ***NOT*** GOING BACK TO THAT PLACE!

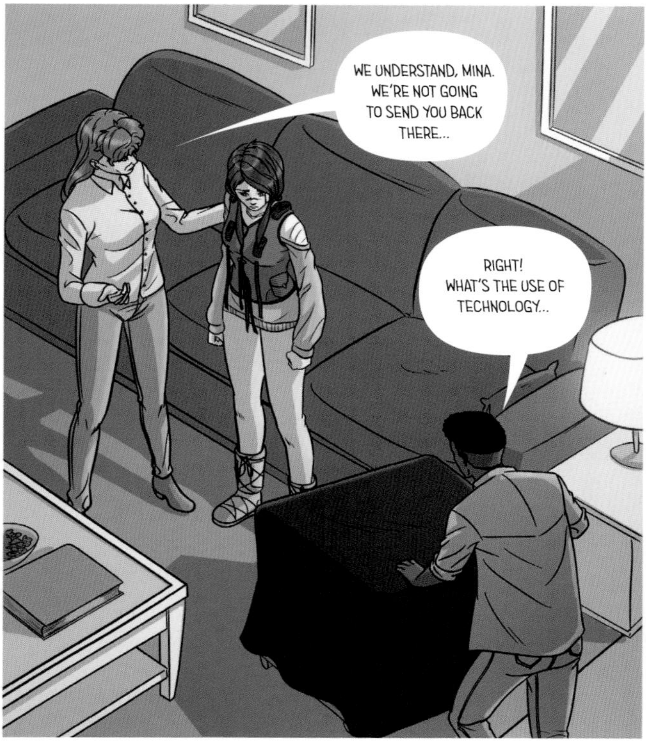
WE UNDERSTAND, MINA. WE'RE NOT GOING TO SEND YOU BACK THERE...
RIGHT! WHAT'S THE USE OF TECHNOLOGY...

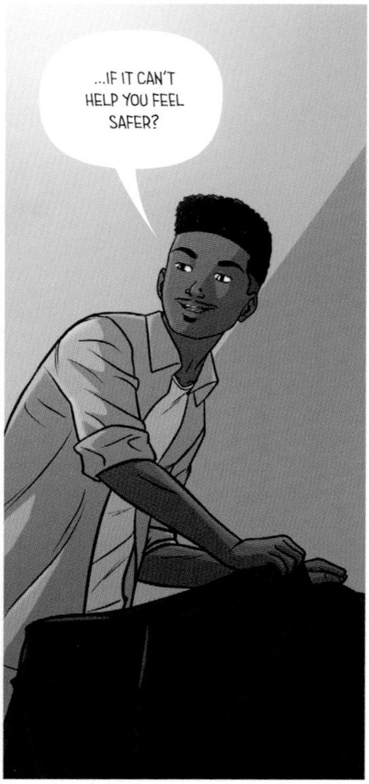
...IF IT CAN'T HELP YOU FEEL SAFER?

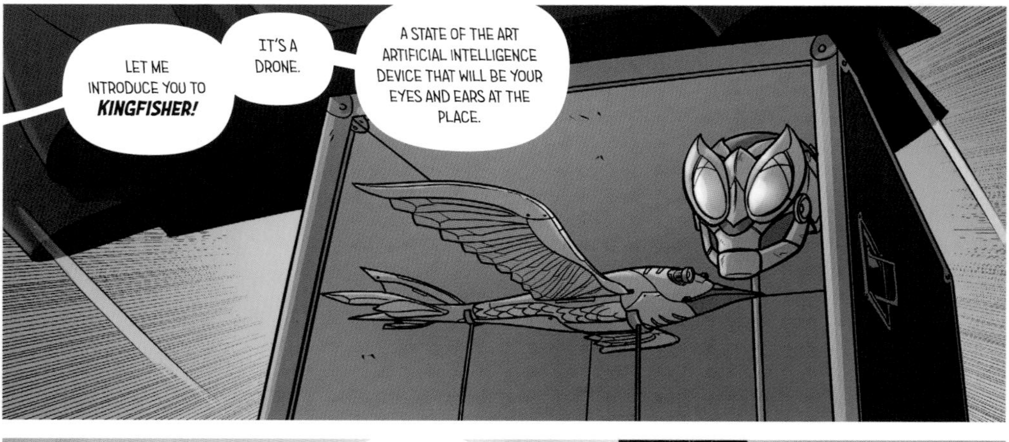
LET ME INTRODUCE YOU TO **KINGFISHER!**
IT'S A DRONE.
A STATE OF THE ART ARTIFICIAL INTELLIGENCE DEVICE THAT WILL BE YOUR EYES AND EARS AT THE PLACE.

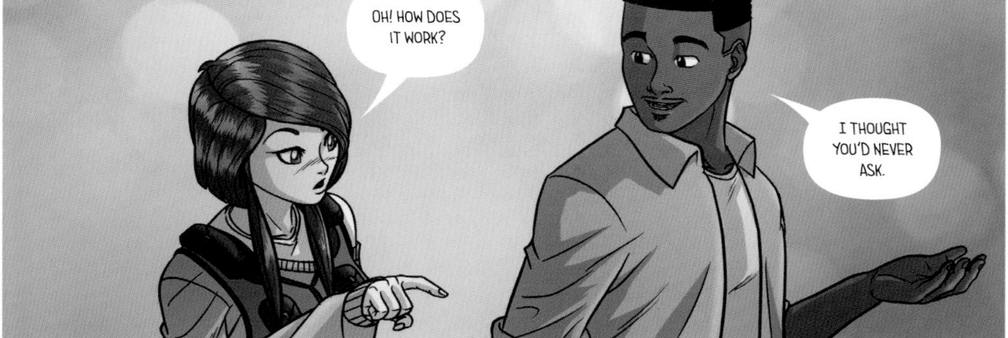
OH! HOW DOES IT WORK?
I THOUGHT YOU'D NEVER ASK.

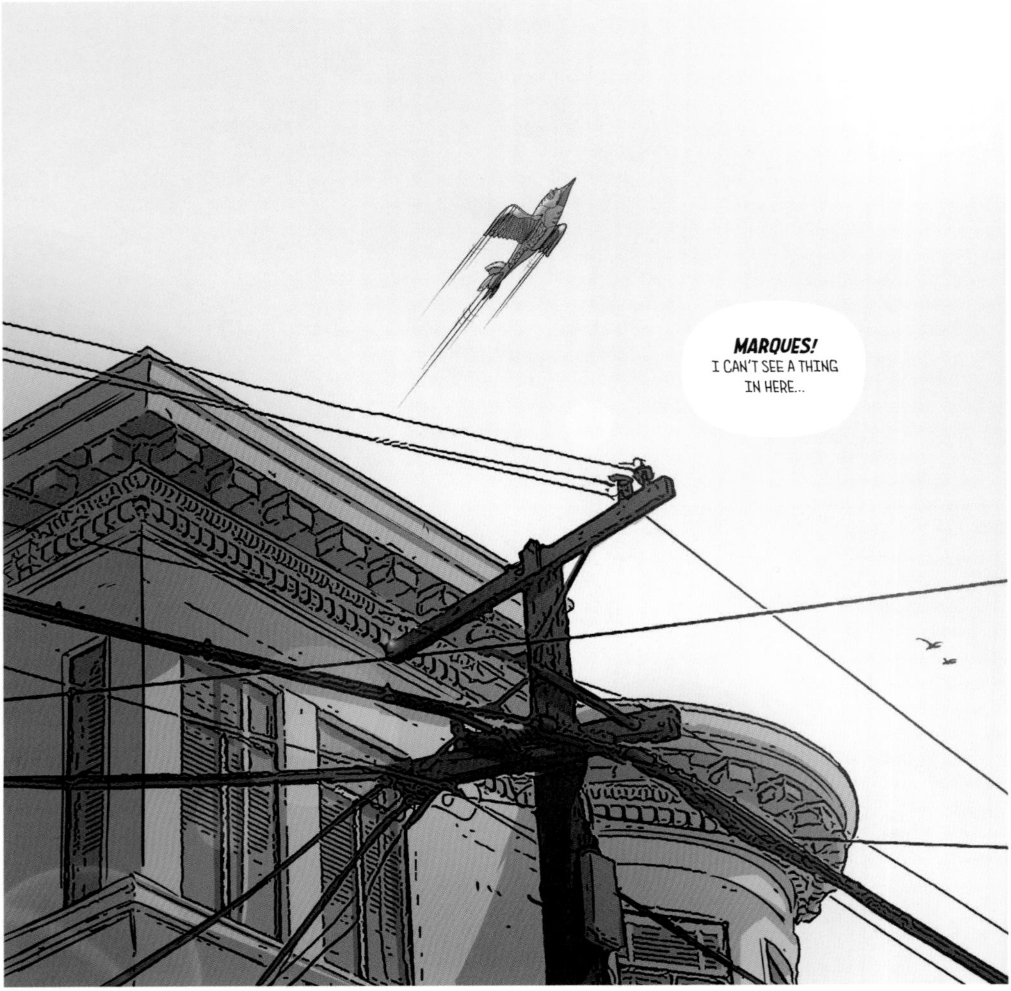
MARQUES! I CAN'T SEE A THING IN HERE...
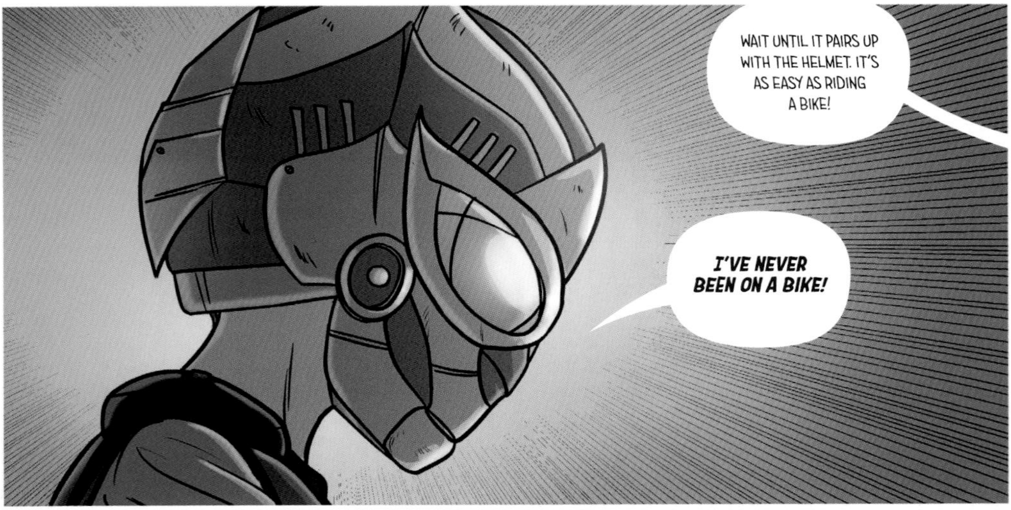
WAIT UNTIL IT PAIRS UP WITH THE HELMET. IT'S AS EASY AS RIDING A BIKE!
I'VE NEVER BEEN ON A BIKE!

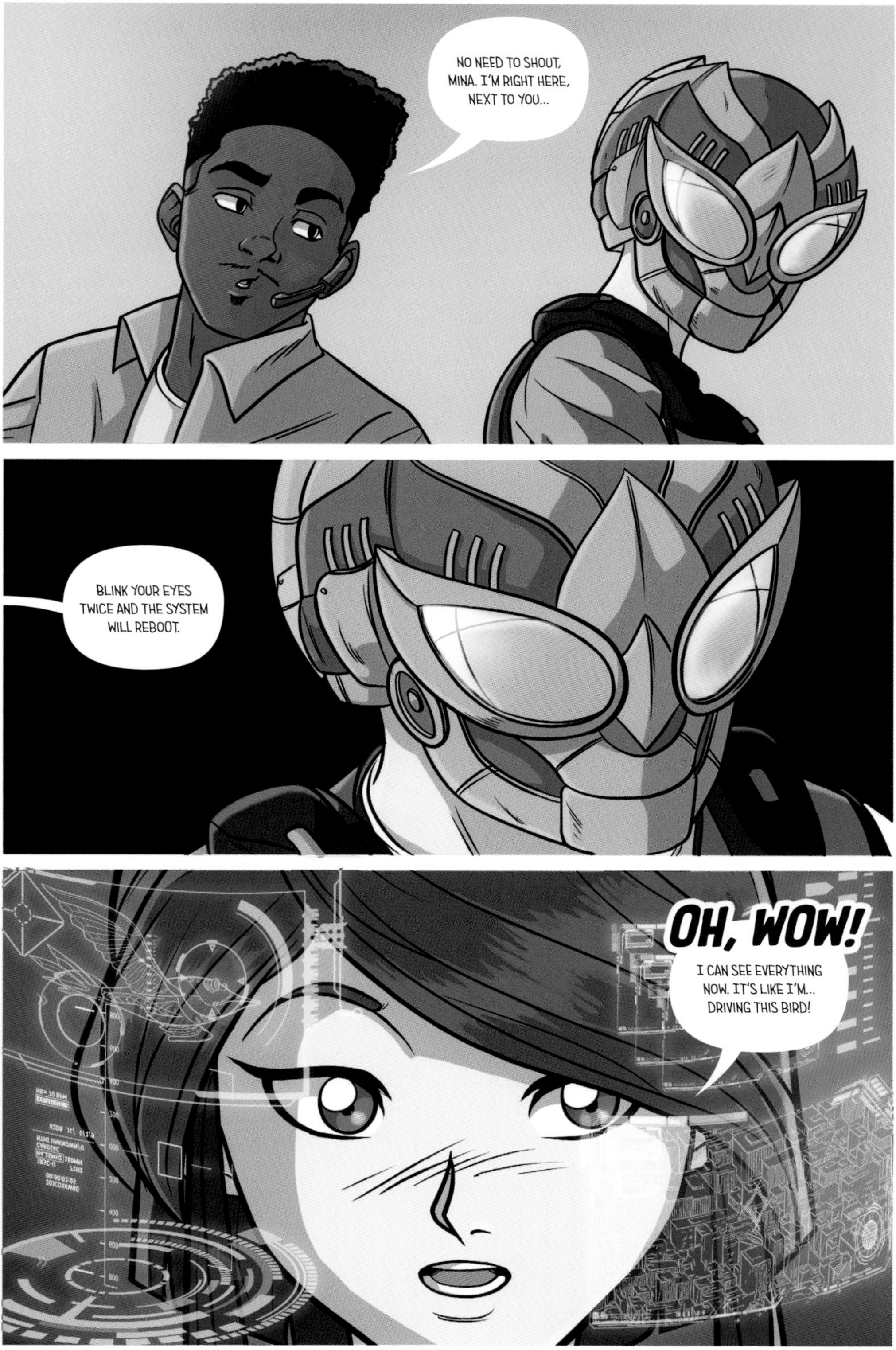
NO NEED TO SHOUT, MINA. I'M RIGHT HERE, NEXT TO YOU...
BLINK YOUR EYES TWICE AND THE SYSTEM WILL REBOOT.
OH, WOW!
I CAN SEE EVERYTHING NOW. IT'S LIKE I'M... DRIVING THIS BIRD!

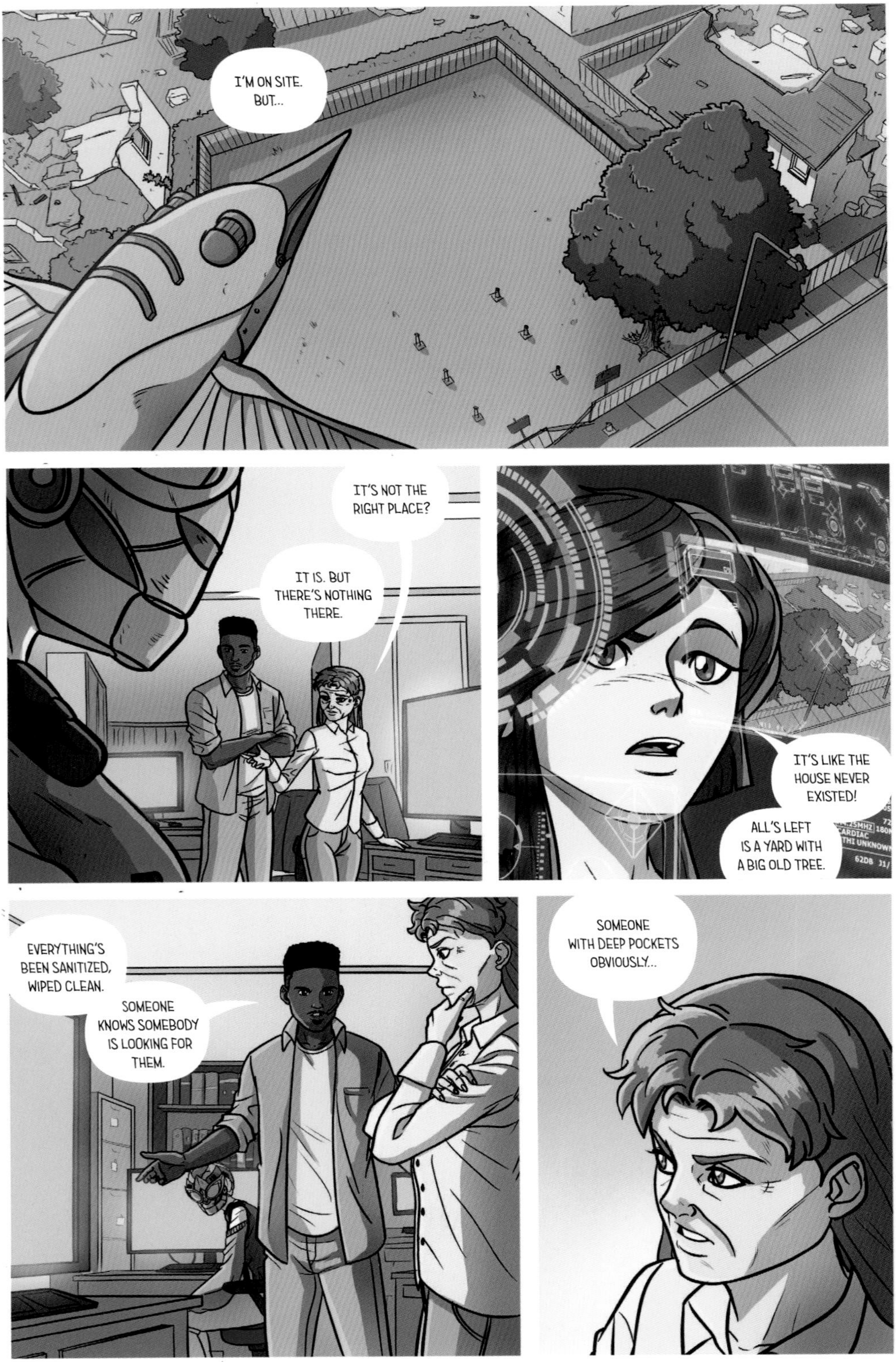

I'M ON SITE. BUT...
IT'S NOT THE RIGHT PLACE?
IT IS. BUT THERE'S NOTHING THERE.
IT'S LIKE THE HOUSE NEVER EXISTED!
ALL'S LEFT IS A YARD WITH A BIG OLD TREE.
EVERYTHING'S BEEN SANITIZED, WIPED CLEAN.
SOMEONE KNOWS SOMEBODY IS LOOKING FOR THEM.
SOMEONE WITH DEEP POCKETS OBVIOUSLY...

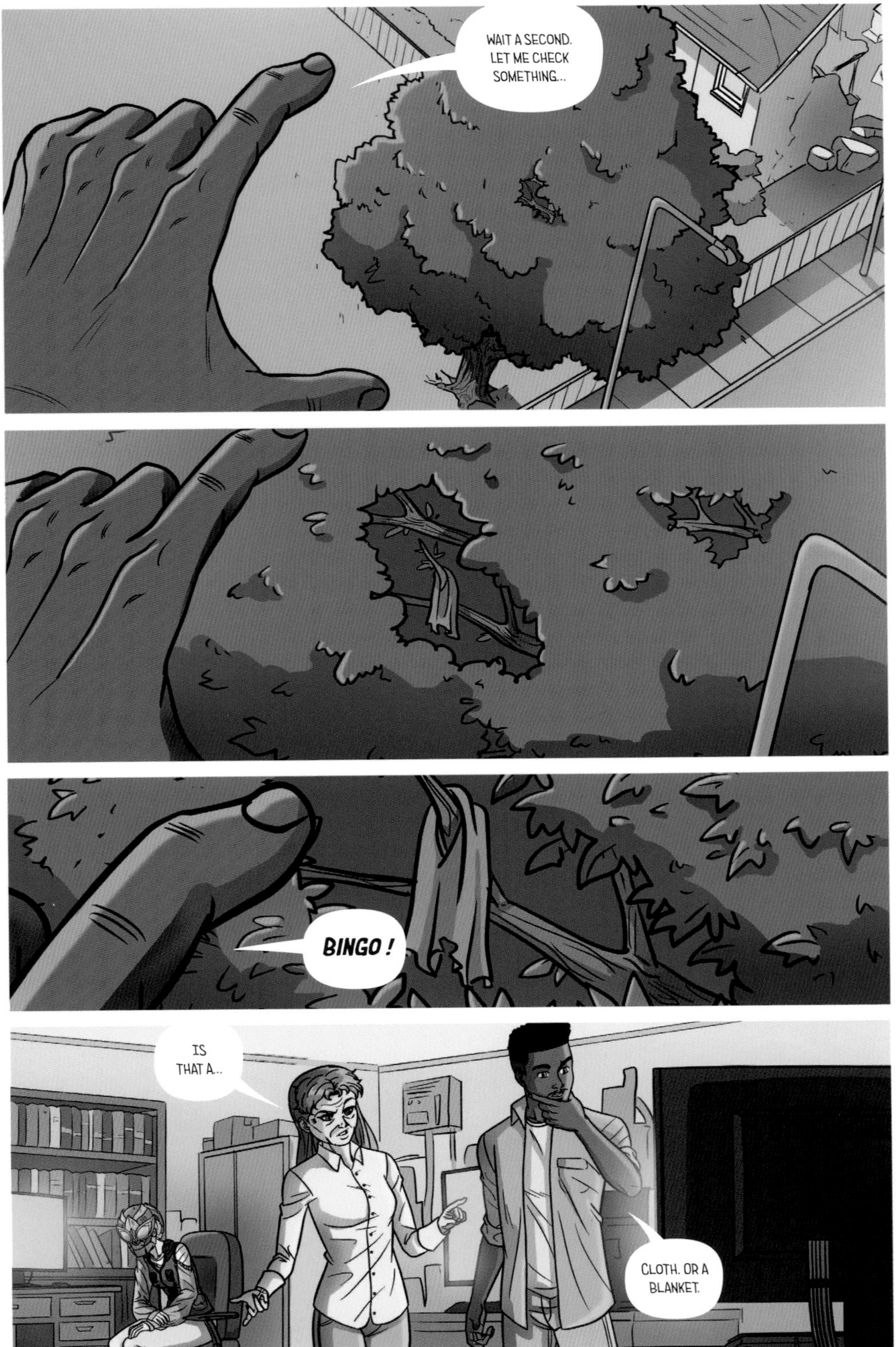
WAIT A SECOND. LET ME CHECK SOMETHING...
BINGO!
IS THAT A...
CLOTH. OR A BLANKET.

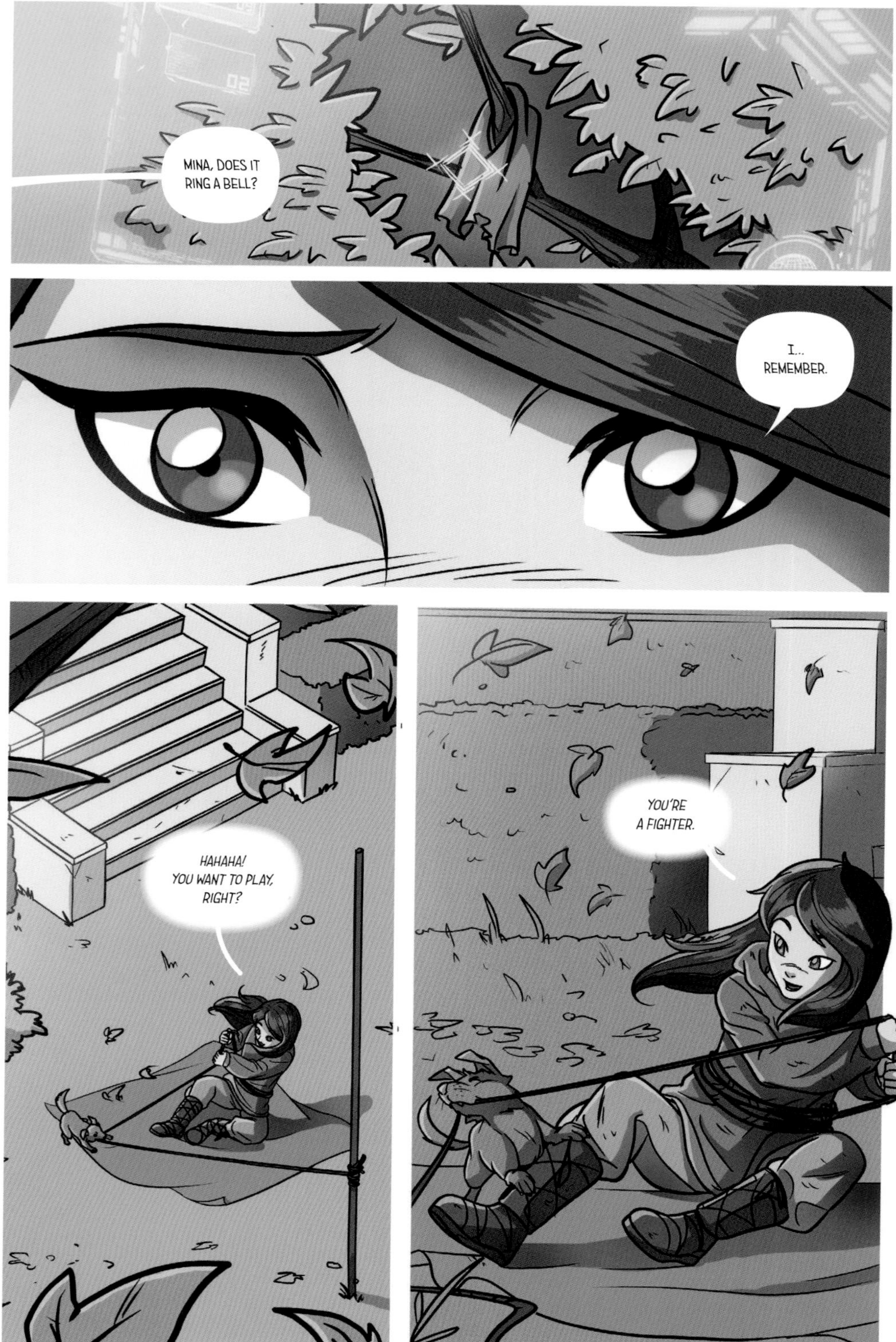
MINA, DOES IT RING A BELL?
I... REMEMBER.
HAHAHA! YOU WANT TO PLAY, RIGHT?
YOU'RE A FIGHTER.

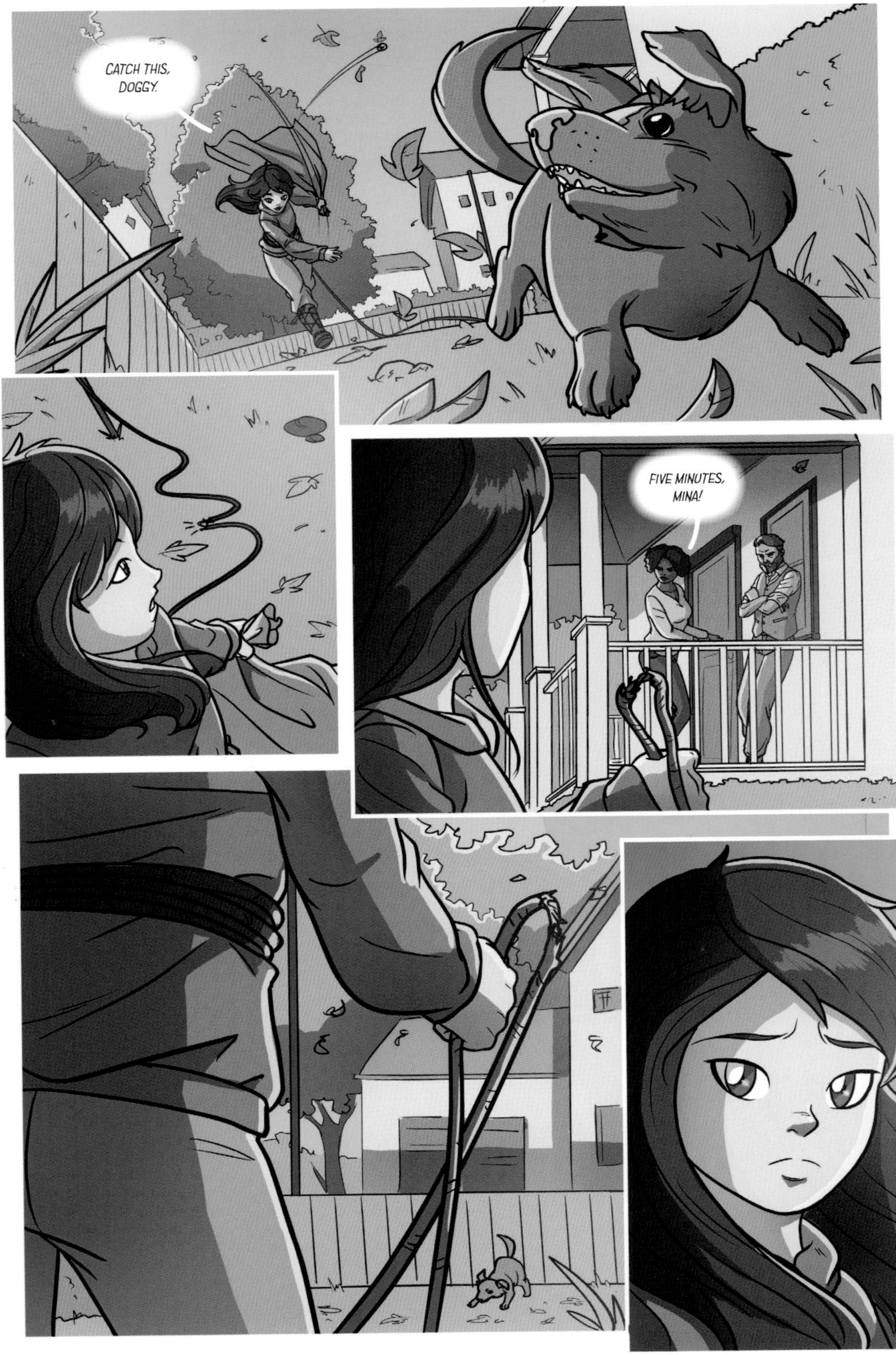
CATCH THIS, DOGGY.
FIVE MINUTES, MINA!

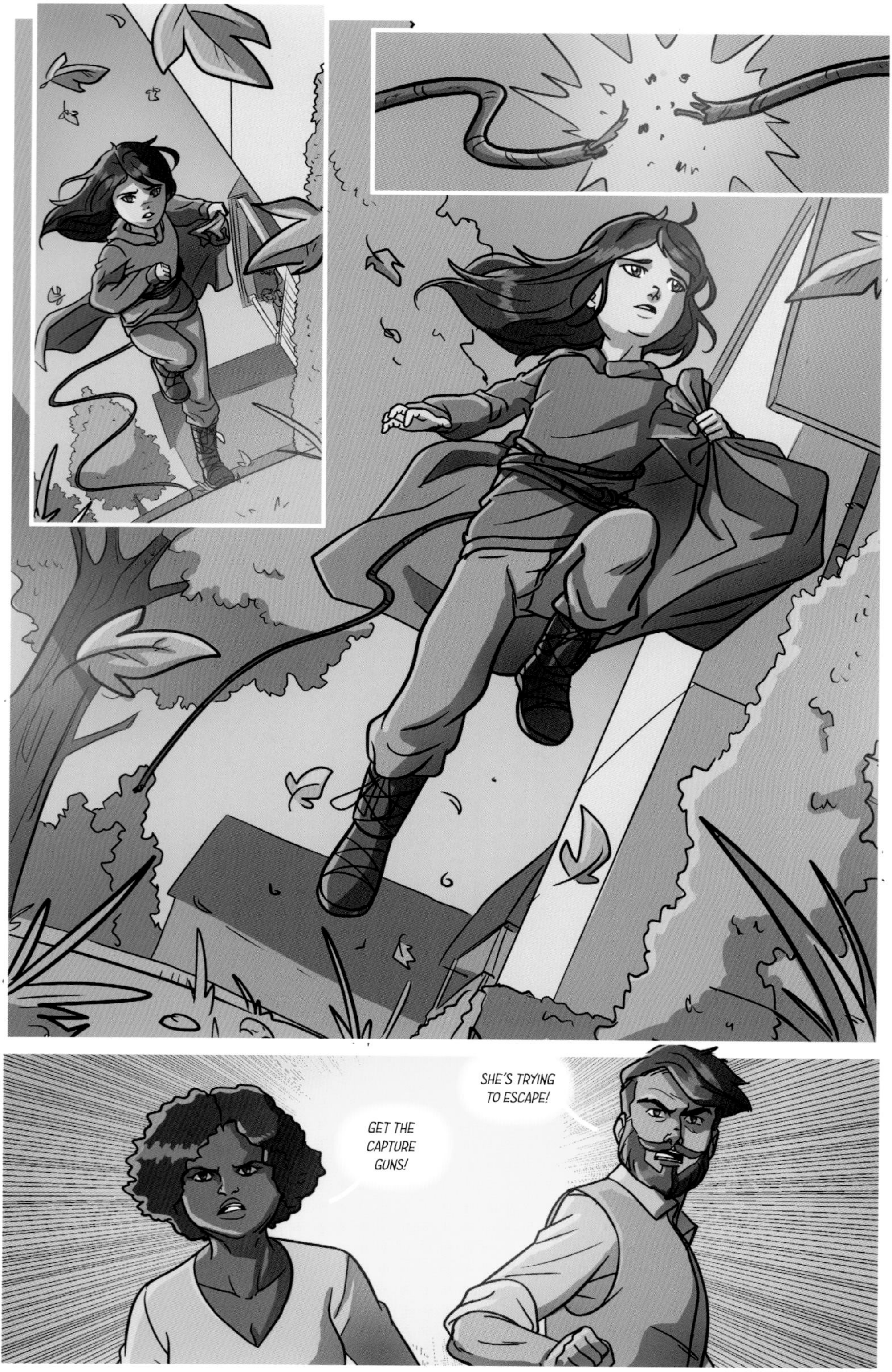
GET THE
CAPTURE
GUNS!
SHE'S TRYING
TO ESCAPE!

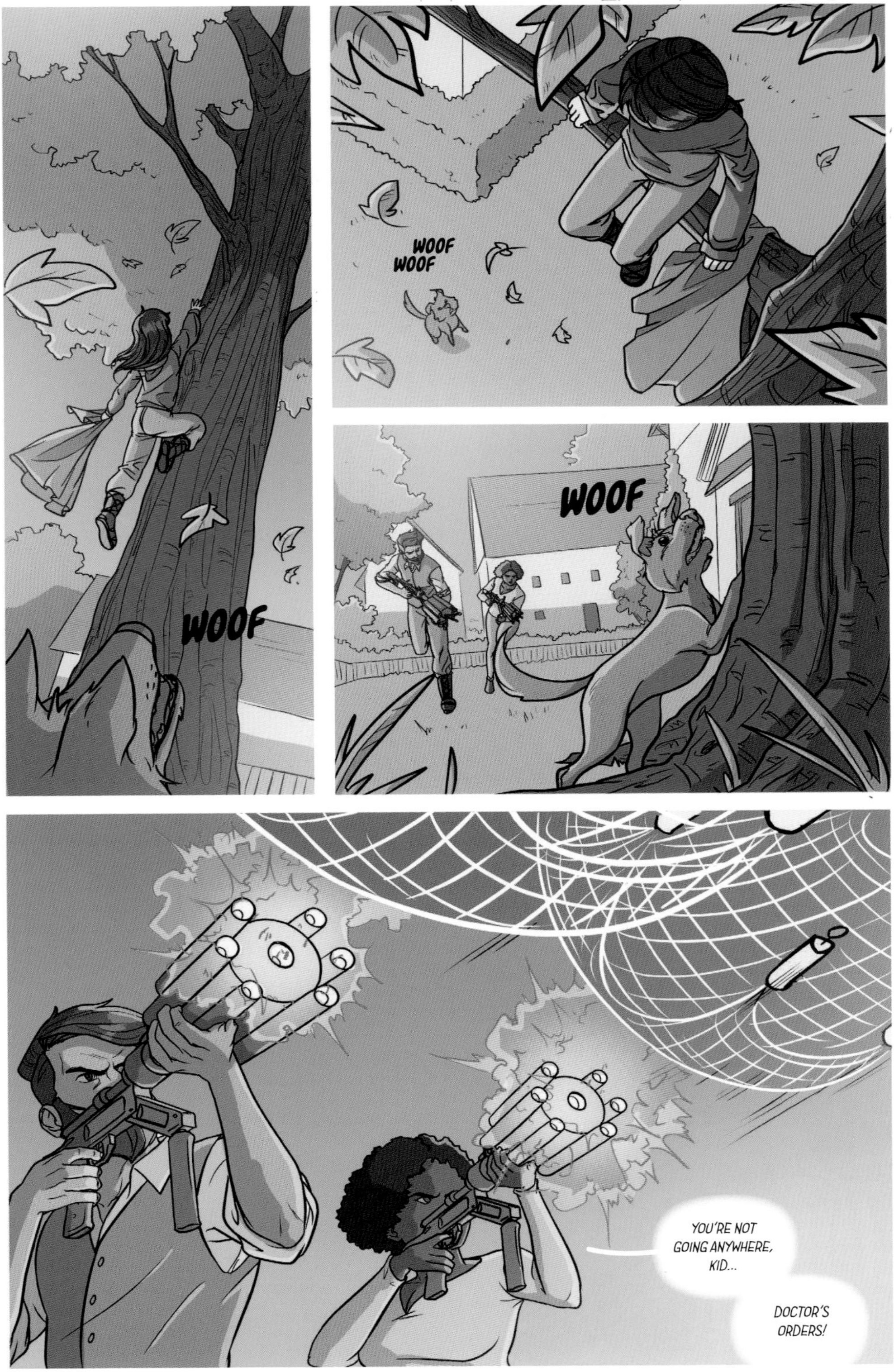
WOOF
WOOF
WOOF
WOOF
YOU'RE NOT GOING ANYWHERE, KID...
DOCTOR'S ORDERS!

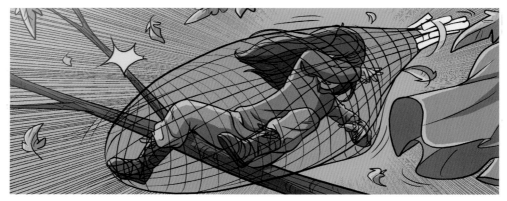

"MINA? DID YOU REMEMBER SOMETHING?"

I WAS THERE...

I TRIED TO ESCAPE WHEN I WAS A LITTLE GIRL.

THIS BLANKET IS MINE.

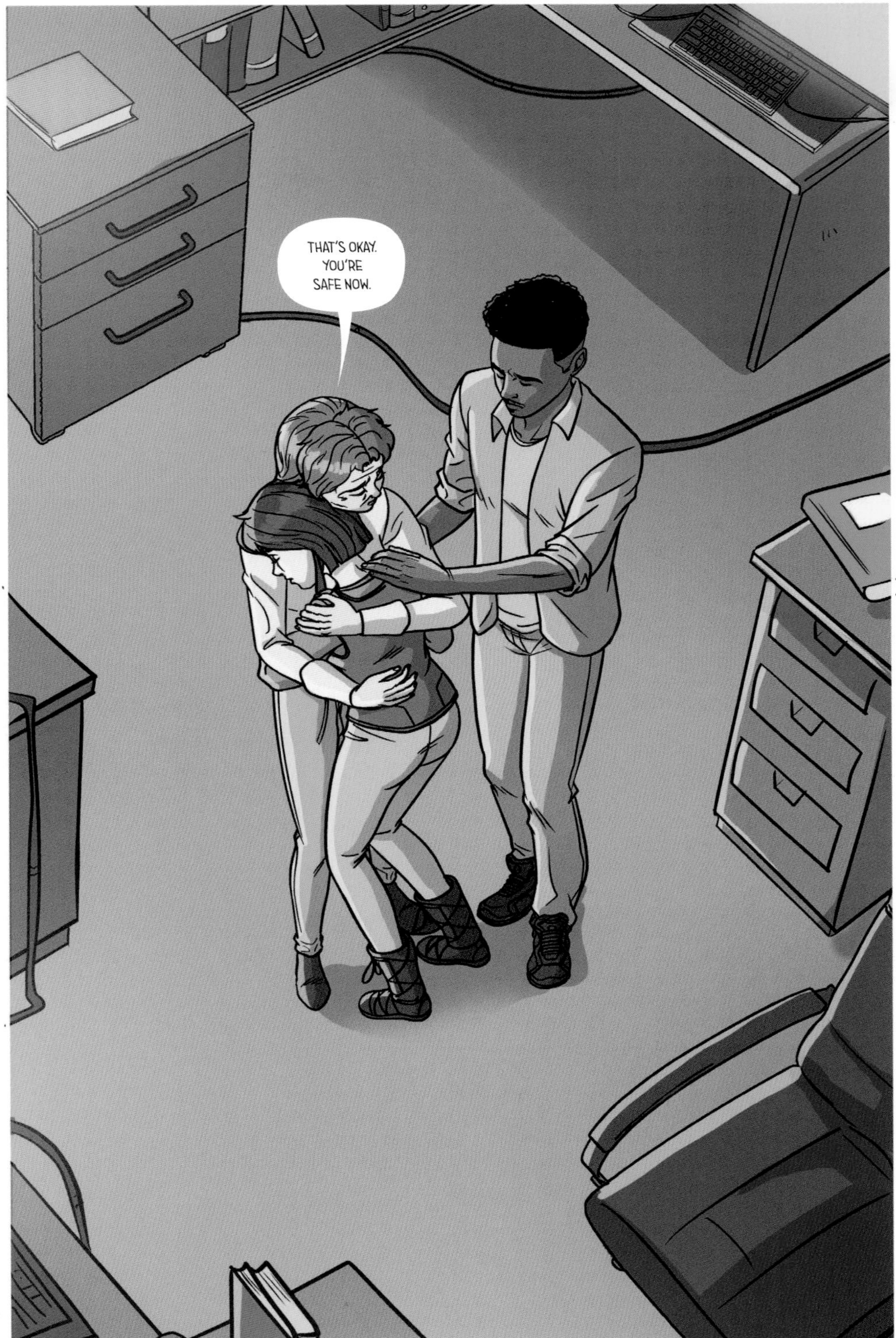
THAT'S OKAY. YOU'RE SAFE NOW.

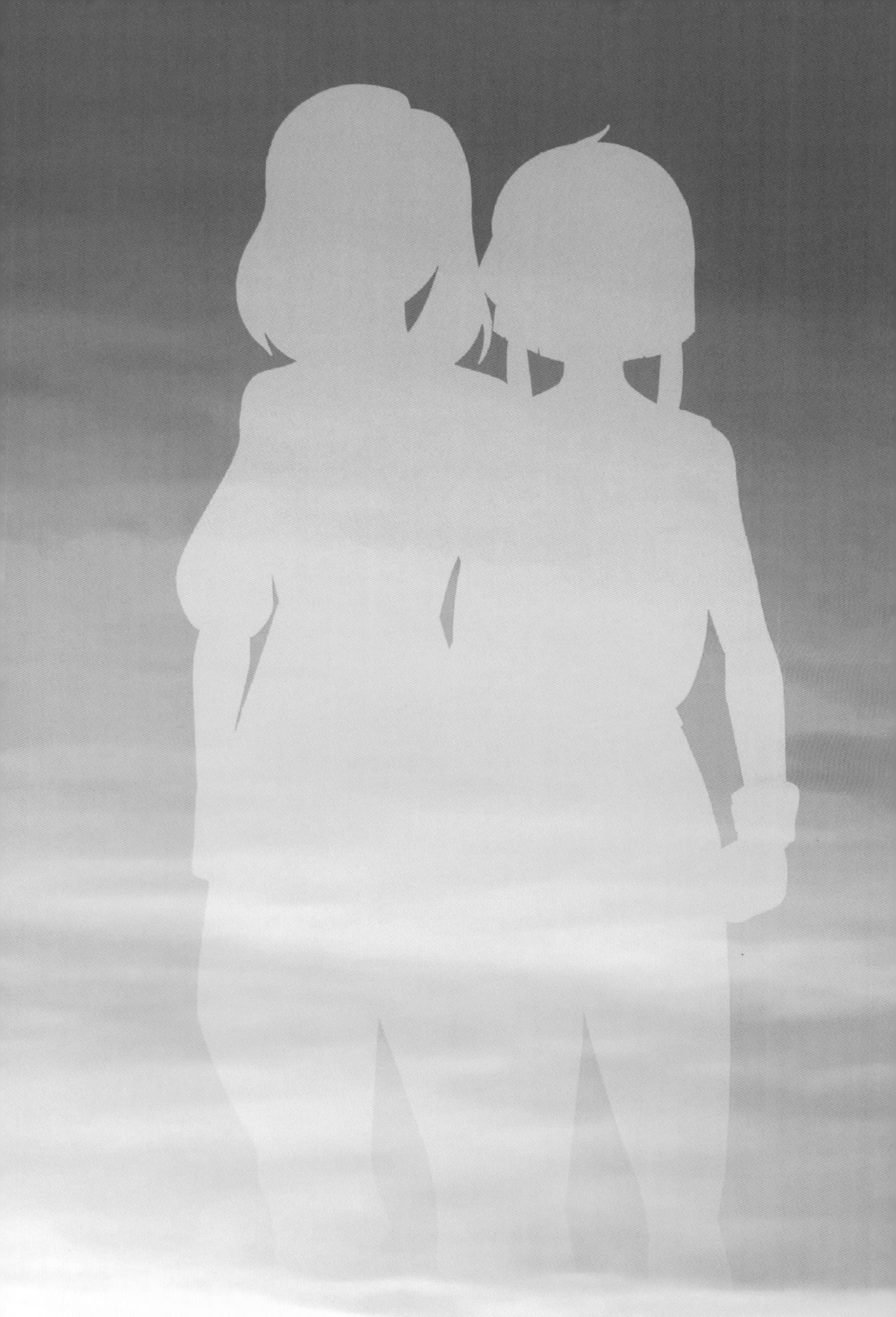

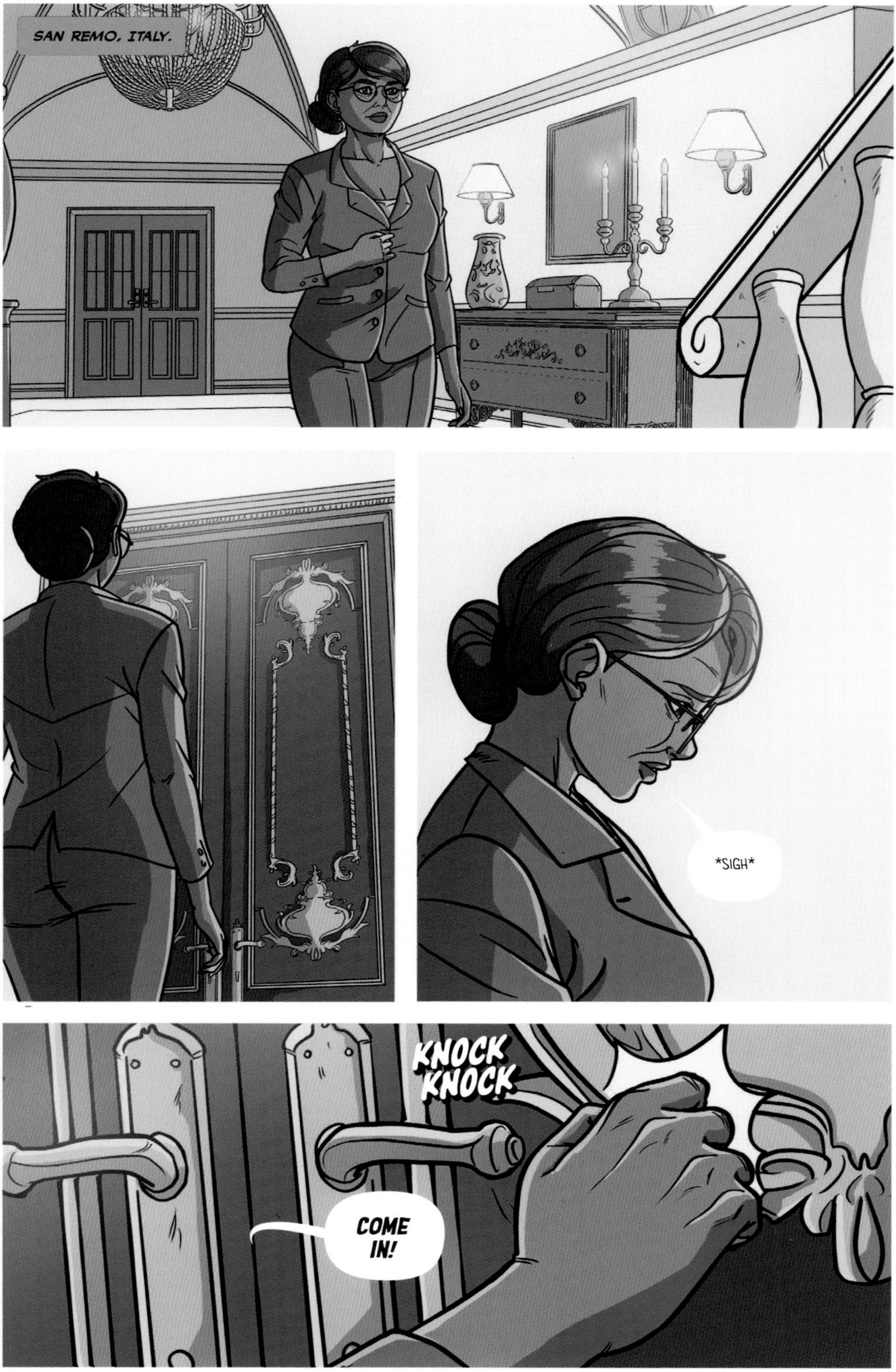
SAN REMO, ITALY.
SIGH
KNOCK KNOCK
COME IN!

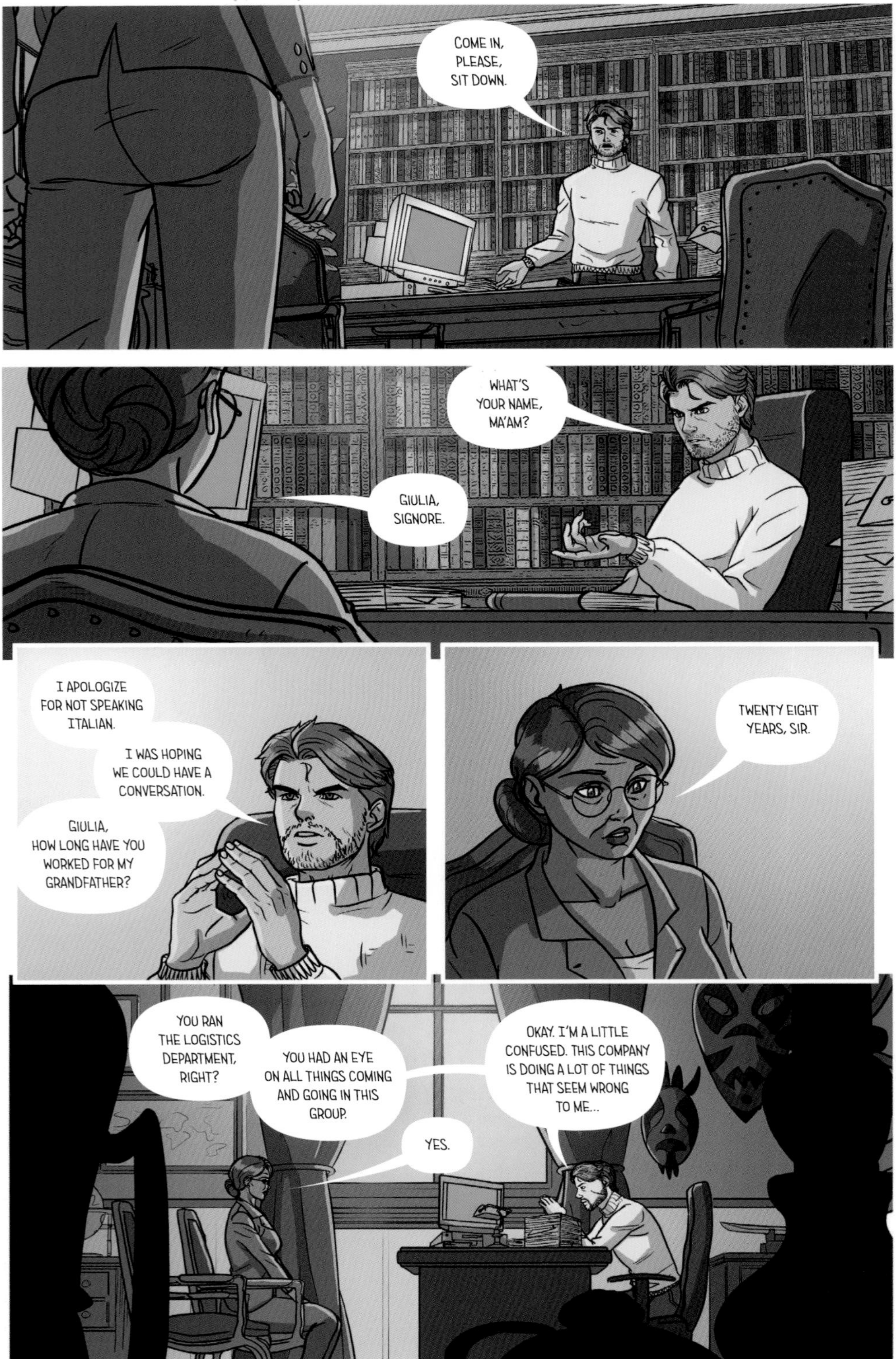
COME IN, PLEASE, SIT DOWN.
WHAT'S YOUR NAME, MA'AM?
GIULIA, SIGNORE.
I APOLOGIZE FOR NOT SPEAKING ITALIAN.
I WAS HOPING WE COULD HAVE A CONVERSATION.
GIULIA, HOW LONG HAVE YOU WORKED FOR MY GRANDFATHER?
TWENTY EIGHT YEARS, SIR.
YOU RAN THE LOGISTICS DEPARTMENT, RIGHT?
YOU HAD AN EYE ON ALL THINGS COMING AND GOING IN THIS GROUP.
OKAY. I'M A LITTLE CONFUSED. THIS COMPANY IS DOING A LOT OF THINGS THAT SEEM WRONG TO ME...
YES.

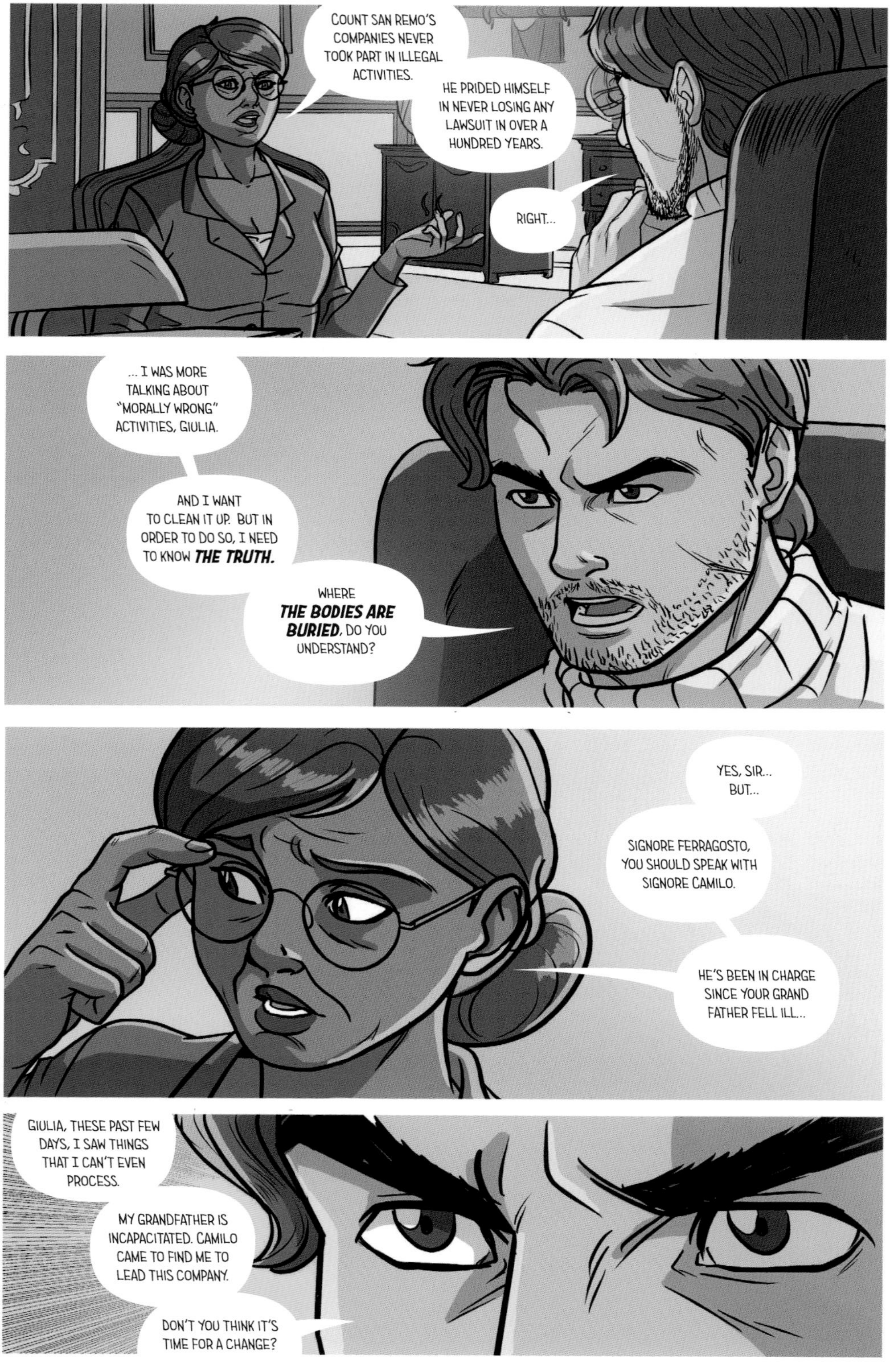
COUNT SAN REMO'S COMPANIES NEVER TOOK PART IN ILLEGAL ACTIVITIES.
HE PRIDED HIMSELF IN NEVER LOSING ANY LAWSUIT IN OVER A HUNDRED YEARS.
RIGHT...
... I WAS MORE TALKING ABOUT "MORALLY WRONG" ACTIVITIES, GIULIA.
AND I WANT TO CLEAN IT UP. BUT IN ORDER TO DO SO, I NEED TO KNOW **THE TRUTH.**
WHERE **THE BODIES ARE BURIED**, DO YOU UNDERSTAND?
YES, SIR... BUT...
SIGNORE FERRAGOSTO, YOU SHOULD SPEAK WITH SIGNORE CAMILO.
HE'S BEEN IN CHARGE SINCE YOUR GRAND FATHER FELL ILL...
GIULIA, THESE PAST FEW DAYS, I SAW THINGS THAT I CAN'T EVEN PROCESS.
MY GRANDFATHER IS INCAPACITATED. CAMILO CAME TO FIND ME TO LEAD THIS COMPANY.
DON'T YOU THINK IT'S TIME FOR A CHANGE?

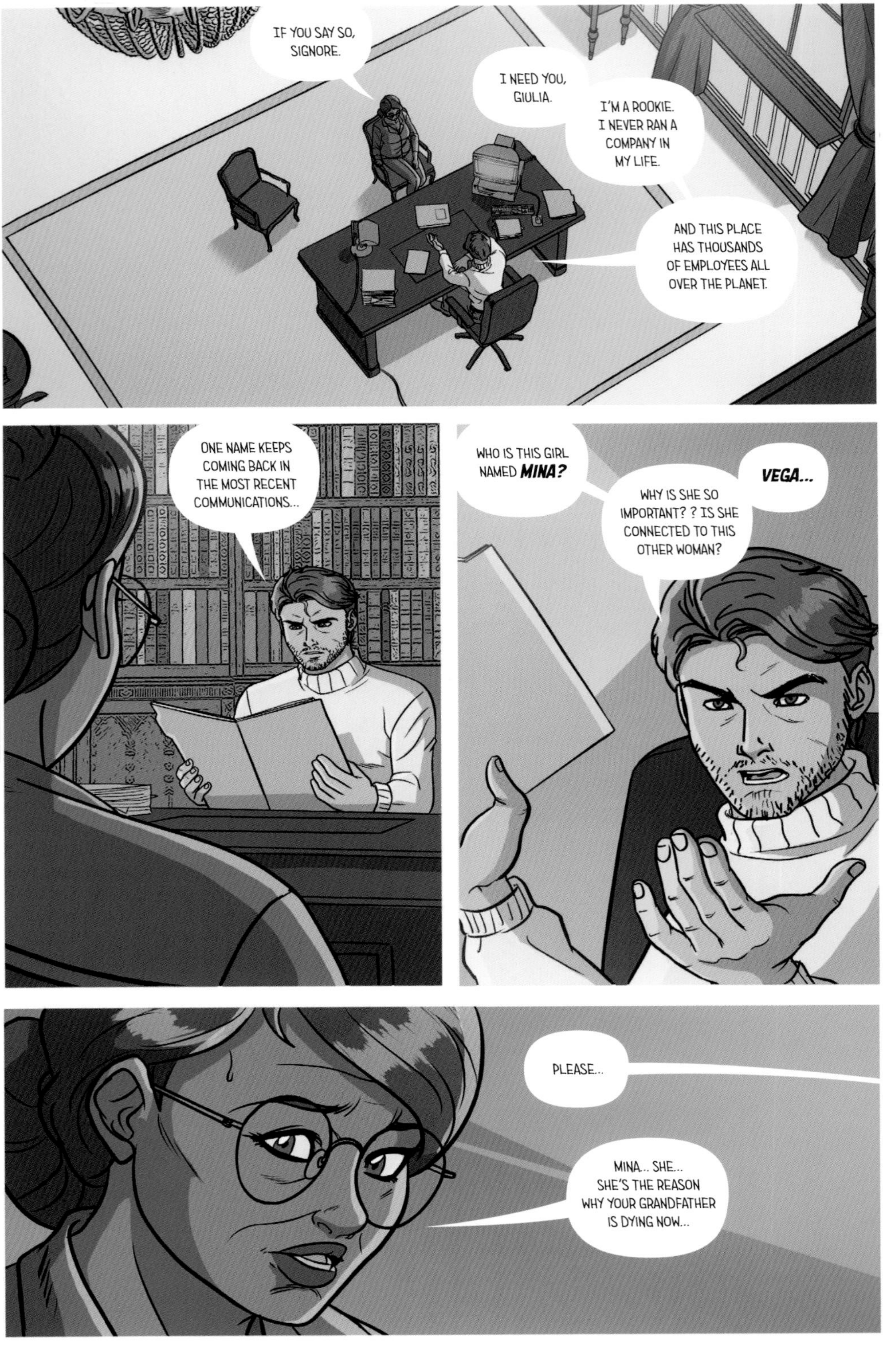
IF YOU SAY SO, SIGNORE.
I NEED YOU, GIULIA.
I'M A ROOKIE. I NEVER RAN A COMPANY IN MY LIFE.
AND THIS PLACE HAS THOUSANDS OF EMPLOYEES ALL OVER THE PLANET.
ONE NAME KEEPS COMING BACK IN THE MOST RECENT COMMUNICATIONS...
WHO IS THIS GIRL NAMED **MINA?**
VEGA...
WHY IS SHE SO IMPORTANT? ? IS SHE CONNECTED TO THIS OTHER WOMAN?
PLEASE...
MINA... SHE... SHE'S THE REASON WHY YOUR GRANDFATHER IS DYING NOW...

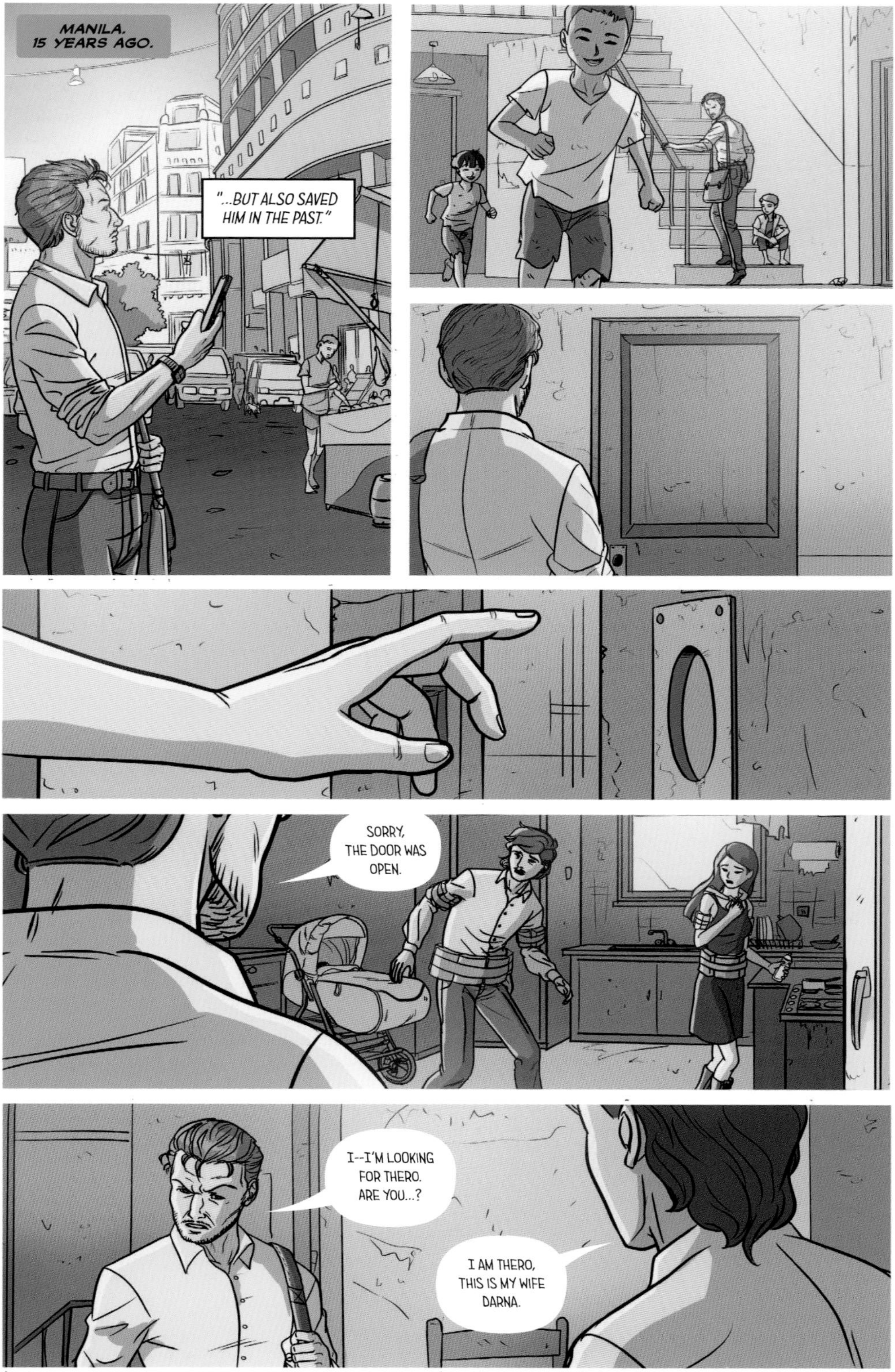
MANILA.
15 YEARS AGO.
"...BUT ALSO SAVED HIM IN THE PAST."
SORRY, THE DOOR WAS OPEN.
I--I'M LOOKING FOR THERO. ARE YOU...?
I AM THERO, THIS IS MY WIFE DARNA.

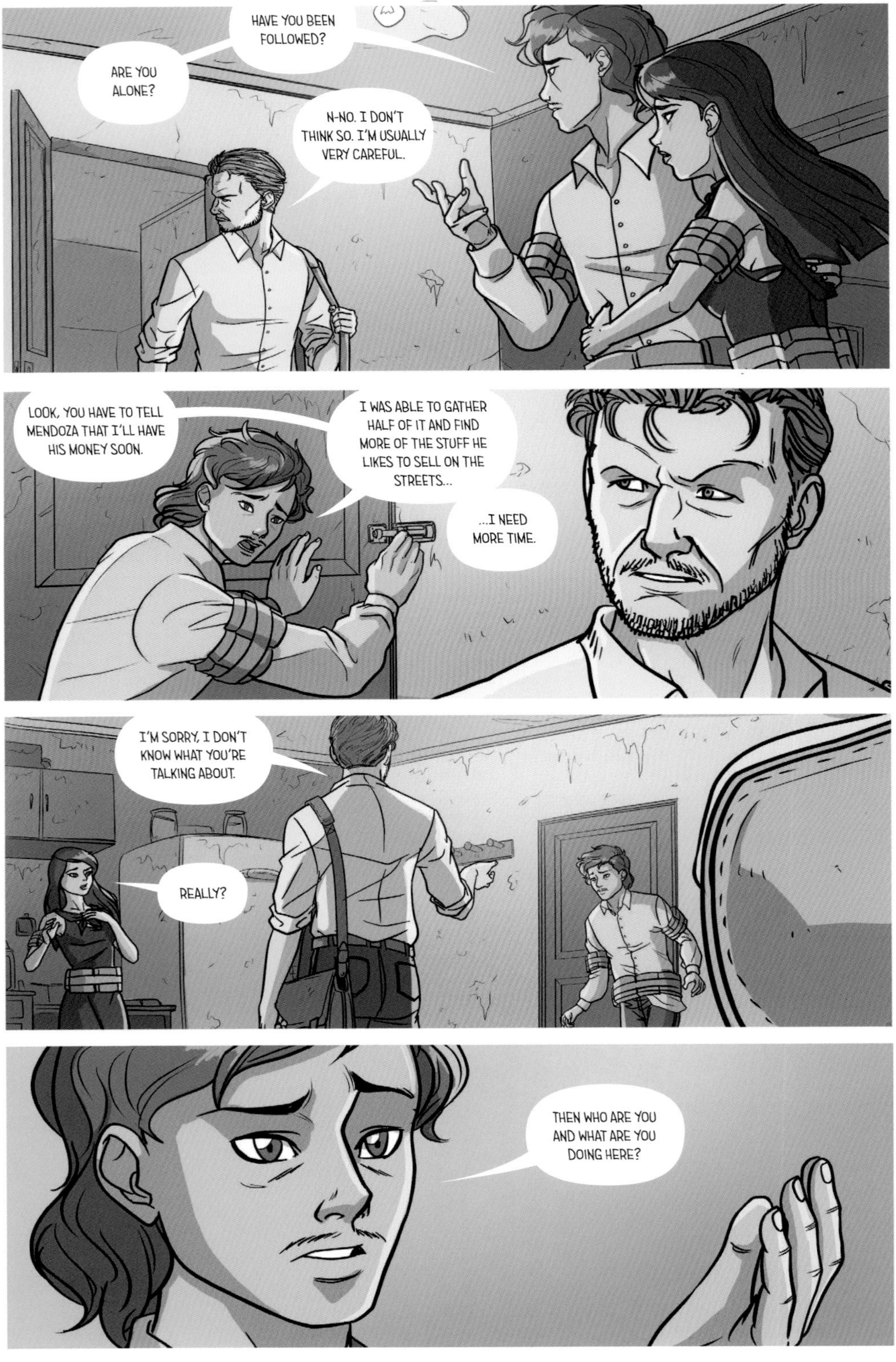
ARE YOU ALONE?
HAVE YOU BEEN FOLLOWED?
N-NO. I DON'T THINK SO. I'M USUALLY VERY CAREFUL.
LOOK, YOU HAVE TO TELL MENDOZA THAT I'LL HAVE HIS MONEY SOON.
I WAS ABLE TO GATHER HALF OF IT AND FIND MORE OF THE STUFF HE LIKES TO SELL ON THE STREETS...
...I NEED MORE TIME.
I'M SORRY, I DON'T KNOW WHAT YOU'RE TALKING ABOUT.
REALLY?
THEN WHO ARE YOU AND WHAT ARE YOU DOING HERE?

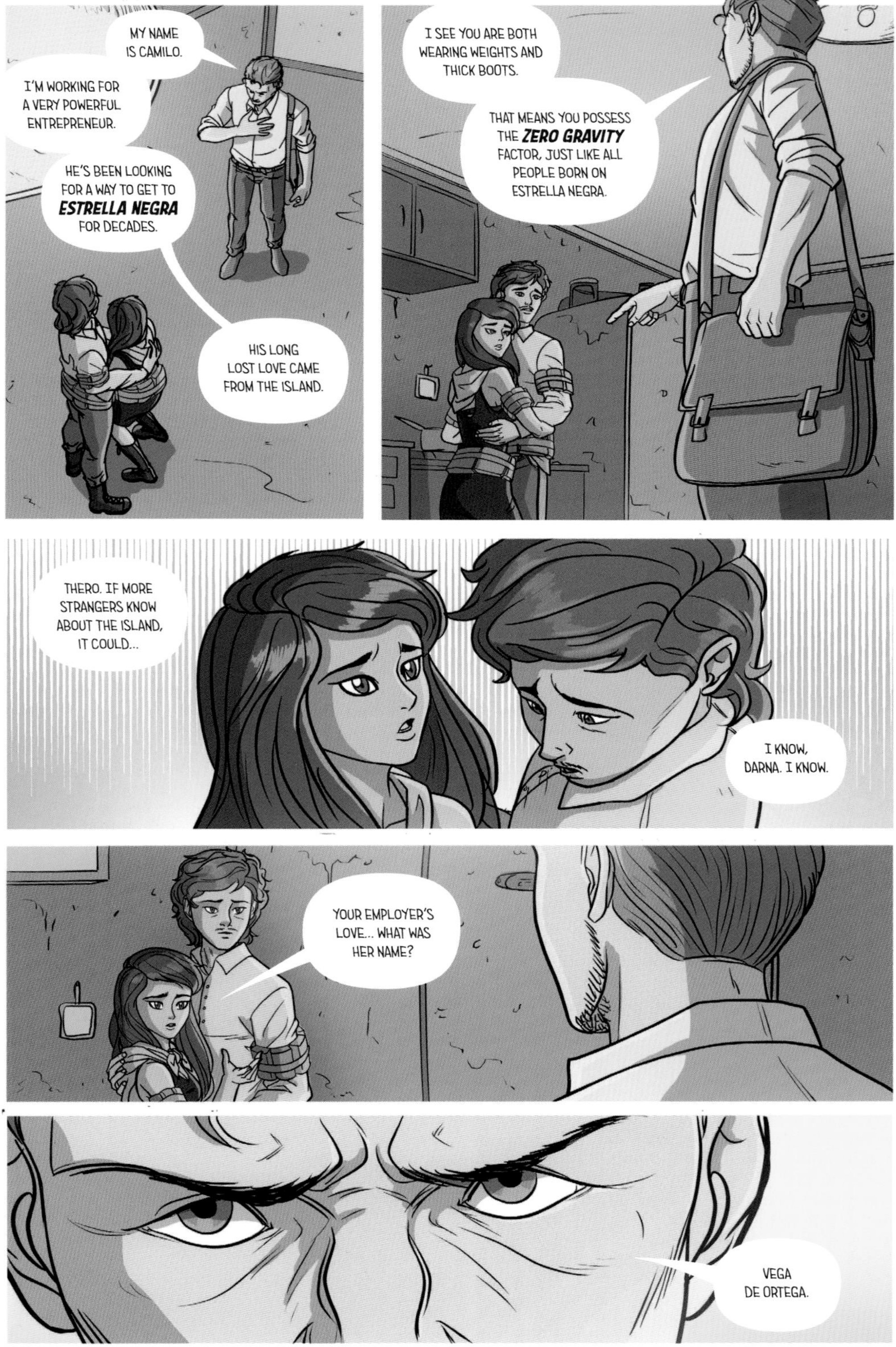
MY NAME IS CAMILO.
I'M WORKING FOR A VERY POWERFUL ENTREPRENEUR.
HE'S BEEN LOOKING FOR A WAY TO GET TO **ESTRELLA NEGRA** FOR DECADES.
HIS LONG LOST LOVE CAME FROM THE ISLAND.
I SEE YOU ARE BOTH WEARING WEIGHTS AND THICK BOOTS.
THAT MEANS YOU POSSESS THE ***ZERO GRAVITY*** FACTOR, JUST LIKE ALL PEOPLE BORN ON ESTRELLA NEGRA.
THERO. IF MORE STRANGERS KNOW ABOUT THE ISLAND, IT COULD...
I KNOW, DARNA. I KNOW.
YOUR EMPLOYER'S LOVE... WHAT WAS HER NAME?
VEGA DE ORTEGA.

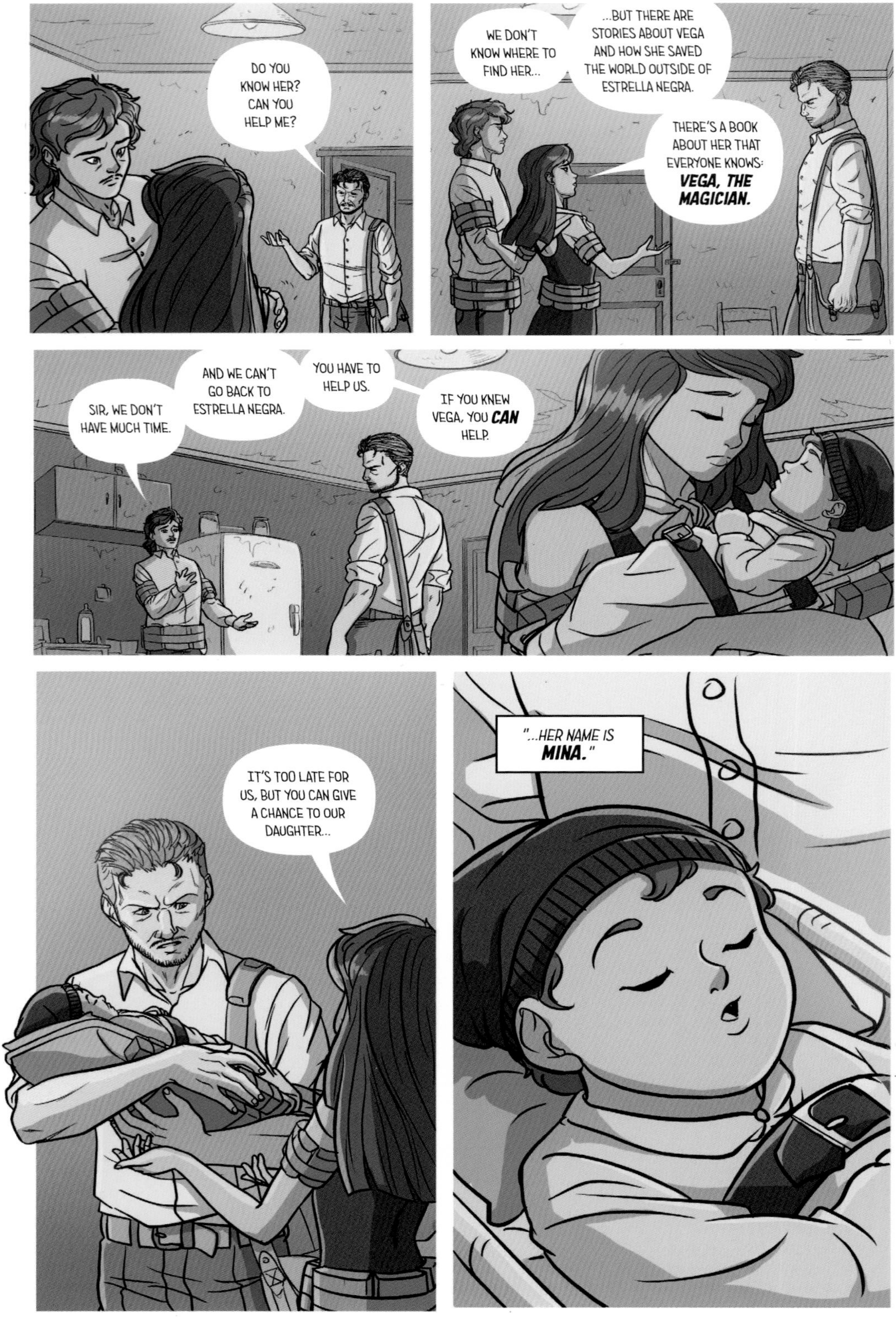
DO YOU KNOW HER? CAN YOU HELP ME?
WE DON'T KNOW WHERE TO FIND HER...
...BUT THERE ARE STORIES ABOUT VEGA AND HOW SHE SAVED THE WORLD OUTSIDE OF ESTRELLA NEGRA.
THERE'S A BOOK ABOUT HER THAT EVERYONE KNOWS: **VEGA, THE MAGICIAN.**
SIR, WE DON'T HAVE MUCH TIME.
AND WE CAN'T GO BACK TO ESTRELLA NEGRA.
YOU HAVE TO HELP US.
IF YOU KNEW VEGA, YOU **CAN** HELP.
IT'S TOO LATE FOR US, BUT YOU CAN GIVE A CHANCE TO OUR DAUGHTER...
"...HER NAME IS **MINA.**"

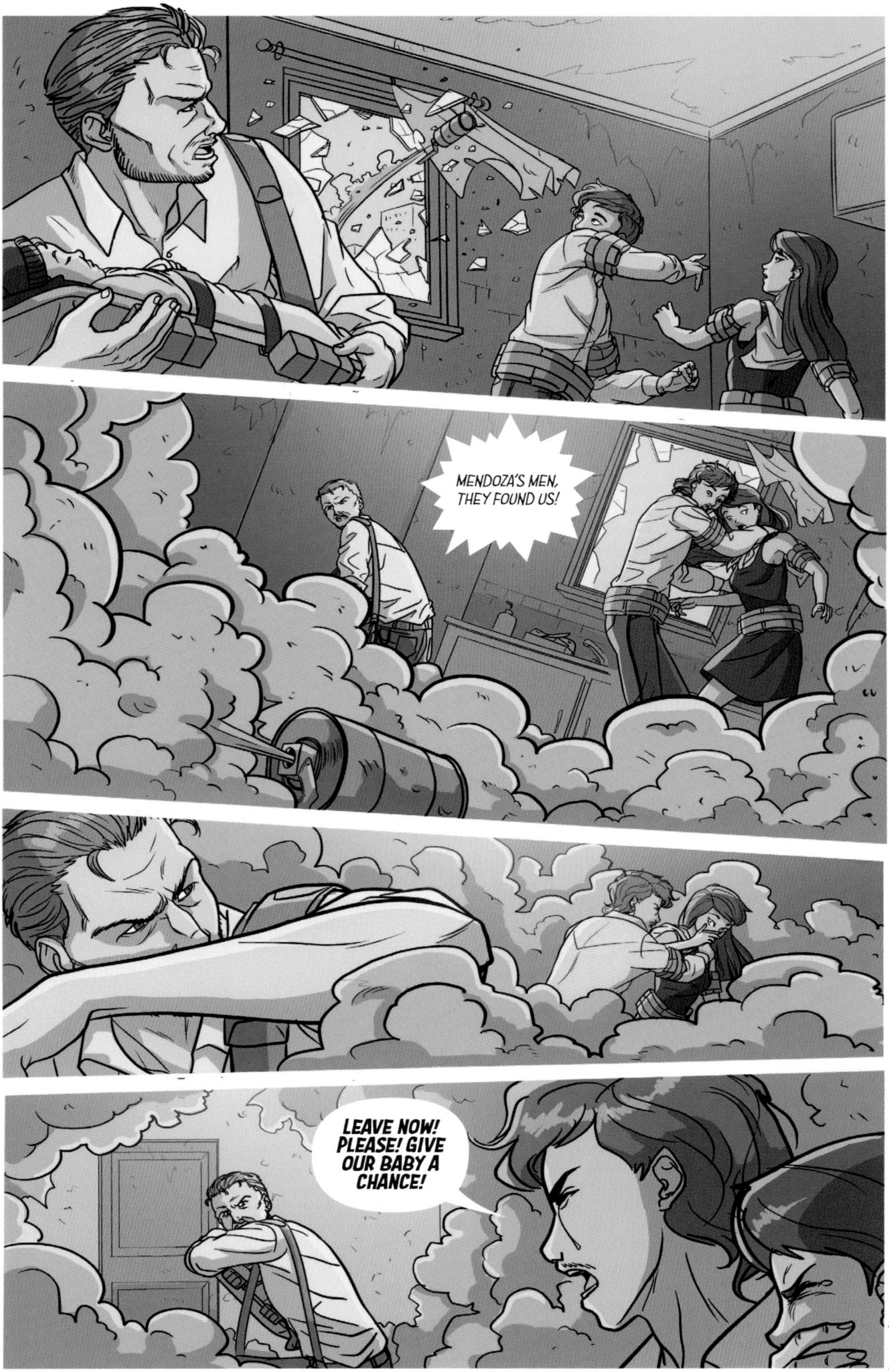
MENDOZA'S MEN, THEY FOUND US!
LEAVE NOW! PLEASE! GIVE OUR BABY A CHANCE!

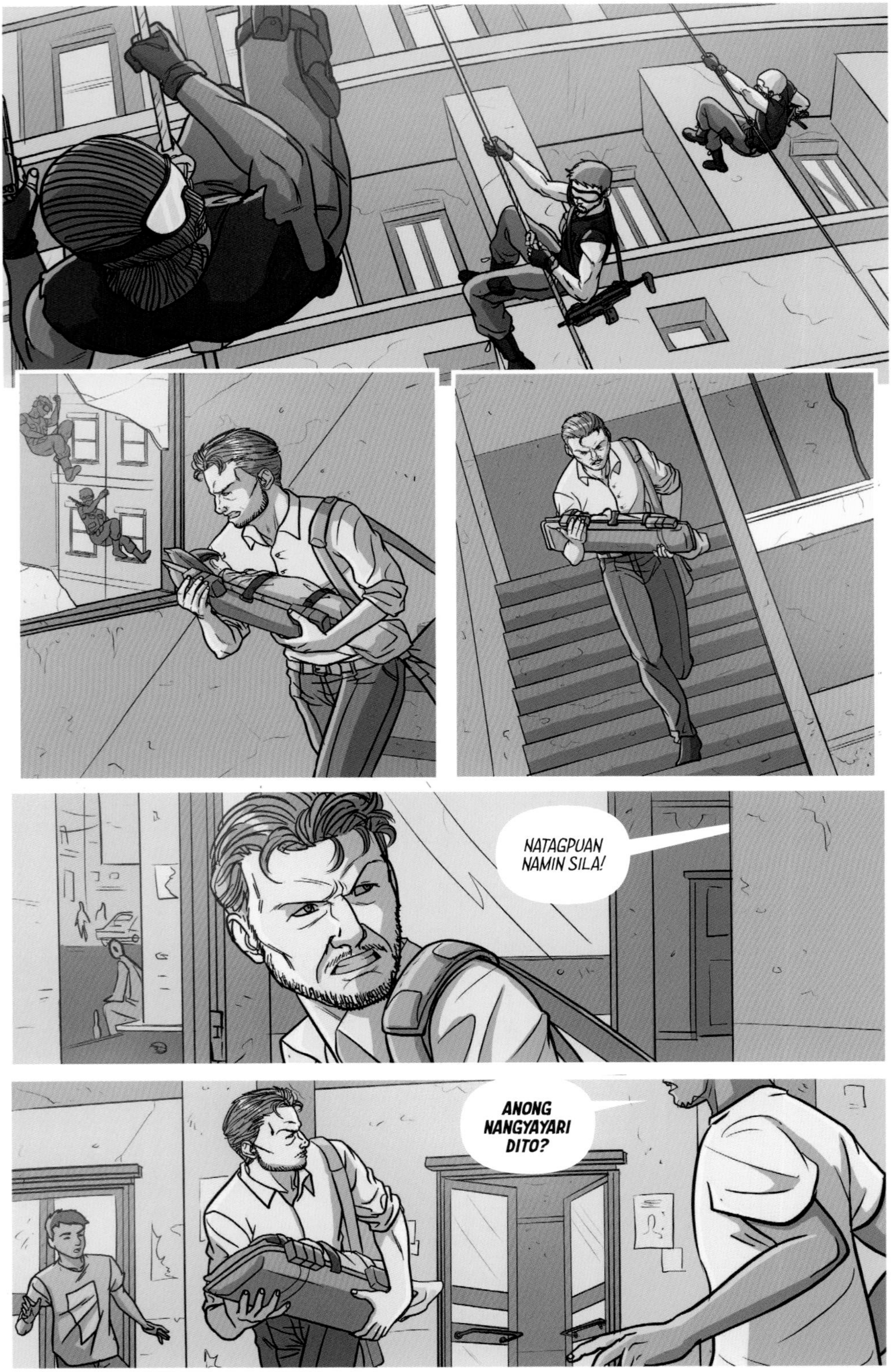
NATAGPUAN NAMIN SILA!
ANONG NANGYAYARI DITO?

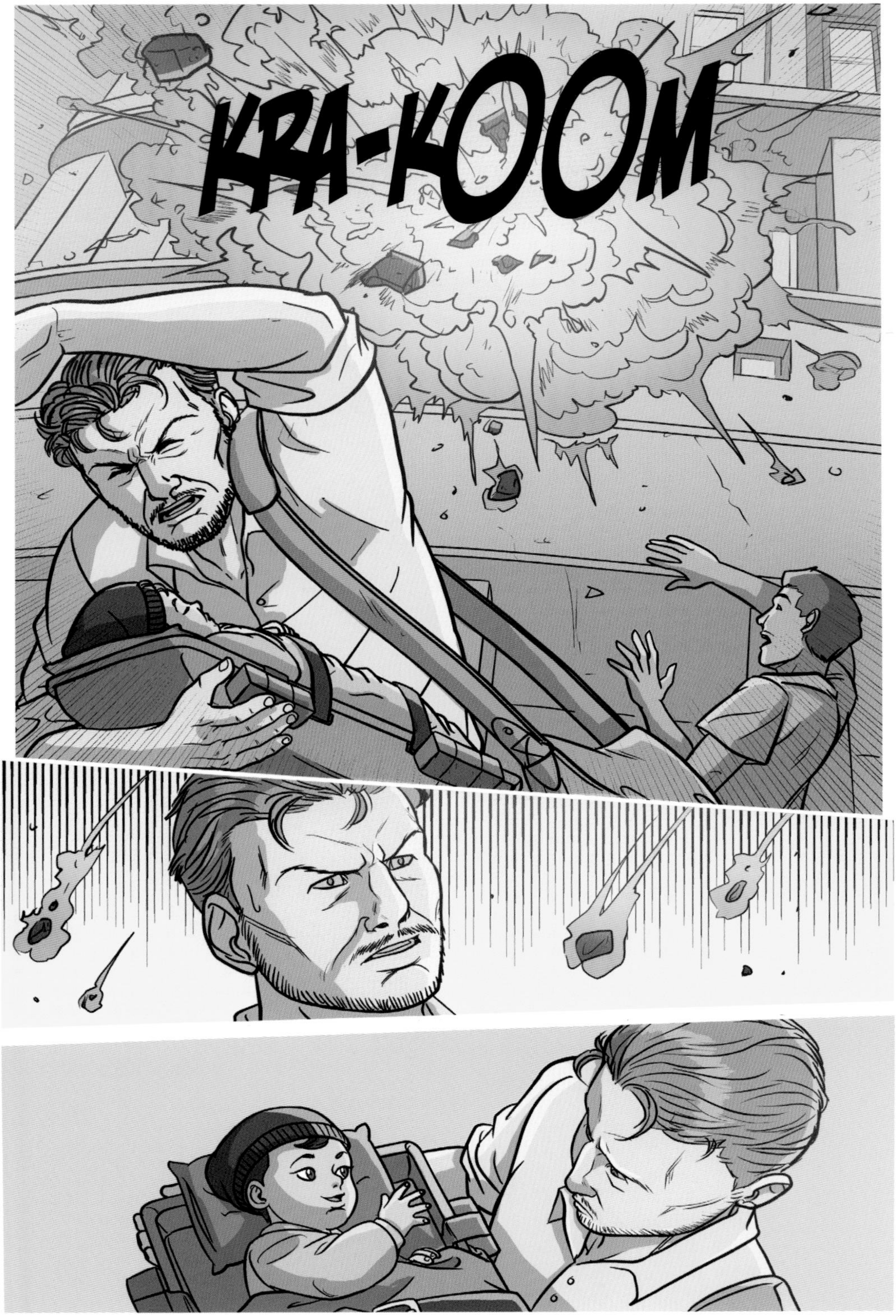
KRA-KOOM

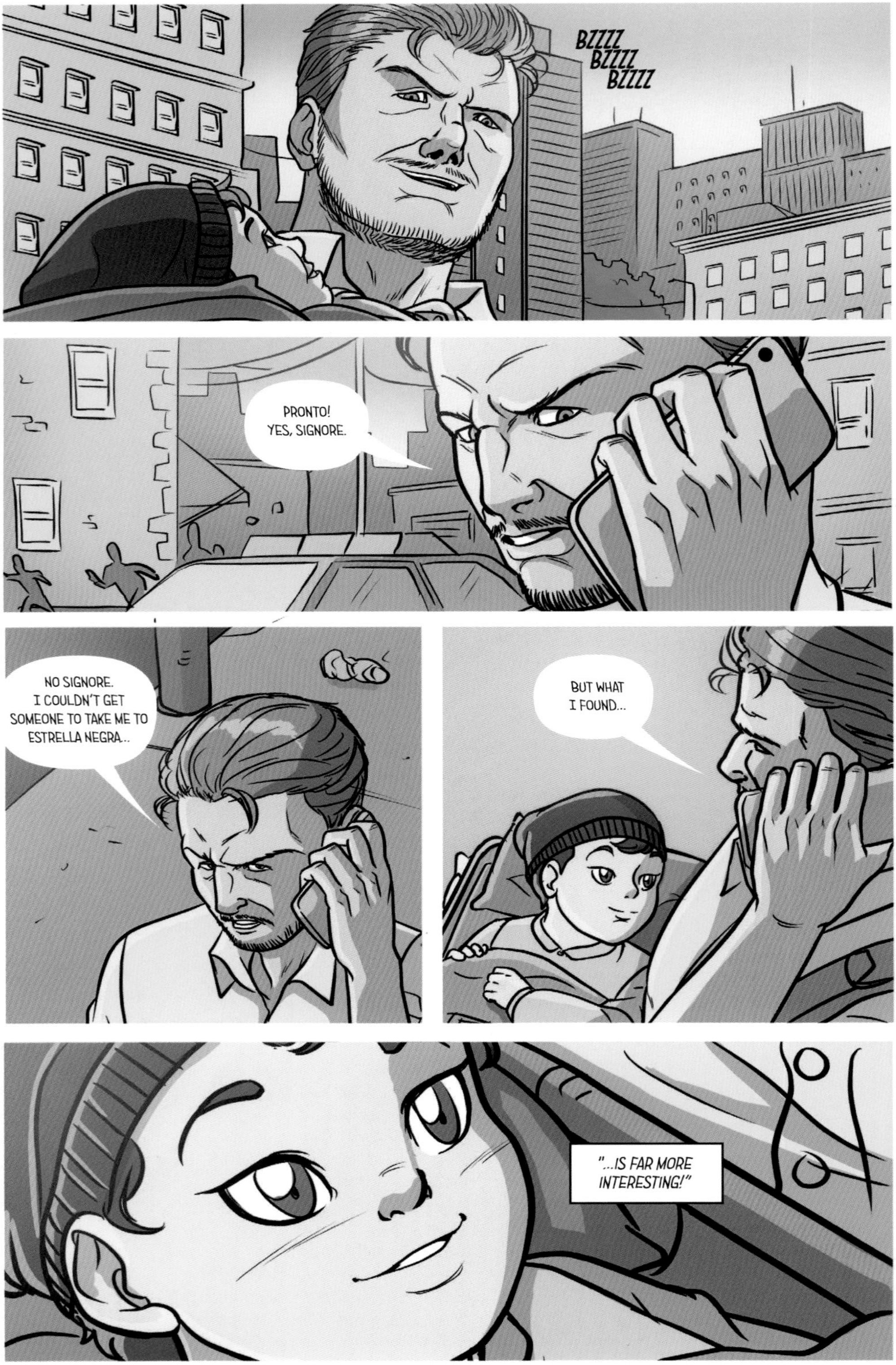
BZZZZ
BZZZZ
BZZZZ
PRONTO! YES, SIGNORE.
NO SIGNORE. I COULDN'T GET SOMEONE TO TAKE ME TO ESTRELLA NEGRA...
BUT WHAT I FOUND...
"...IS FAR MORE INTERESTING!"

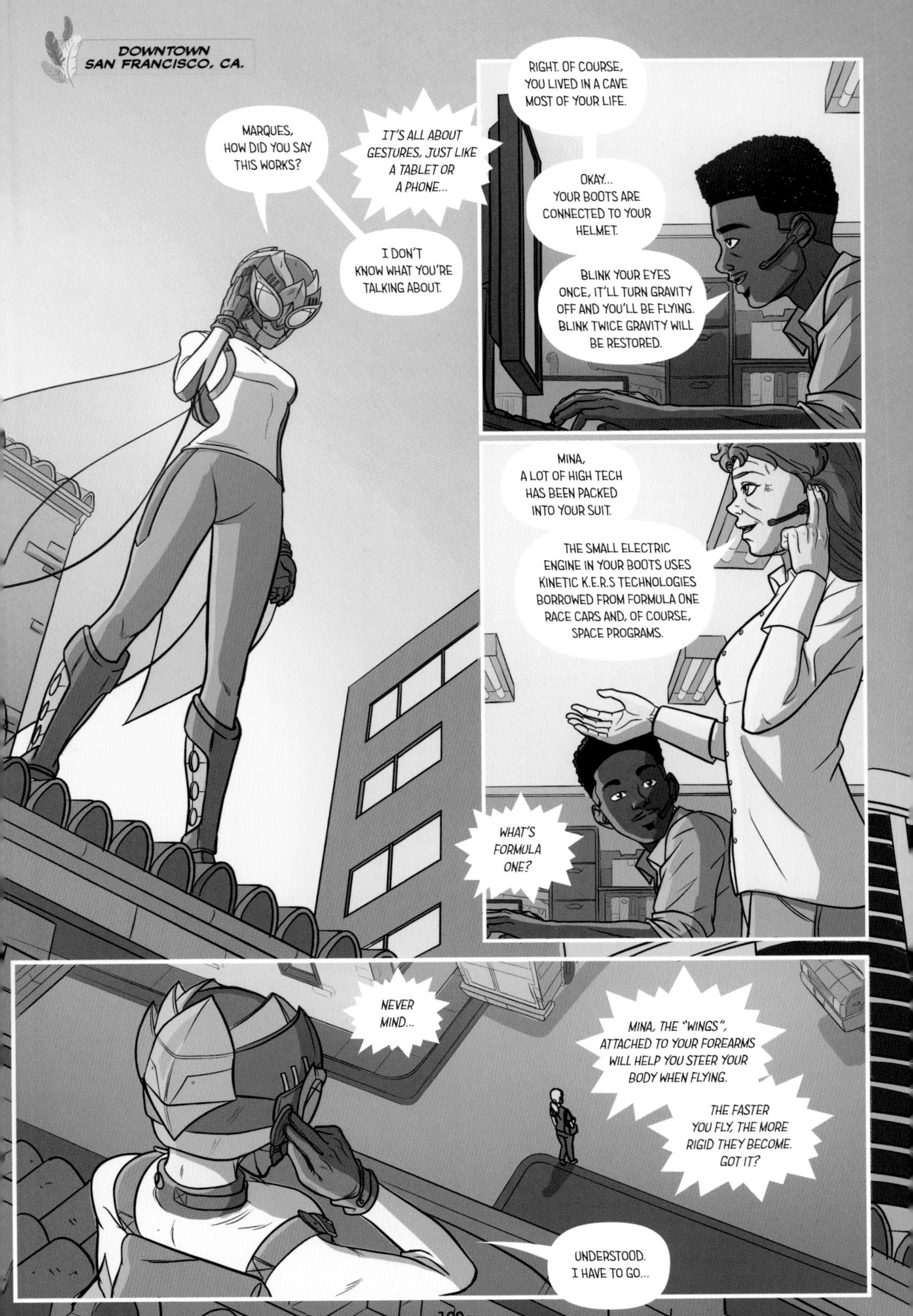
DOWNTOWN SAN FRANCISCO, CA.
MARQUES, HOW DID YOU SAY THIS WORKS?
IT'S ALL ABOUT GESTURES, JUST LIKE A TABLET OR A PHONE...
I DON'T KNOW WHAT YOU'RE TALKING ABOUT.
RIGHT. OF COURSE, YOU LIVED IN A CAVE MOST OF YOUR LIFE.
OKAY... YOUR BOOTS ARE CONNECTED TO YOUR HELMET.
BLINK YOUR EYES ONCE, IT'LL TURN GRAVITY OFF AND YOU'LL BE FLYING. BLINK TWICE GRAVITY WILL BE RESTORED.
MINA, A LOT OF HIGH TECH HAS BEEN PACKED INTO YOUR SUIT.
THE SMALL ELECTRIC ENGINE IN YOUR BOOTS USES KINETIC K.E.R.S TECHNOLOGIES BORROWED FROM FORMULA ONE RACE CARS AND, OF COURSE, SPACE PROGRAMS.
WHAT'S FORMULA ONE?
NEVER MIND...
MINA, THE "WINGS", ATTACHED TO YOUR FOREARMS WILL HELP YOU STEER YOUR BODY WHEN FLYING.
THE FASTER YOU FLY, THE MORE RIGID THEY BECOME. GOT IT?
UNDERSTOOD. I HAVE TO GO...

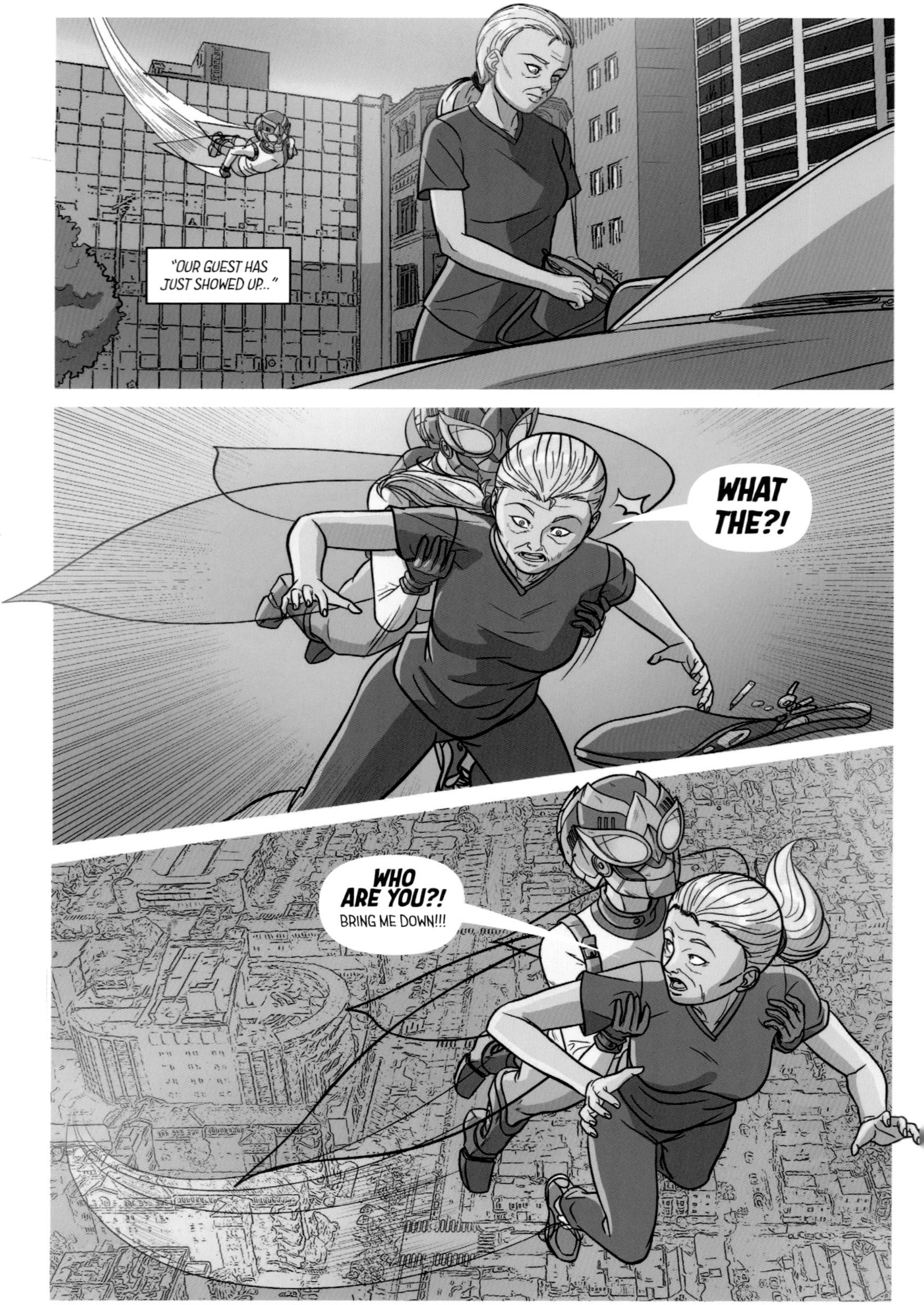
"OUR GUEST HAS JUST SHOWED UP..."
WHAT THE?!
WHO ARE YOU?! BRING ME DOWN!!!

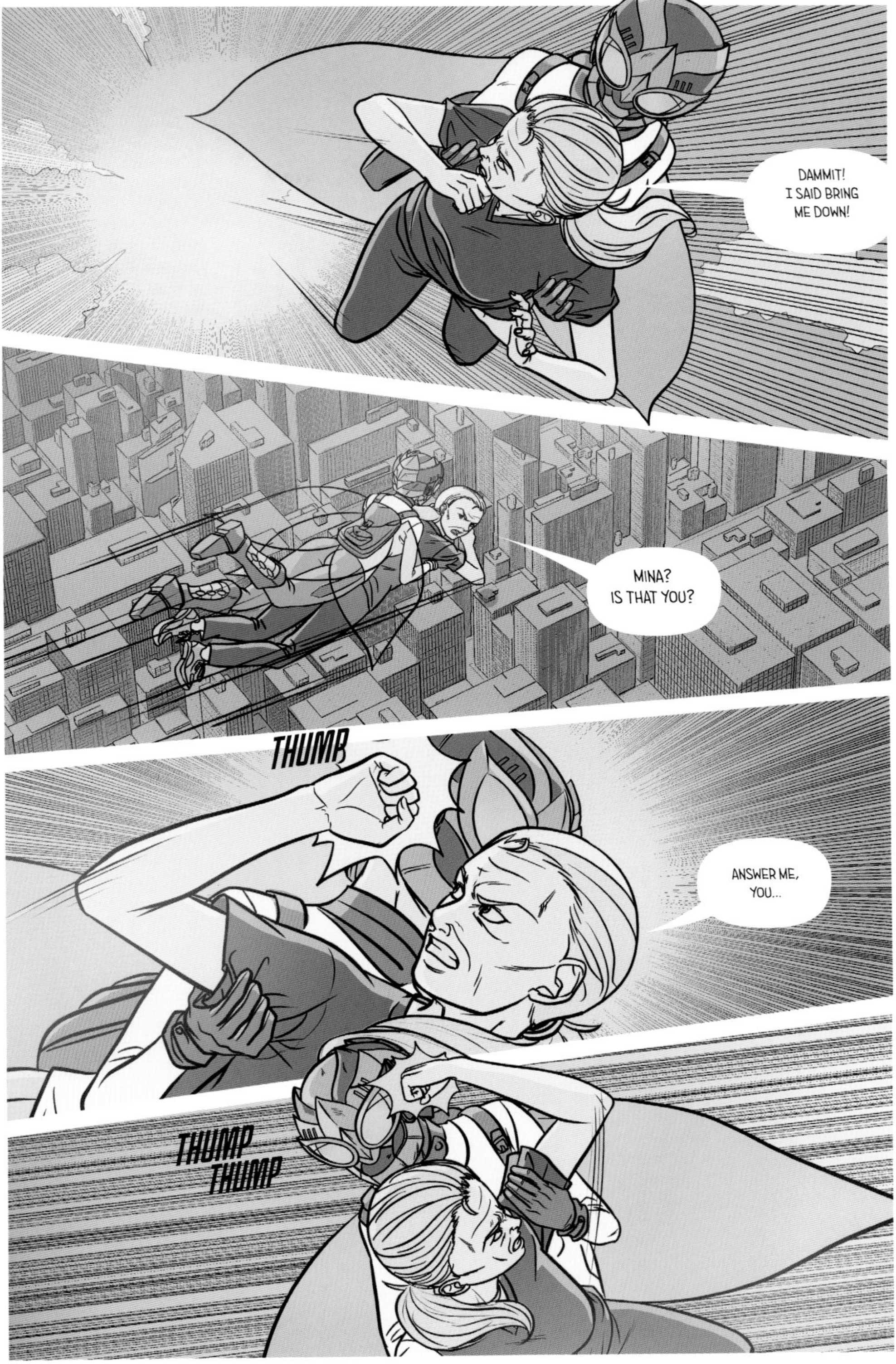
DAMMIT! I SAID BRING ME DOWN!
MINA? IS THAT YOU?
THUMP
ANSWER ME, YOU...
THUMP THUMP

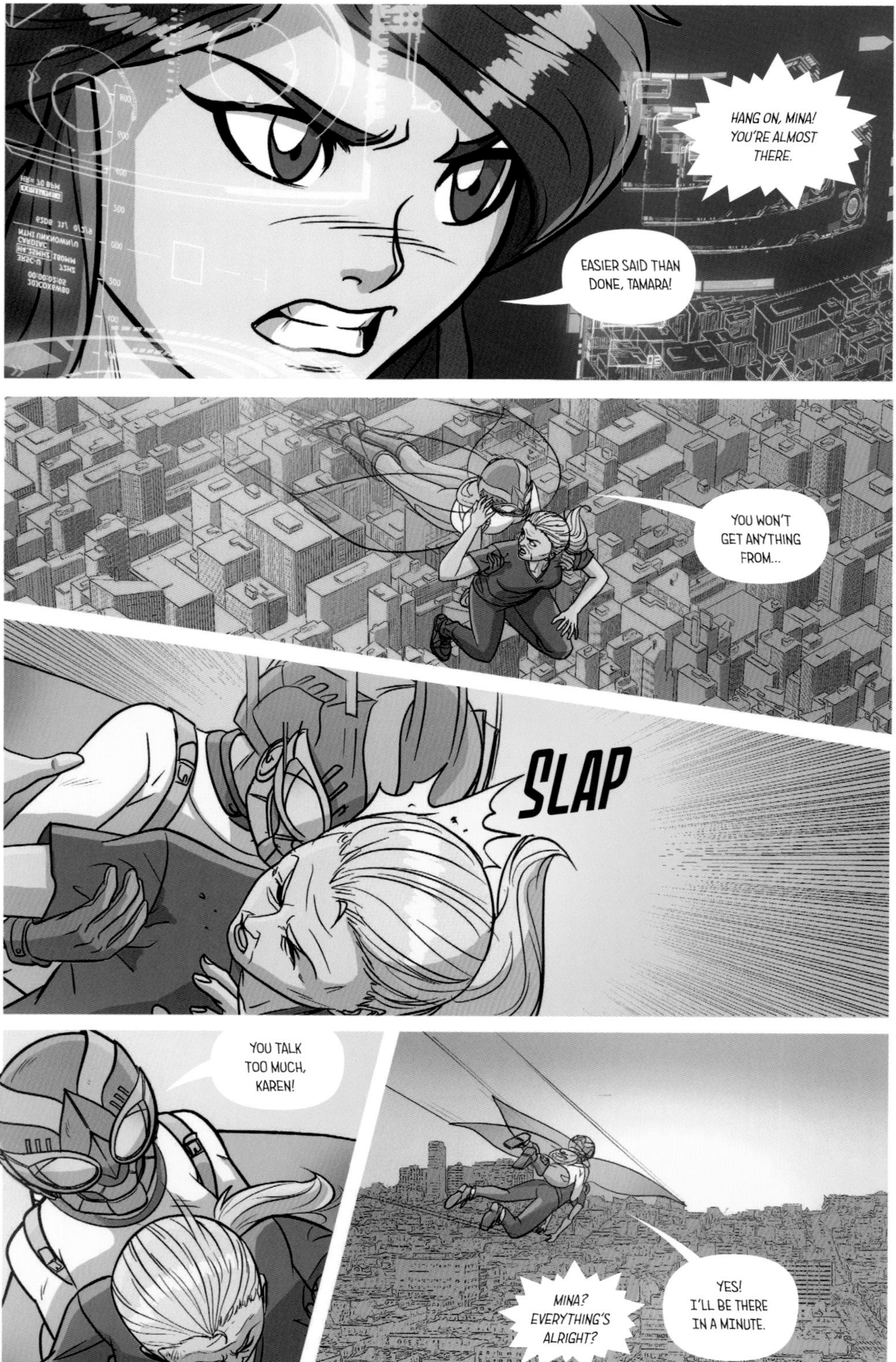
HANG ON, MINA! YOU'RE ALMOST THERE.
EASIER SAID THAN DONE, TAMARA!
YOU WON'T GET ANYTHING FROM...
SLAP
YOU TALK TOO MUCH, KAREN!
MINA? EVERYTHING'S ALRIGHT?
YES! I'LL BE THERE IN A MINUTE.

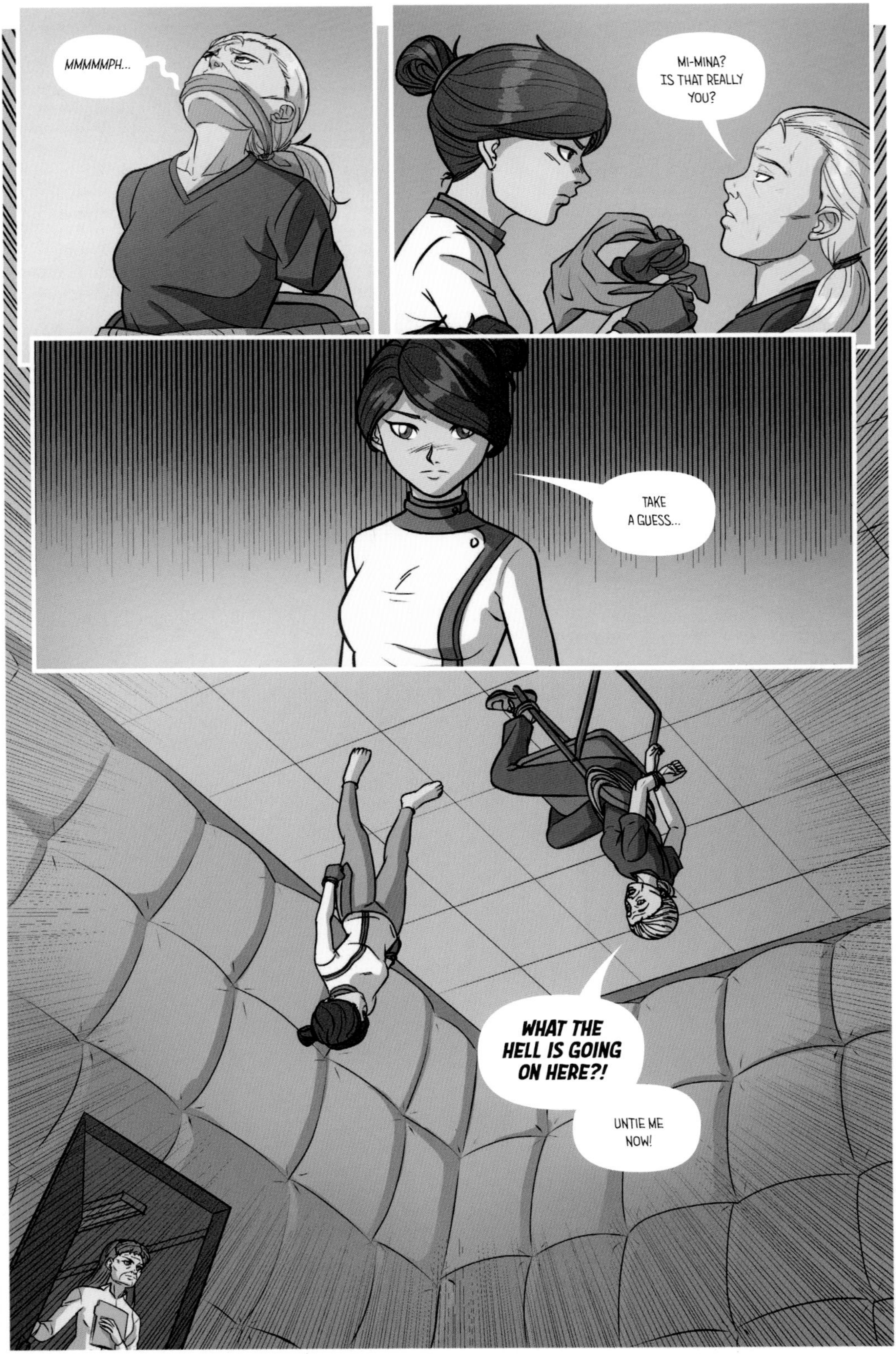
MMMMMPH...
MI-MINA? IS THAT REALLY YOU?
TAKE A GUESS...
WHAT THE HELL IS GOING ON HERE?!
UNTIE ME NOW!

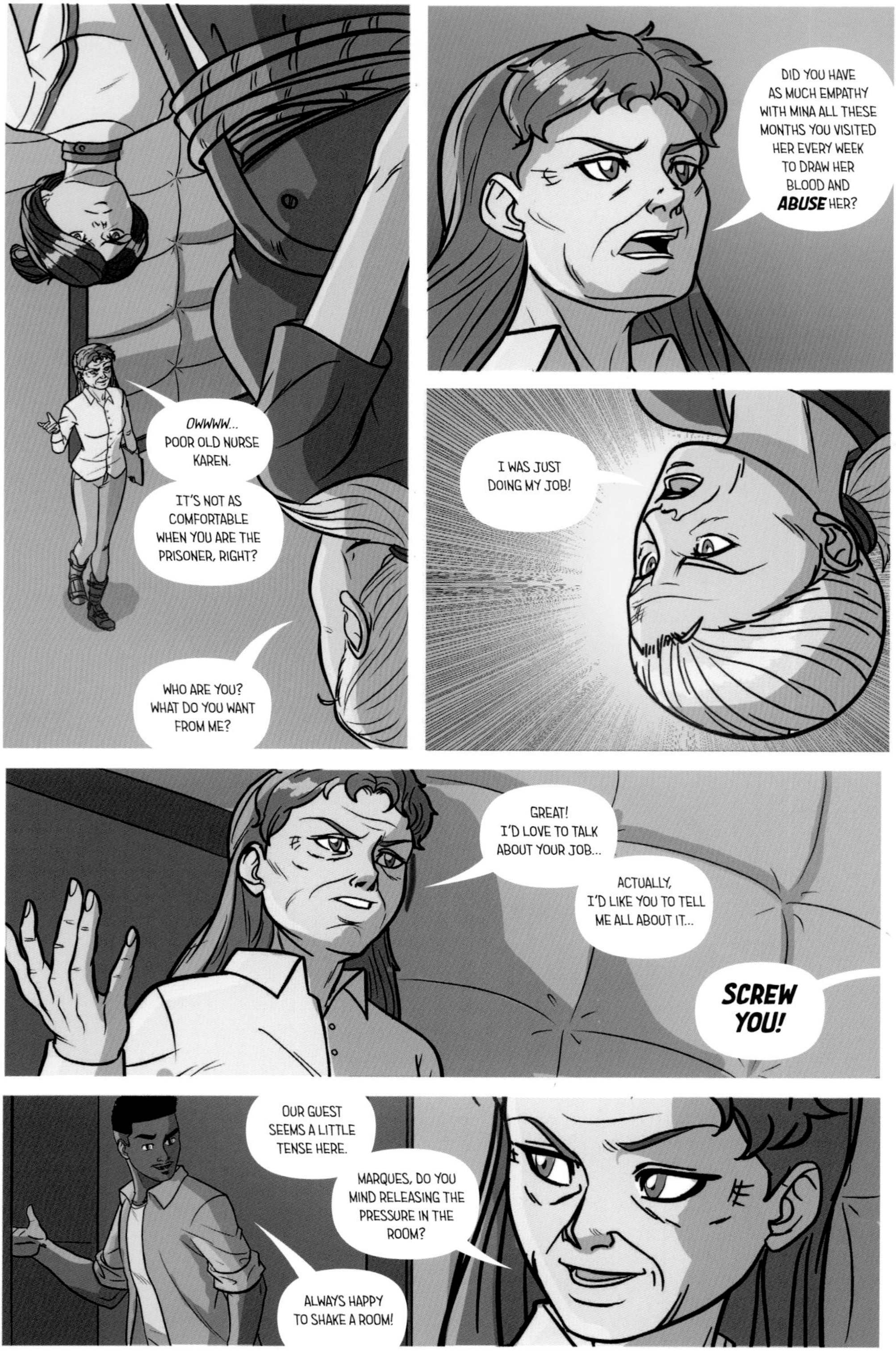
OWWWW... POOR OLD NURSE KAREN.
IT'S NOT AS COMFORTABLE WHEN YOU ARE THE PRISONER, RIGHT?
WHO ARE YOU? WHAT DO YOU WANT FROM ME?
DID YOU HAVE AS MUCH EMPATHY WITH MINA ALL THESE MONTHS YOU VISITED HER EVERY WEEK TO DRAW HER BLOOD AND ABUSE HER?
I WAS JUST DOING MY JOB!
GREAT! I'D LOVE TO TALK ABOUT YOUR JOB...
ACTUALLY, I'D LIKE YOU TO TELL ME ALL ABOUT IT...
SCREW YOU!
OUR GUEST SEEMS A LITTLE TENSE HERE.
MARQUES, DO YOU MIND RELEASING THE PRESSURE IN THE ROOM?
ALWAYS HAPPY TO SHAKE A ROOM!

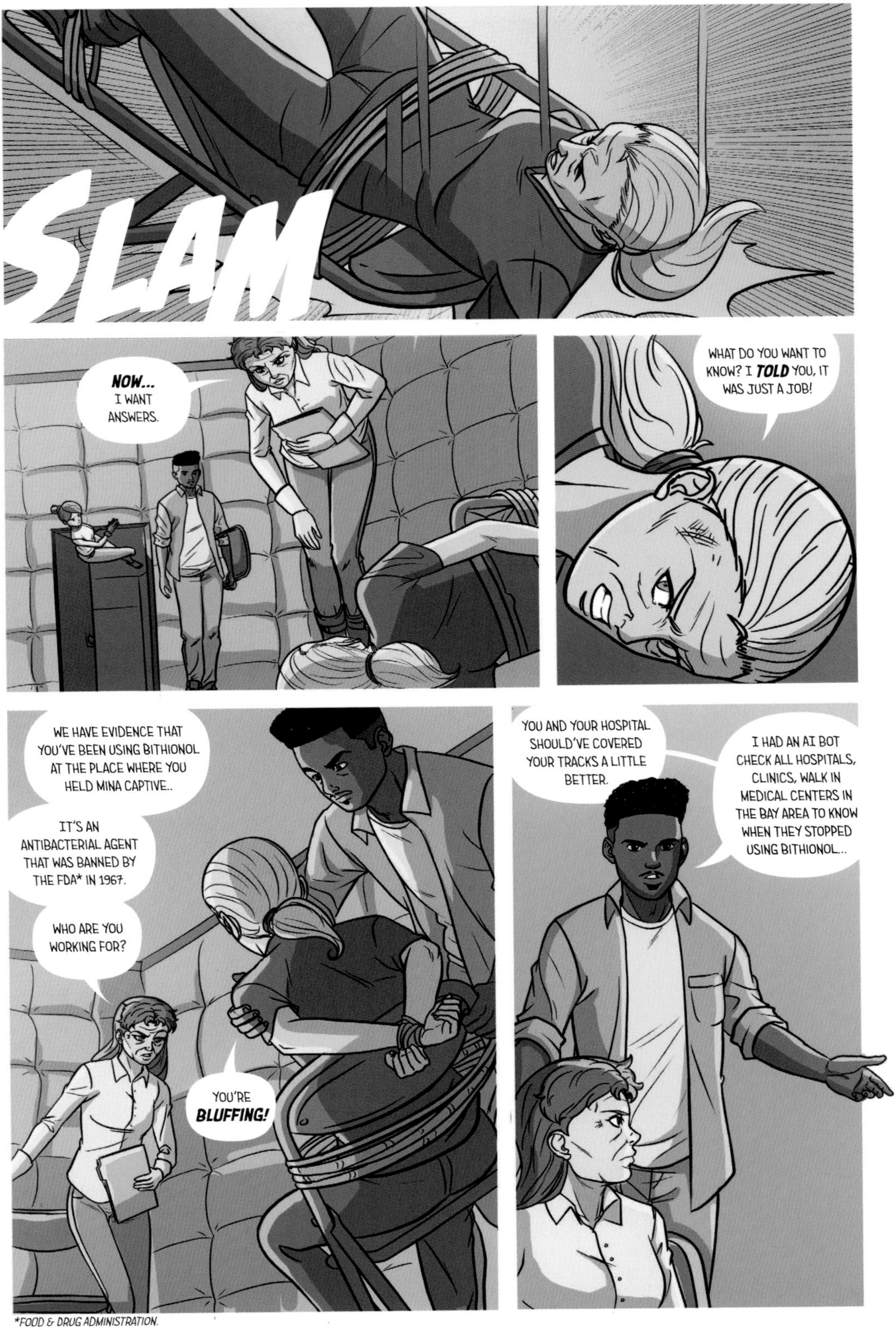
SLAM
NOW... I WANT ANSWERS.
WHAT DO YOU WANT TO KNOW? I TOLD YOU, IT WAS JUST A JOB!
WE HAVE EVIDENCE THAT YOU'VE BEEN USING BITHIONOL AT THE PLACE WHERE YOU HELD MINA CAPTIVE..
IT'S AN ANTIBACTERIAL AGENT THAT WAS BANNED BY THE FDA* IN 1967.
WHO ARE YOU WORKING FOR?
YOU'RE BLUFFING!
YOU AND YOUR HOSPITAL SHOULD'VE COVERED YOUR TRACKS A LITTLE BETTER.
I HAD AN AI BOT CHECK ALL HOSPITALS, CLINICS, WALK IN MEDICAL CENTERS IN THE BAY AREA TO KNOW WHEN THEY STOPPED USING BITHIONOL..

*FOOD & DRUG ADMINISTRATION.

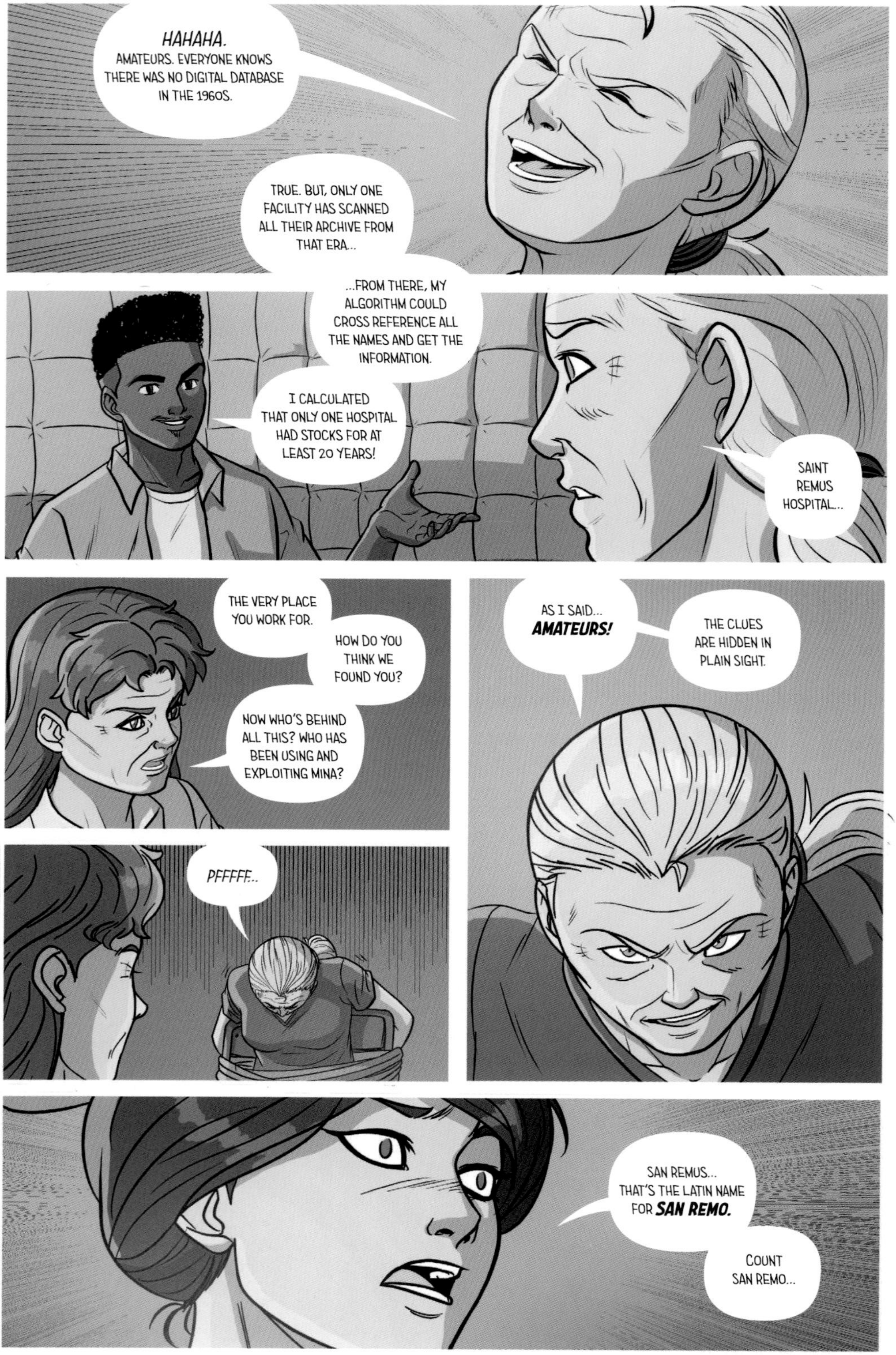
HAHAHA. AMATEURS. EVERYONE KNOWS THERE WAS NO DIGITAL DATABASE IN THE 1960S.
TRUE. BUT, ONLY ONE FACILITY HAS SCANNED ALL THEIR ARCHIVE FROM THAT ERA...
...FROM THERE, MY ALGORITHM COULD CROSS REFERENCE ALL THE NAMES AND GET THE INFORMATION.
I CALCULATED THAT ONLY ONE HOSPITAL HAD STOCKS FOR AT LEAST 20 YEARS!
SAINT REMUS HOSPITAL...
THE VERY PLACE YOU WORK FOR.
HOW DO YOU THINK WE FOUND YOU?
NOW WHO'S BEHIND ALL THIS? WHO HAS BEEN USING AND EXPLOITING MINA?
PFFFFF...
AS I SAID... AMATEURS!
THE CLUES ARE HIDDEN IN PLAIN SIGHT.
SAN REMUS... THAT'S THE LATIN NAME FOR SAN REMO.
COUNT SAN REMO...

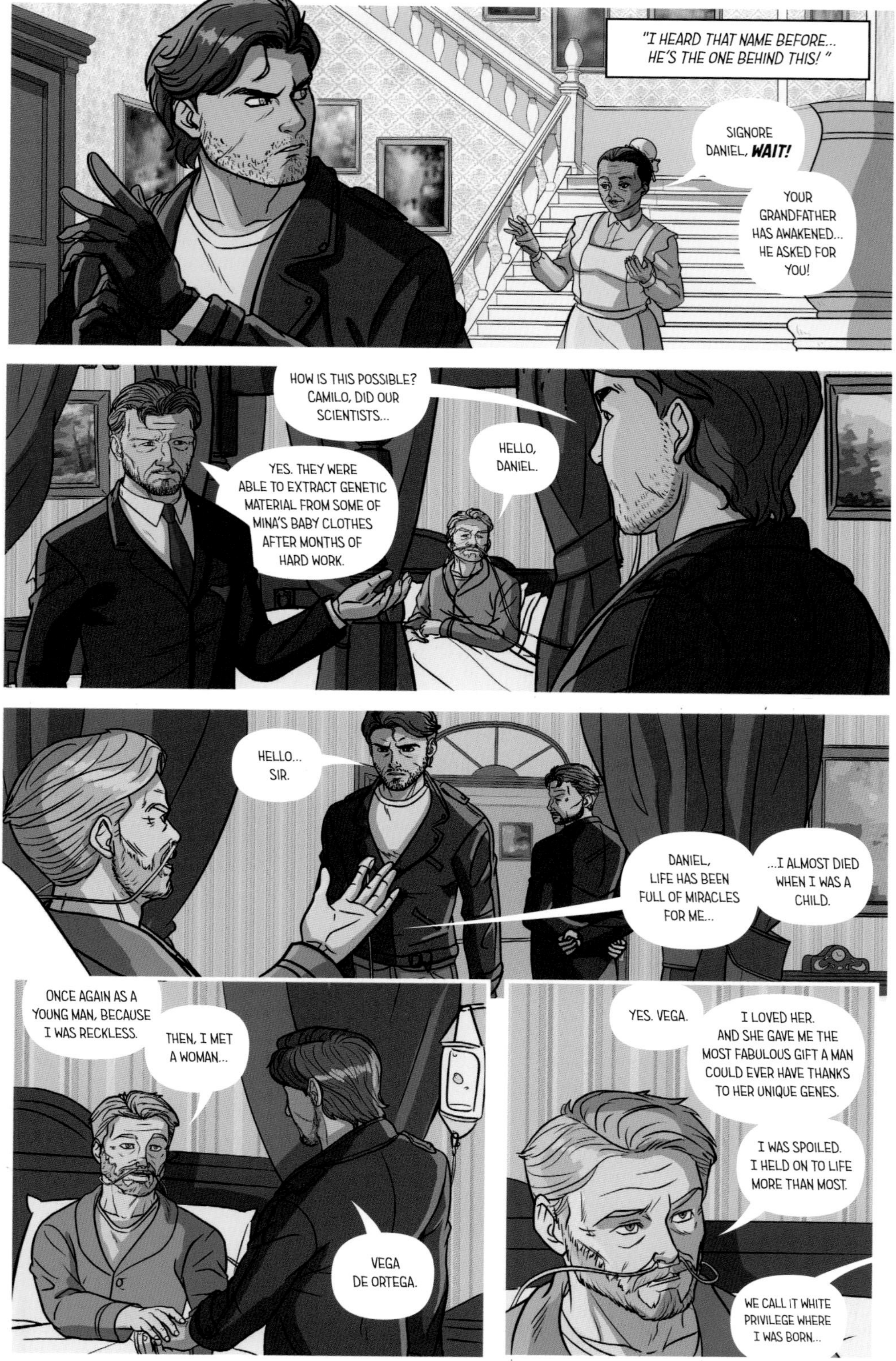
"I HEARD THAT NAME BEFORE... HE'S THE ONE BEHIND THIS!"
SIGNORE DANIEL, **WAIT!**
YOUR GRANDFATHER HAS AWAKENED... HE ASKED FOR YOU!
HOW IS THIS POSSIBLE? CAMILO, DID OUR SCIENTISTS...
YES. THEY WERE ABLE TO EXTRACT GENETIC MATERIAL FROM SOME OF MINA'S BABY CLOTHES AFTER MONTHS OF HARD WORK.
HELLO, DANIEL.
HELLO... SIR.
DANIEL, LIFE HAS BEEN FULL OF MIRACLES FOR ME...
...I ALMOST DIED WHEN I WAS A CHILD.
ONCE AGAIN AS A YOUNG MAN, BECAUSE I WAS RECKLESS.
THEN, I MET A WOMAN...
VEGA DE ORTEGA.
YES. VEGA.
I LOVED HER. AND SHE GAVE ME THE MOST FABULOUS GIFT A MAN COULD EVER HAVE THANKS TO HER UNIQUE GENES.
I WAS SPOILED. I HELD ON TO LIFE MORE THAN MOST.
WE CALL IT WHITE PRIVILEGE WHERE I WAS BORN...

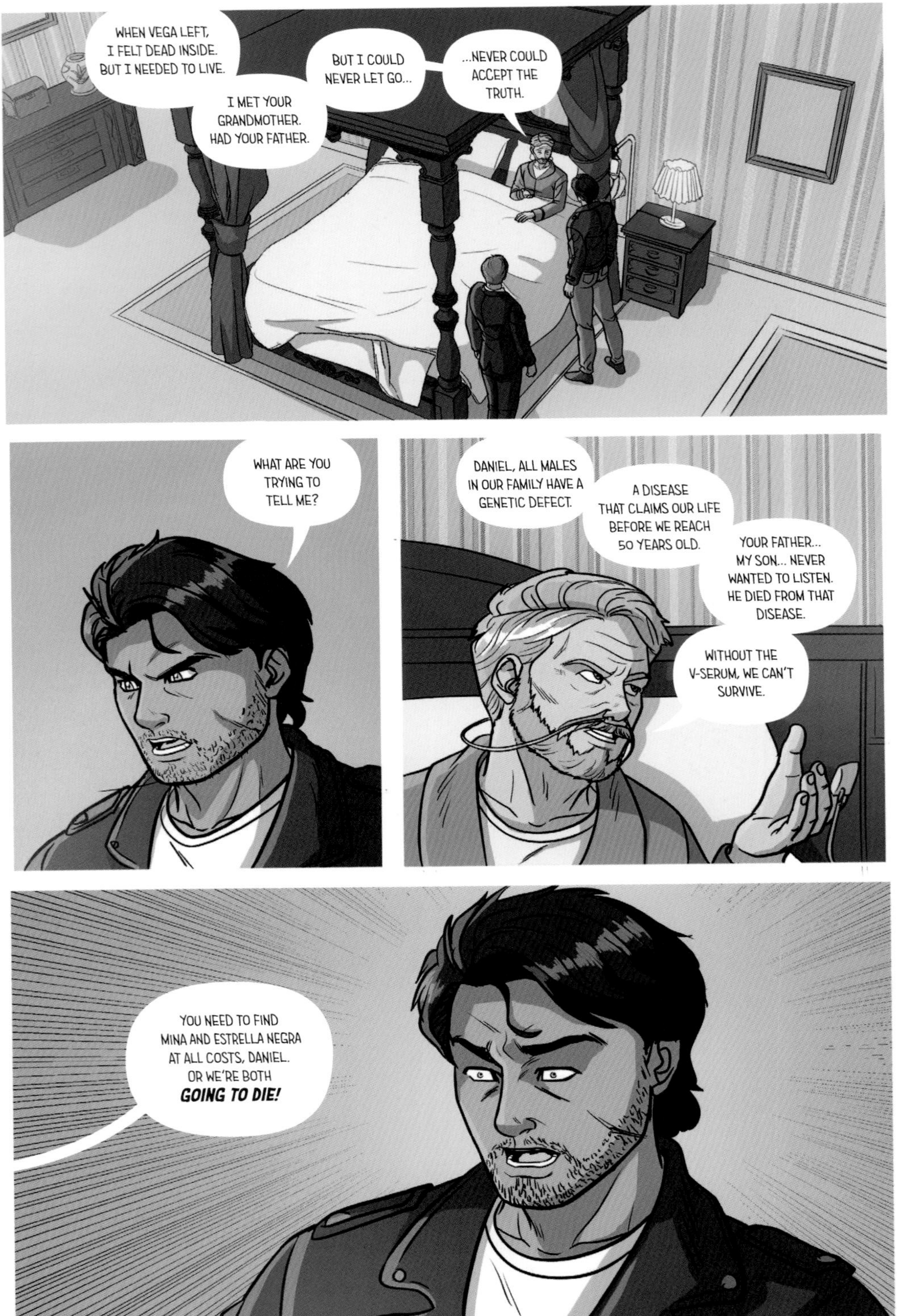
WHEN VEGA LEFT, I FELT DEAD INSIDE. BUT I NEEDED TO LIVE.
I MET YOUR GRANDMOTHER. HAD YOUR FATHER.
BUT I COULD NEVER LET GO...
...NEVER COULD ACCEPT THE TRUTH.
WHAT ARE YOU TRYING TO TELL ME?
DANIEL, ALL MALES IN OUR FAMILY HAVE A GENETIC DEFECT.
A DISEASE THAT CLAIMS OUR LIFE BEFORE WE REACH 50 YEARS OLD.
YOUR FATHER... MY SON... NEVER WANTED TO LISTEN. HE DIED FROM THAT DISEASE.
WITHOUT THE V-SERUM, WE CAN'T SURVIVE.
YOU NEED TO FIND MINA AND ESTRELLA NEGRA AT ALL COSTS, DANIEL. OR WE'RE BOTH ***GOING TO DIE!***

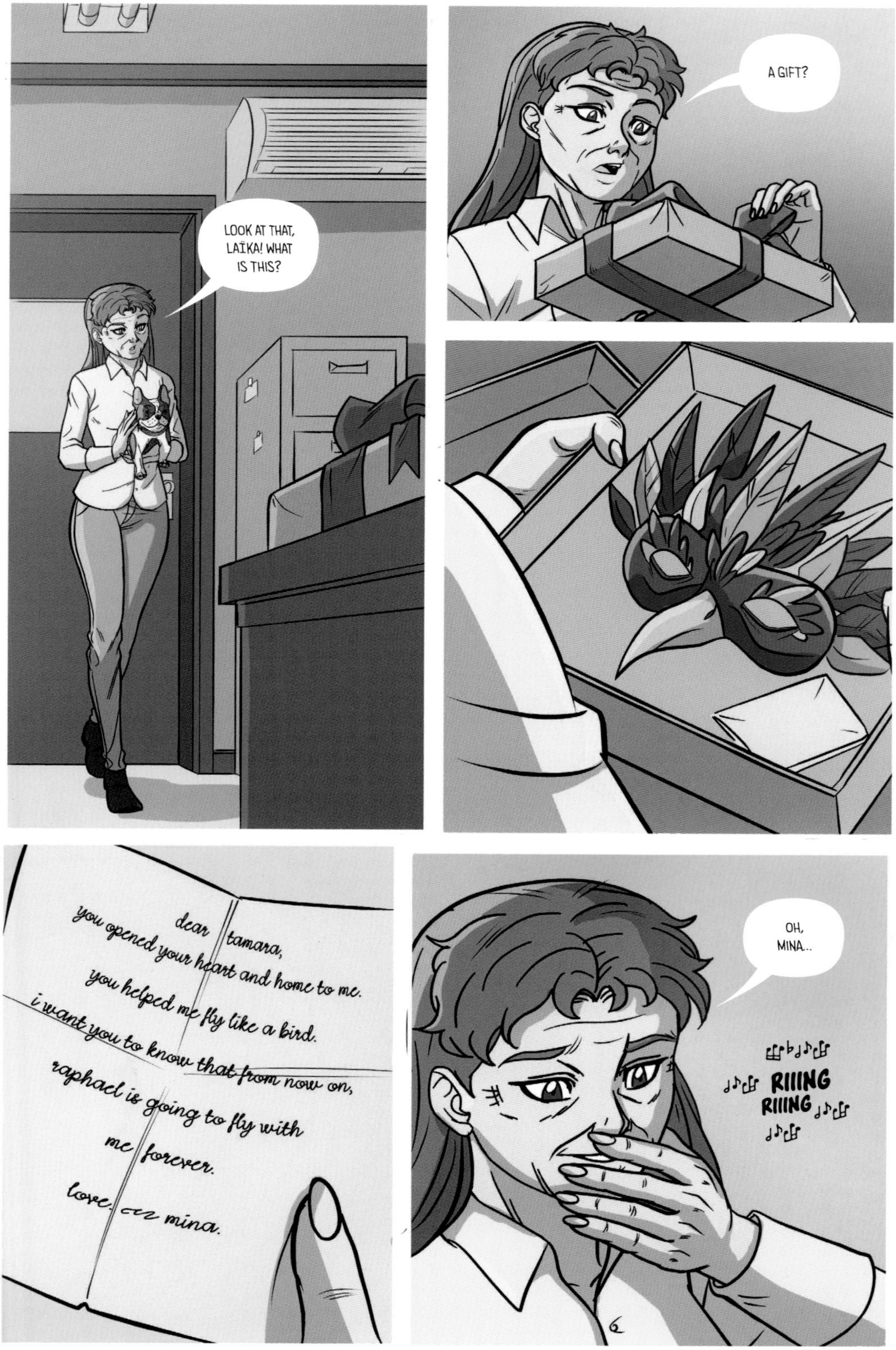
LOOK AT THAT, LAÏKA! WHAT IS THIS?
A GIFT?
dear tamara,
you opened your heart and home to me.
you helped me fly like a bird.
i want you to know that from now on,
raphael is going to fly with me forever.
love, mina.
OH, MINA..
RIIING RIIING

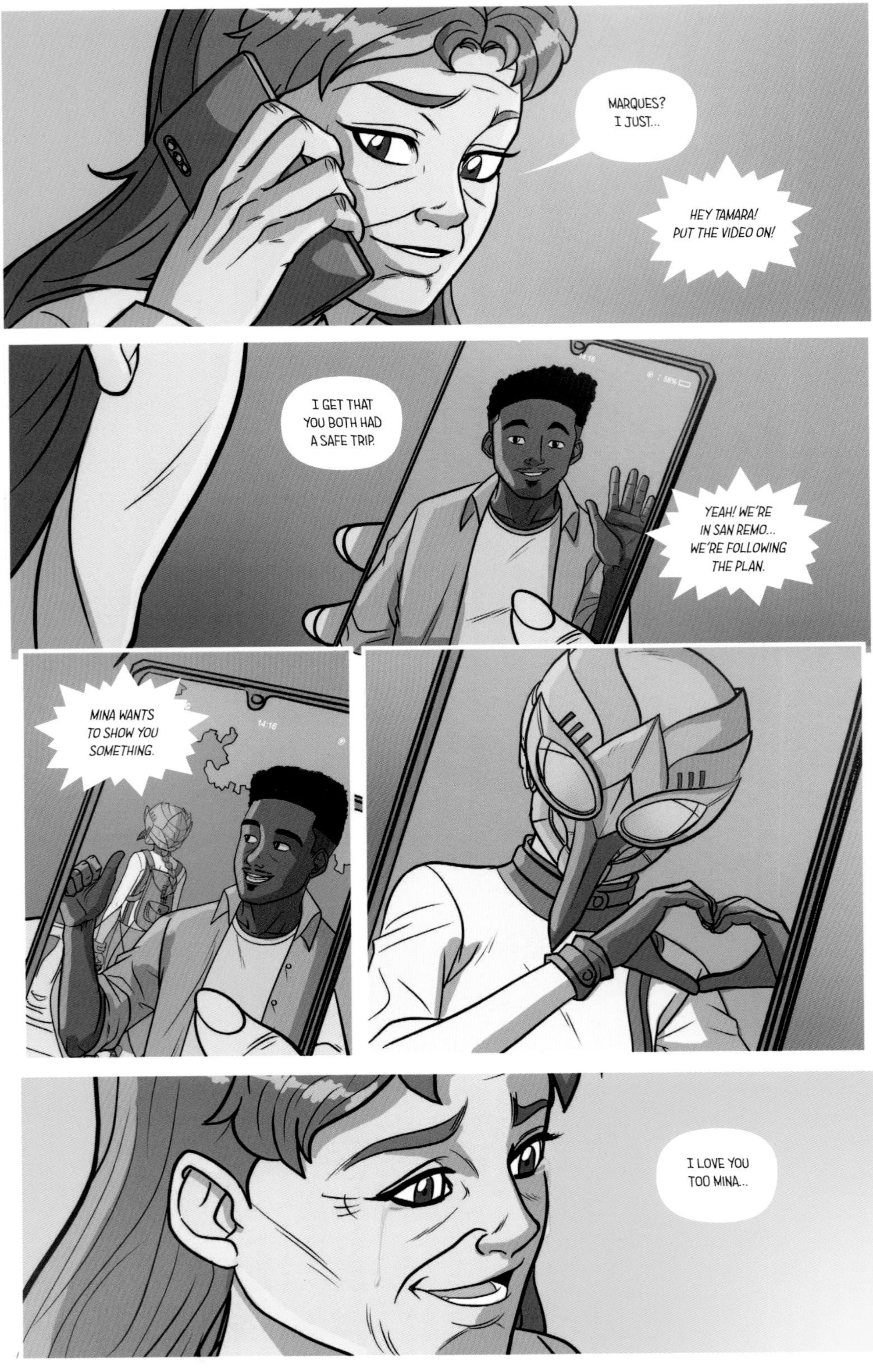
MARQUES? I JUST...
HEY TAMARA! PUT THE VIDEO ON!
I GET THAT YOU BOTH HAD A SAFE TRIP.
YEAH! WE'RE IN SAN REMO... WE'RE FOLLOWING THE PLAN.
MINA WANTS TO SHOW YOU SOMETHING.
I LOVE YOU TOO MINA...

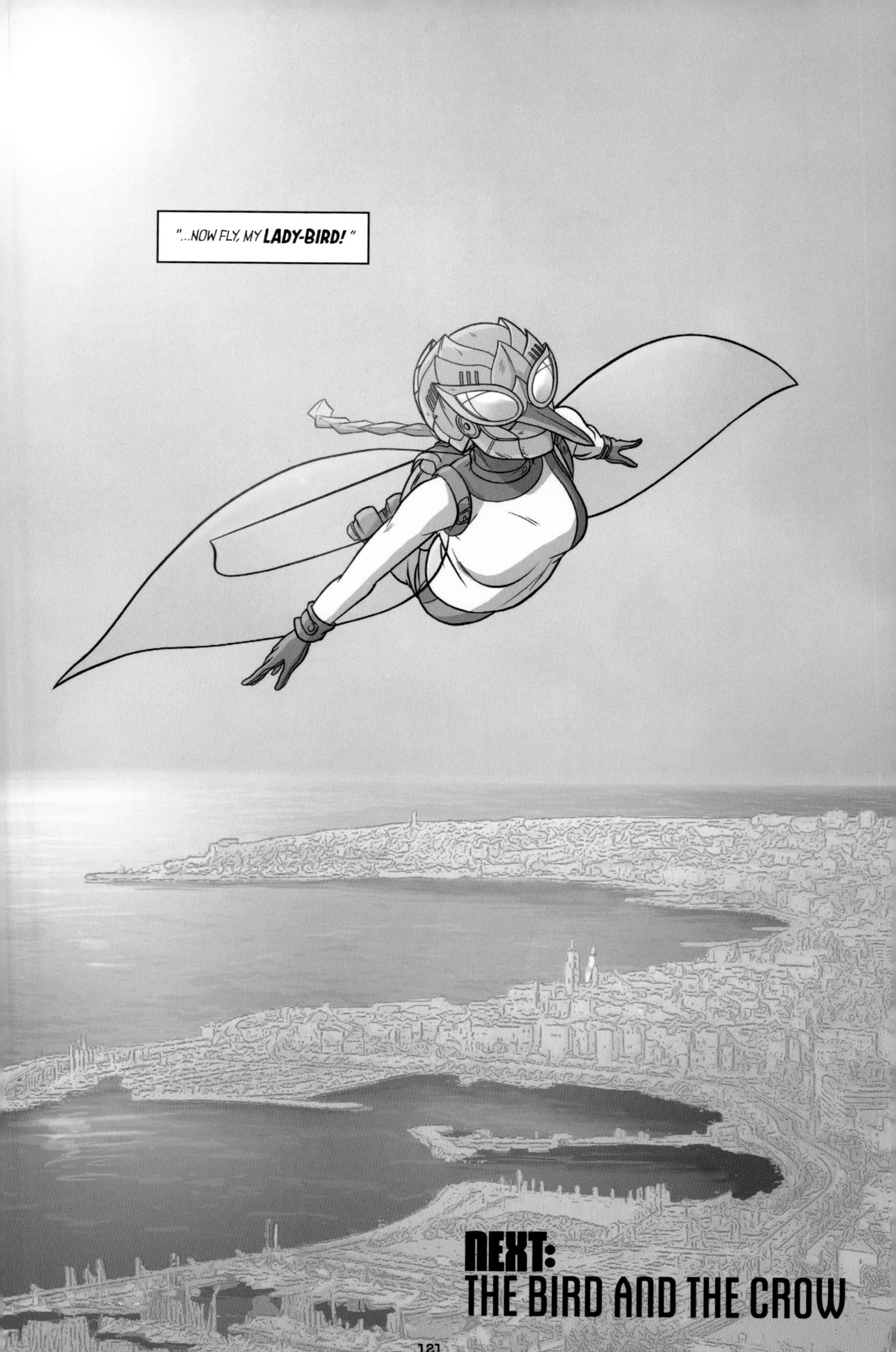
"...NOW FLY, MY **LADY-BIRD!**"
NEXT:
THE BIRD AND THE CROW

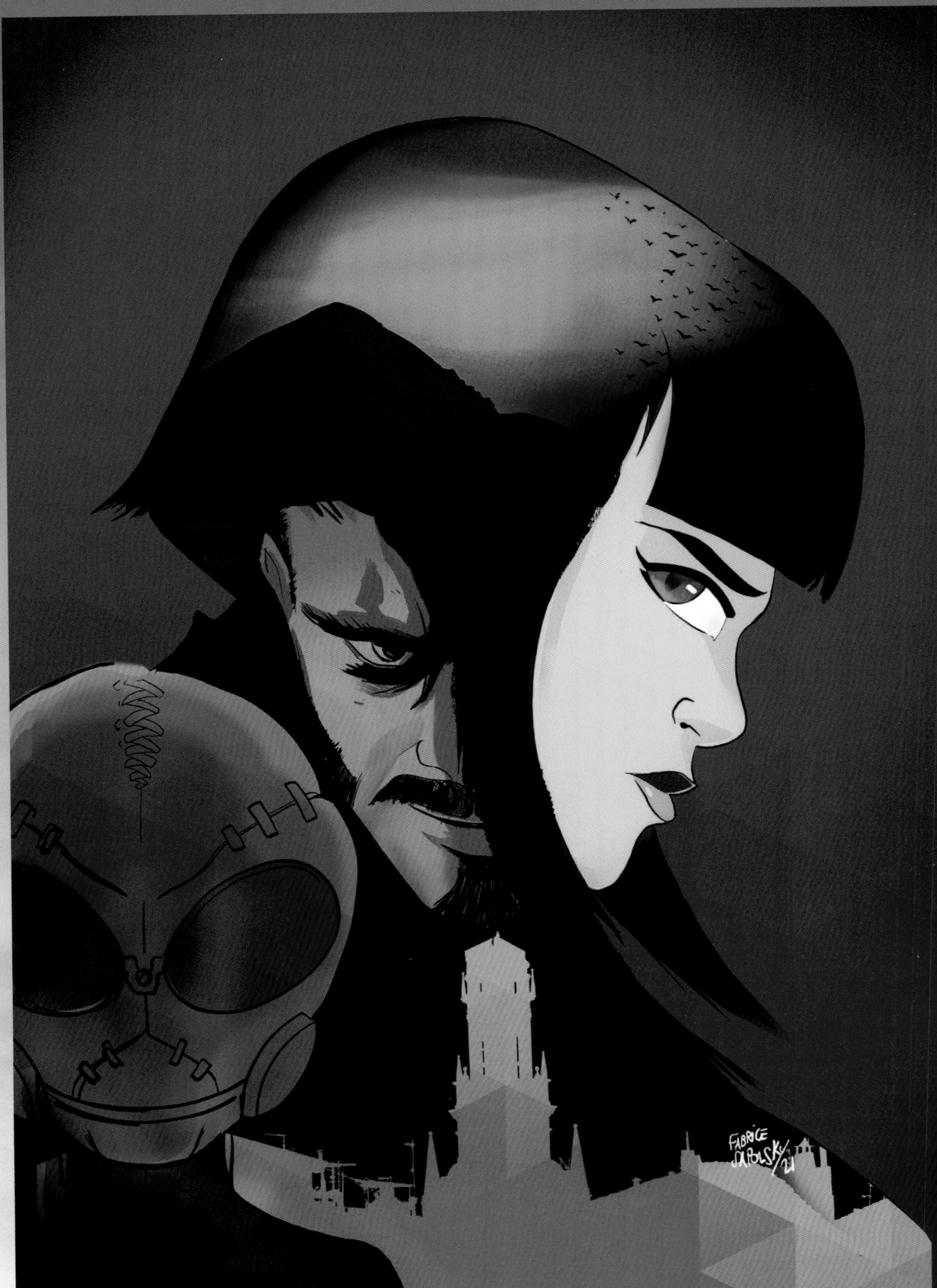
FABRICE SAPOLSKY/21

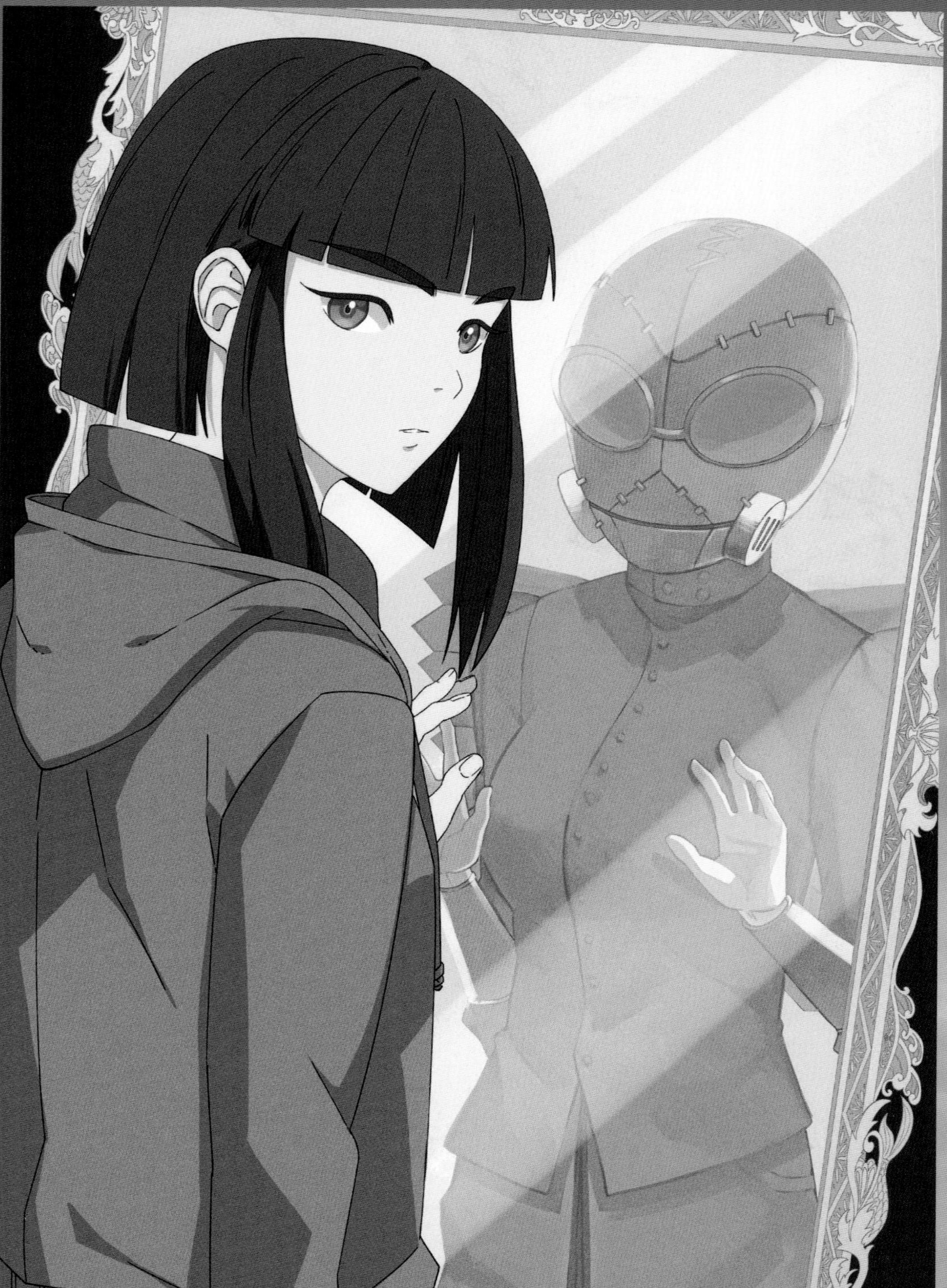